The Language of Czech and Polish Civil Law Contracts: A Comparative Study Based on Corpus Research

Anna Szuster

The Language of Czech and Polish Civil Law Contracts: A Comparative Study Based on Corpus Research

PETER LANG

Lausanne - Berlin - Bruxelles - Chennai - New York - Oxford

Library of Congress Cataloging-in-Publication
This book has been requested for registration in the Library of Congress
CIP catalog of the Library of Congress.

Bibliographic Information published by the Deutsche Nationalbibliothek
The Deutsche Nationalbibliothek lists this publication in the Deutsche Nationalbibliografie; detailed bibliographic data is available in the internet at http://dnb.d-nb.de.

This publication was financially supported by the Faculty of Arts at the University of Ostrava.

ISBN 978-3-631-90898-3 (Print)
E-ISBN 978-3-631-90875-4 (E-PDF)
E-ISBN 978-3-631-91070-2 (E-PUB)
10.3726/b21323

Published by Peter Lang GmbH, Berlin, Deutschland

info@peterlang.com - www.peterlang.com

Abstract: The work, entitled *The Language of Czech and Polish Civil Law Contracts: A Comparative Study Based on Corpus Research*, is devoted to aspects of the field of specialised translation. It consists of three main parts: two theoretical sections and a research section with conclusions summing up the work. The first theoretical section, entitled *Methodological Assumptions*, provides an overview of the current state of translation studies. The main trends are presented, along with profiles of scholars working in the field. In relation to corpus research, translation studies methodology is also described (corpus-based translation studies), along with the main tools of corpus analysis, and the concept of a corpus is explained with an indication of the typological division of corpora. This part contains a description of two national corpora: a Czech one and a Polish one.The second section of the work, also theoretical, entitled *Specialised Translation Process*, focuses on the translation process from an external point of view (that of the client/ordering party) and from an internal point of view (that of the translator), discussing the tools, techniques and strategies used in specialised translation (parallel texts, glossaries, CAT tools, searching for equivalents using domestication and foreignization strategies). The topical issues of machine translation and post-editing, highly discussed in the translator community, are addressed, along with quality requirements and professional liability aspects in specialised translation.The third section of the work focuses on research. It consists of a corpus analysis of selected contracts creating obligations. The analysis was conducted with an emphasis on the search for the presence of universals of translation as defined in the proposition put forward by Mona Baker. The research was carried out using tools such as an original corpus of civil law contracts, the EUR-Lex reference corpus of legal and legislative texts, original texts, and parallel texts. A community survey was also included in the research methods. The work ends with conclusions.

Keywords: corpus research, corpus-based translation studies, corpus, equivalence, translation

Table of Contents

Introduction

On 1 May 2004, Poland (and nine other countries, including the Czech Republic) joined the European Union through the Accession Treaty. This fact marked the beginning of many transformations on numerous levels: from political, economic, and social, to cultural and technological. The world around us and the way citizens function in it have changed. Poland's opening up to other EU countries was also linked to changes in the area of the flow of goods and services, as well as the adaptation of the Polish legal system to EU requirements. As a consequence of these developments, the translation of texts has become a necessity and the translation profession has gained importance. Practical application of the translated texts showed that obtaining a good translation requires the work of an experienced and responsible translator with a range of competencies appropriate to the profession. The translation of specialised texts, whether in the field of law, economics, or finance, requires not only the completion of philological studies and an excellent command of the language, but also knowledge of various fields of economics, legal, or financial regulations, knowledge of the diversity of legal systems and, above all, the ability to prepare the right tools and use the right strategies during the translation process.

Although 17 years have passed since Poland and the Czech Republic joined the European Union, many questions and concerns still arise about the training of future translators and how to develop adequate translation skills so that the translations they produce meet EU requirements and, above all, are error-free. Translator training is not only about knowledge of language, translation strategies, and techniques, but also about making future students of translation aware of the responsibilities and impact of the profession.

This work, entitled *The Language of Czech and Polish Civil Law Contracts: A Comparative Study Based on Corpus Research*, is devoted to the problems of specialised texts in practical terms, the broadly understood translator's workflow, as well as a comparative analysis of the texts of contractual *agreements* functioning in different legal systems – Czech and Polish.

The main objective of this study is to examine whether so-called translation universals – in the sense of the hypothesis put forward by Mona Baker – exist in specialist translations in the Czech-Polish language pair. A secondary aim of this work is to present the translation tools and techniques used by translators of specialised texts, as well as the ways in which translation strategies are chosen and the translator's work is prepared.

The subject of the work is the translation techniques and strategies used in Czech-Polish translations of civil law contractual agreements. The research material in this work is a comparative corpus of civil law contract texts created by the author using Sketch Engine. The legal system of the source language is the Czech legal system, and the legal system of the target language is the Polish legal system. The research also used the reference corpus of EU legal texts EUR-Lex as a reference, Polish and Czech civil codes, as well as texts of civil law contracts functioning in the Czech and Polish legal systems without any intention of translation.

The work consists of three parts: a theoretical part consisting of two chapters, and a research part with conclusions.

The first part of the paper is theoretical in nature and is devoted to the methodological assumptions of the presented research project. The starting point is a review of previous translation studies, discussing the main trends in translation studies together with an indication of the profiles of their authors and representatives. A significant part of the discussion has been devoted to issues of corpus-based translation studies as a methodology for translation research. Although the paper is based on Slavic texts, the author also drew on research from the Anglo-Saxon research area. The work makes use of corpus research; therefore, this section also includes an explanation of what a corpus is, an outline of the idea of corpus research, and an indication and description of the types of corpora along with their purposes. An attempt has been made to justify why corpora deserve the attention of the translator of specialised texts, and how the translator can use them independently and even build them up and create further tools from them, such as glossaries. This leads on to the next section of the paper, in which the author describes the tools for implementing corpus-based research. As already noted, the research for this work was carried out using Sketch Engine, while the type of materials and how they were selected are described later in the work.

The second chapter of the work reflects the author's research interests. An in-depth understanding of the translator's craft, the role of the environment, and the process of translating specialised texts itself provided the impetus to reflect on opportunities to improve translation skills and competencies. This part of the work addresses the most topical issues in the translation community, namely machine translation, post-editing, and translation quality, in light of the PN EN 17100: 2015 standard of professional liability. The author shares the view that organisations and associations of translators play a significant role both in the professional work of translators as individuals and in the development of national procedures and policies through which quality standards of translation are maintained. This part of the work is based on a wealth of experience gained through many years of work as a translator of specialised texts, participation in conferences, field meetings, and interviews conducted in the community of specialised translators, and in the community of recipients of such translations. Issues of translation strategies such as foreignisation and domestication or the role of parallel texts during translation work and glossary development are also addressed.

The third part of the work – the research chapter – is empirical in nature and includes a presentation of the material obtained through corpus-based research. Six types of civil law contracts are the subject of this research. The author cites authentic texts without the intention of translation, characterising how they function in each legal system. She then carries out a comparative analysis, looking for differences and similarities in the areas of phraseology, terminology, syntax, and key concepts. The effect of the analysis is not only to provide a terminological base, but also to obtain information on the characteristic aspects of a given agreement, taking into account the legal system in which it operates and, consequently, how it is translated. Part three also presents the results of the research carried out using an email questionnaire and the in-depth interview method. Based on the assumption that translations of specialised texts are tools for realising the concepts and plans of translation clients, a community interview was carried out by e-mail and telephone among certified translators, lawyers, notaries, and entrepreneurs who commission translations of specialised texts. They were asked what the strengths and weaknesses of translating specialised texts are from the point of view of the end user. Respondents commented on the difficulty of receiving the translation, as well as the quality of the translation, which is very important to them. This is because the translation itself is not the problem, the crux of the matter is the issue of quality, which has a number of consequences for the user.

The research material for this study was collected between 2018 and 2021. A significant part of the work was written during two fellowship programmes. The first of these was the PROM programme, a 10-day stay at the Jan Długosz University of Humanities and Sciences in Częstochowa, during which the author conducted library research and gave a lecture to students on professional translation and the practice of translating specialist texts.

The second programme was a six-month research stay in cooperation with the University of Warsaw (scholarship from the Ministry of Education, Youth and Sports of the Czech Republic). As part of this programme, the author had the opportunity to learn about the methodology of corpus research at the Warsaw Faculty of Polish Studies, as well as to collect research material and meet with academics specialising in research within the same subject area. Aiming to ensure that the material for the section of the work dealing with machine translation, post-editing, translation practice, and the professional responsibility of translators is as up to date a reflection of the situation of the translation community as possible, the author collected this material over a three-year period at various industry conferences. They were: the Translation and Localization Conference in Warsaw KTLC (2018, 2019, 2020, and 2021), the Conference of the Directorate-General for Translation in Brussels Translating Europe Forum (2019, 2020, 2021), the Conference of the Lublin Translators' Association and the Maria-Curie Skłodowska University in Lublin *Konferencja z pozytwnym przesłaniem* (2021), the Conference of the Polish Society of Sworn and Specialised Translators (TEPIS) (2021), and the Czech Union of Interpreters and Translators (JTP) *Jeronýmovy dny* (2020, 2021). The above activities were complemented by the author's active participation in six academic conferences.

1 Methodological assumptions

1.1. The current state of translation studies

The art of translation is of interest to many eminent scholars. The 20th century brought a number of interesting, often surprising, and groundbreaking theories in this area. Since this work is devoted to the issues of translation and interlingual and intercultural communication, the author has decided to present an overview of the main trends and theories concerning this topic and to recall the most important researchers in contemporary translation studies.

There are two books that are well-known to a Polish audience interested in translation issues. The first is a paper from the second half of the 1990s by Alicja Pisarska and Teresa Tomaszkiewicz, entitled *Współczesne tendencje przekładoznawcze*. The second is *Współczesne teorie przekładu* by Piotr Bukowski and Magda Heydel. Both works describe the development of the most important translation theories of the 20th century. Bukowski and Heydel also wrote the noteworthy book *Polska myśl przekładoznawcza*, which was published in 2013 by the Jagiellonian University Publishing House.

It is impossible to think of a contemporary work devoted to translation studies without reference to Roman Jakobson. His article (Jakobson, 1959) on the linguistic aspects of translation marked the beginning of a new phase of research. Roman Jakobson coined the term 'equivalence-in-difference', and he also believed that any cognitive experience can be expressed in any existing language (Bukowski, Heydel, 2009: 45). He also created the concept of distinguishing three types of translation: intra-linguistic, interlinguistic and intersemiotic. His work stated that translation is the transfer of symbols, and symbols are interpreted by means of other symbols, that translation is a matter of words and an element of the linguistic tradition, and that linguistic theories of translation are based on comparisons between the structures of the source language and the target language (Pisarska, Tomaszkiewicz, 1996: 13).

A figure whose activities and research stimulated the discussion of translation in linguistic and anthropological-cultural terms was Eugene A. Nida.

A central concept in his theory is equivalence (Nida, after: Bukowski, Heydel, 2009: 9), which will appear in the considerations later in this work. Nida called his theory the 'science of translation'. Nida's notion of dynamic (functional) equivalence means that the translator focuses not so much on the source text itself, but on how it will be received in the target language. Nida believed that the essence of translation rests in reproducing in the target language the most accurate natural equivalent of the content conveyed in the original language, first in terms of meaning and then in terms of style (Pisarska, Tomaszkiewicz, 1996: 14).

Another figure worth mentioning besides Nida is the Czech researcher Jiří Levý, a well-known linguist and translation theorist who wrote the famous 1963 work *The Art of Translation*. In it, Levý argues that the interpreter's job is a decision-making process, during which he or she must choose one solution from the many options available. By substituting one linguistic material for another in the translation process, the translator is forced to shape all the linguistic artistic devices used in the text independently (Levý, after: Bukowski, Heydel, 2009: 80).

The German field of translation studies, inspired by Nida's theory, was moving towards the study of equivalence. The strand of linguistic research known as *Übersetzungswissenschaft* was represented by Wolfram Wilss and Werner Koller, while the so-called Leipzig School included researchers such as Otto Kade, Gert Jäger, and Albrecht Neubert. *Übersetzungswissenschaft* sought to apply the principles of the mathematical sciences to its research into questions of equivalence, thereby rejecting traditional translation theory. Wilss, investigating the process of translation, which he called transfer, started from a communicative model of translation operations (Pisarska, Tomaszkiewicz, 1996: 24).

Another German scholar, Hans Vermeer, who countered the claim 'that translation is primarily a matter of language' (ibid.), also developed an important theory on translation. In his understanding, translation is largely a cross-cultural transfer. The translator must not only be proficient in the foreign language but also have a broad knowledge of the target language's culture, as language is an integral part of it, and it is impossible to translate a text without adequate erudition. The creator of skopos theory argues that an essential feature of translation is its purpose. The researcher treats the text holistically, against the background of the culture in which it functions.

Translation studies from the French academic field have emphasised the extra-linguistic sphere, namely the communicative context and the different types of texts. Maurice Pergnier, a representative of French sociolinguistic research, focused on the problems of translation in the context of a communicative situation. A context mediating meaning is a context in terms of the situation parameter as well as a strictly textual context (Pisarska, Tomaszkiewicz, 1996: 28).

> This setting of translation issues shifts the focus from an interest in linguistic problems or language comparison towards an analysis of the meaning of the text. Understood in this way, translation and the analysis of its impact on the recipient is an act of communication, and the field that provides the tools of analysis for the translation researcher is sociolinguistics (Pisarska, Tomaszkiewicz, 1996: 29).

This view of the problem of translation was also shared by another French researcher, Jean Delisle. The so-called Paris School, of which Delisle was a representative, developed an interpretive theory of translation, based on similar assumptions to those considering the contribution of communication theory and pragmatics to the translation model. Here, Danica Seleskovitch, who formulated theories based on her own professional experiences as a conference and simultaneous interpreter, played an important role. Consequently, the central point of her interest is 'the thought mechanisms of the translator, who interprets the meaning of the original, on the basis of linguistic signs, as well as on the basis of his own knowledge, feelings and experiences [...] translation is not analysed from a comparative point of view as a finished product, but as a creative process' (Pisarska, Tomaszkiewicz, 1996: 30).

Within the circle of French linguistic research, the names of three more well-known researchers should be noted: Jean-Claude Margot, Jean-René Ladmiral, and Henri Meschonnic. They are united by basing their theses and theories on their own experiences in the translation profession. Margot believes that 'translation should be faithful to the source text, the target language and the recipient of the translation' (Pisarska, Tomaszkiewicz, 1996: 30). The textual approach is also shared by Ladmiral, who in turn defines translation as an act of communication at the speech level. He recognises that it must be taken into account that the translator, in the process of translation, performs an act of interpretation of the source text and translatological choices. Meschonnic, on the other hand, argues that translation is a translinguistic activity. It also opposes Nida's approach, in which content dominates over form. In Meschonnic's view, the process of translation requires both elements (content and form) to be taken into account equally.

In linguistic research in the 1980s, it is worth pointing out the Sapir-Whorf hypothesis, known as the principle of linguistic relativism. According to this claim, translation is completely impossible due to the impossibility of transferring concepts and cultures (Pisarska, Tomaszkiewicz, 1996: 33).

The opposite of the principle mentioned above, on the other hand, is the theory formulated by Noam Chomsky and the generative grammar school. Chomsky created the rule of linguistic universals. It says that everything can be translated into another language because 'translation takes place at the surface level – it is a "recoding" of non-linguistic and universal deep structures that are common to all languages despite surface differences' (Pisarska, Tomaszkiewicz, 1996: 33). The degree of translatability has been the subject of much debate from then until now and is closely linked to the position of the text in its specific culture.

When talking about German-language non-linguistic research dedicated to the issue of translation, the hermeneutic theory should be mentioned. Hermeneutic theory focuses primarily on the process of text interpretation aimed at understanding the foreign sense – interpretation here means the translation of the foreign sense into an intelligible one (Bukowski, Heydel, 2009: 26). The main researchers of this direction are the philosophers Edmund Husserl, creator of the concept of *Lebenswelt*, and Hans-Georg Gadamer, creator of the concept of *Horizontverschmelzung*. Their work led to a philosophical movement that focused on the reader's reception of translation, but the work was overwhelmingly concerned with literary translation.

Gadamer's influence can also be seen in two other German scholars: Fritz Paepcke and Radegundis Stolze. The result of their investigations was to define the nature of the translator as an active and creative reader, with an emphasis on comprehension, which should not mean passive reception of the text (Bukowski, Heydel, 2009: 35).

In the field of British hermeneutics, it is worth mentioning the name of George Steiner and his 1957 work *After Babel*, as well as Peter Newmark, who focuses on two elementary principles in his reflections on translation: truth and accuracy. He created so-called translation rules, such as transference, cultural equivalence, literal translation of the most common collocations, literal translation, functional equivalence, descriptive equivalence, and a strategy combining these two types of equivalence (Pisarska, Tomaszkiewicz, 1996: 36). Newmark has made numerous pragmatic claims about translation. He was a proponent of the thesis that 'a good translation is a literal translation, accurate and economical, compact and economical as possible' (ibid.: 36). He also takes the view that the interpreter builds his or her interpreting skills only through professional practice and that teaching translation itself is about discussions, analysis of examples, mutual listener-presenter learning, and the collection of characteristic exemplifications.

A strong trend that emerged in the 1960s was the so-called manipulist school.[1] It has had a significant impact on contemporary translation research. Some of the earliest theorists of this group, the vast majority of whom were researchers from the Netherlands and Israel,[2] were James Holmes and Susan Bassnett. This strand originated in comparative literary studies, focusing on the development of descriptive and systemic research on translation. Holmes advocated the rejection of the 'theory' and 'science' of translation. He believed that they were not suitable for describing the specifics of translation, and postulated the establishment of a new field, namely *translation studies* as we know it today (Bukowski, Heydel, 2009: 21). Theo Hermans (2007, after: Heydel, 2009: 22) writes in his work that 'every translation presupposes some degree of manipulation of the original text'. He also argues that 'total equivalence is the death of translation'.

Two other researchers who should be mentioned when talking about manipulators are Itamar Even-Zohar and his student Gideon Toury. In the work of these Israeli scholars, the focus has essentially shifted from the equivalence of the translation to the question of its relevance to the

---

1 The name of the movement was coined after the publication of the book by Theo Hermans, *The Manipulation of Literature. Studies in Literary Translation* (1985). According to manipulists views, translation is always to some extent a manipulation of the source text for certain purposes (after: Pisarska, Tomaszkiewicz, 1996: 38).

2 We can also mention names such as: José Lambert, Gideon Toury, André Lefevere, Theo Hermans, and Ria Vanderauwera.

original on the one hand, and its acceptability within the target context and its norms on the other. The concept of acceptability became central to these two researchers. Furthermore, Toury advocates that norms decisively shape equivalence (Even-Zohar, Toury, after: Bukowski, Heydel, 2009: 22).

French scholar Antoine Berman, like the American Lawrence Venuti, advocates 'foreignisation', i.e., maintaining maximum fidelity to the original text by adopting a strategy of alienation in translation. Berman is an opponent of translation, which, as a result of 'deformative tendencies', eliminates what in the original text yields to the logic of the target language – what 'experiences' or puts it to the test. Venuti, too, presents the thesis of the 'invisibility' of interpreters in his work. Through the use of certain strategies, interpreters make the reader feel that he or she is interacting with the original work and that there is no visible interference from the translator. Berman and Venuti believe that the translator should produce what is known as an alienating translation, emphasising the linguistic and cultural differences between the source and target texts, trying to preserve as faithfully as possible the features of the source text (Bukowski, Heydel, 2009: 25).

Closely linked to the manipulist movement is the concept of the so-called cultural turn. This phenomenon was described in their 1998 paper by Susan Bassnett and André Lefevere. The translator and his or her work act as mediators involved in the creation of an image of the alien in the process of intercultural communication.

> This mediation takes place within the prevailing structures of power, national interests, religious systems and economics, which the translator is subjected to at various levels [...] the text and linguistic aspects move to the periphery and the translator, his multiple entanglements and the ideological effect of his work become the centre [...] (Bukowski, Heydel, 2009: 25).

Bassnett also believes that after the cultural turn in translation studies, the time has come for a translationist turn in cultural studies. The cultural turn has given rise to the sociology of translation.

In the field of sociology, Pierre Bourdieu has made an important contribution to the development of translation theory. He created the categories of cultural capital, habitus, and field. His research influenced Anthony Pym, whose theory is referenced in this work's section on perspectives in translation.

The establishment of the field of translation studies as an autonomous discipline was, in turn, suggested by the British researcher Mary Snell-Hornby. Her proposed model, called integrative, postulates translation studies as an integrated and independent discipline, covering all types of translation, from literary to technical. In such an approach, translation studies draws on the achievements of many scientific disciplines, however, it is a separate discipline and should therefore develop its own research methods, based on its own specificities and not on external models and conventions (Pisarska, Tomaszkiewicz, 1996: 45).

Snell-Hornby proposed four hypotheses for integrated studies. The first presupposes, at the very least, a mutual interest on the part of the practitioner translator and the translation researcher in the space between their respective fields of activity, languages, or cultures. The second anticipates the opposite field of interest in relation to linguistics, extending its interest from the micro to the macro level. The third envisages the removal of rigid divisions in translation studies, and the emergence of prototypology in place of typology and spectrum in place of dichotomy. The fourth implies removing the isolation of phenomena in translation studies and shifting the focus of interest to the study of networks of connections and relations, emphasising their relevance in the context of text, situation, and culture (Pisarska, Tomaszkiewicz, 1996: 47).

In addition to the linguistic theories and phenomena themselves, the thought processes that occur during the translation process are also of interest to researchers. While translation was previously seen in terms of a product, later research has focused on the process of translation by a specific translator under specific conditions (Pisarska, Tomaszkiewicz, 1996: 52). Researchers such as Paul Kussmaul, Hans Hönig, and Wolfgang Lörschner conducted psycholinguistic research on translation processes. However, their studies were carried out in Germany, Finland, and Canada. The research used so-called thinking-aloud protocols. The results clarified, among other things, the understanding of the translated text, the differences between novice and experienced translators, as well as their perception of the translation process. Hönig's research focuses primarily on associative and translational competence, the subjectivity of understanding, the nature of mental and associative processes, and intuition. Combining elements of semantics, scenes and frameworks with protocols for speaking aloud, Paul

Kussmaul explores creativity. The research and its results serve primarily didactic and methodological purposes and are used in translator education (Pisarska, Tomaszkiewicz, 1996: 52).

Feminist translation seems interesting and somewhat surprising. In this philosophy, translation is compared to the core of motherhood, and thus has the task of giving the text life and endowing it with care. The feminist strand of translation studies was initiated by feminist writers who address gender and grammatical type in their discussions. They rejected the opposition between the masculine and feminine worlds, elements of masculinity and femininity, father and mother, and patriarchal and matriarchal relations.[3] A representative of the feminist translation trend was Luise von Flotow.[4]

Contemporary linguistic research is constantly evolving. It is worth looking at the achievements of Maria Tymoczko, Mona Baker, or the Polish researcher Elżbieta Tabakowska. The field of contemporary translation studies includes work on corpus-based translation studies, which is discussed in more detail in the next chapter.

Translation studies is a wonderful journey into a world where language as a tool of communication unites people (although sometimes also divides them), allows them to learn previously unknown facts, and explore the secrets of knowledge. Knowledge of languages allows people to communicate with each other, discover the world, and get to know each other, a value with extraordinary impact and power. There are as many points of view as there are researchers. While one may disagree with them, debate them, or pay tribute to them, one must take into account that many scholars have devoted their time, and often their entire lives, to the study of translation. Whatever our opinion of them, they open up a range of new opportunities for translators, including translators of specialised texts. And the multitude of theories, movements, and research undertaken only testifies to what an interesting and complex phenomenon translation is.

---

3 It is worth recalling at this point the work of Walter Benjamin (2018) *The Task of the Translator*, which initiated this interpretation of translation.

4 For more on feminist translation, see the work of Pisarska and Tomaszkiewicz.

1.2. Corpus translation studies as a methodology for translation research

This work follows the most up-to-date trends in the field of translation studies, in particular, corpus-based translation studies, which is described later in the work. Lucja Biel (2015) states that corpus-based translation studies is the result of the linguistic interests of translation scholars. It is interdisciplinary, as it draws on the tools of corpus linguistics, cognitive linguistics, discourse analysis, Michael Halliday's systemic-functional grammar, ethnolinguistics, and neurolinguistics. In the 21st century, we benefit from the scientific achievements of linguists who lived in times that are now distant to us, in a different reality, including that of language. Nowadays, the world is changing at a very fast pace, and the ubiquitous computerisation, which has extended to practically every area of life, has not left linguistics unaffected.

The linguistics within which this work is thematically situated is computer-based corpus linguistics. Its inception dates back to the 1950s, while the rapid growth of the field occurred in the 1970s and 1980s. A new discipline, called corpus linguistics, then emerged (Lewandowska-Tomaszczyk, 2005b: 9)[5]. Barbara Lewandowska-Tomaszczyk (2005b), in a collective work on corpus linguistics[6], states that the impetus for the emergence of this field was a new view of grammar (different from Chomsky's previous conception),[7] inspired by the research of William Labov (ibid.: 10).[8] As a result

5 Łukasz Piątkowski, a Germanist, states in his work on corpus linguistics that it gained the status of a scientific discipline in the 1990s. He refers in this regard to the work of P. Baker, *Sociolinguistics and Corpus Linguistics*, Edinburgh 2010, p. 5.

6 It is one of the first works (if not the first) in Poland dedicated to the topic of corpus linguistics.

7 Lewandowska-Tomaszczyk points to native speaker intuition in Chomsky's terms, defined as the idealised ability of a language user to make unambiguous judgements about the grammaticality of context-free sentences, thus in terms of the generative model. In Labov's case, on the other hand, the concept of probability was used.

8 Labov's interests (1996, after: Lewandowska-Tomaszczyk, 2005b: 10) focused on grammar as a system of social communication, taking into account the more or less frequent use of certain linguistic forms and constructions.

of Labov's research, the focus began to be 'on linguistic usus, usage, viewed in terms of the frequency of occurrence of a form' (ibid.: 10). The timing was favourable for this type of research, as it was a moment of development in information technology, computers, and computer software. Thanks to the new equipment and the use of appropriate applications, linguists have been able to collect extensive research material and analyse it quickly and efficiently. The result of this work was the emergence of computational linguistics, a field at the interface of linguistics and computer science.

> Computer linguistics deals with the computer processing (analysis) and production (synthesis) of natural language. The main focus of computational linguistics is so-called *language* technology, which includes the understanding and generation of speech, the development of knowledge representation systems within the framework of so-called *ontologies*, machine *translation* or computational lexicography (Lewandowska-Tomaszczyk, 2005b: 11).

Łukasz Piątkowski (2018: 2), on the other hand, argues that the main goal of computational linguistics is to analyse large amounts of linguistic data in a short period of time, using new technologies.

The new field of linguistics has given researchers the opportunity to use computational tools to collect a huge amount of research material that would have taken a lot of time to analyse using traditional methods. Computers have enabled research to be carried out more efficiently and effectively. Corpus linguistics, which is a branch of computational linguistics, deals with the analysis of language collected in language corpora (Lewandowska-Tomaszczyk, 2005b: 11).[9] Lewandowska-Tomaszczyk asks to what extent corpus linguistics represents a new type of linguistics and to what extent it represents a new method of collecting, storing, and retrieving linguistic data. Leaving this question unresolved, he identifies two types of action within this new field. Corpus linguistics, as understood by Lewandowska-Tomaszczyk (2005b: 12), can mean both 'activities at the interface between computer science and linguistics, i.e., the production of new tools for the analysis of language and the possibilities of using these

---

9 The definition of a language corpus as well as the types of corpora will be described in detail later in the paper. Lewandowska-Tomaszczyk (2005b: 13) defines a corpus as 'a collection of authentic linguistic texts, spoken and written, representing different varieties, styles and text types'.

tools', as well as using them 'to discover new properties and features of language, which in turn produces a new conception of language itself'.

Nowadays, we have become so accustomed to the existence of corpora and working with them that one can repeat after the creators of the National Corpus of the Polish Language that 'without access to a corpus it is impossible today to carry out linguistic research, write dictionaries or textbooks of foreign languages, create search engines taking into account the Polish variety, computer translators or other programs of advanced language technology' (NKJP: National Corpus of Polish Language, 2020).

Corpus analysis is used in both qualitative and quantitative research (Lewandowska-Tomaszczyk, 2005b; Malak, 2011; Pawłowski, 2001; Piątkowski, 2018), and provides a range of possibilities and tools for doing so.[10] Corpus-based methods can be applied to a wide range of fields, for example, translation studies, cultural studies, and even glottodidactic studies (Lenko-Szymańska, Gruszczyńska, 2016), as 'corpus data are an irreplaceable source of information for researchers representing a wide range of different disciplines dealing with language, from purely theoretical research to natural language processing' (ibid.: 1).

In Poland, there are still few publications on corpus-based research and a lack of tools for its implementation. In Anglo-Saxon or even Czech research circles, the subject of corpus research is of great interest – there are numerous publications devoted to the tools and techniques of their implementation.[11]

In choosing a methodology to conduct the research for this work, the author drew on both Polish research and foreign works in the field of corpus

---

10 German language area researcher Elżbieta Dziurewicz (2015, after: Piątkowski, 2018: 133) argues that in linguistic research, corpus-based analyses have applications in lexicography, in traductology, in language learning, in sociolinguistics, in text linguistics, and in pragmatics, but also in traditional linguistics: morphology, syntax, and phraseology.

11 A noteworthy paper by researcher Kinga Wąsińska from the University of Silesia is entitled *Corpus Linguistics – an attempt to evaluate new research tools on the basis of the book Corpus Linguistic for Grammar. A Guide for Research by Christian Jones and Daniel Waller* (London-New York 2015, 201 p.). Wąsińska describes corpus-based research from a glottodidactic perspective using the reading of English researchers as an example.

research. The methodology adopted is corpus-based translation studies as interpreted by Biel in her 2015 article *Corpus-based Translation Studies*. She classifies this methodology as follows:

> On Holmes' map of translation studies, corpus-based translation studies can be placed among basic research *(pure translation studies)* in the so-called *descriptive* or empirical stream *(descriptive translation studies)*, but also among applied research (e.g., the use of corpora in translation didactics). In the classification of major research streams proposed by Marco, which includes the text-descriptive model, the cognitive model, the cultural model and the sociological model, corpus-based translation studies fits into the text-descriptive model. Hatim, on the other hand, classifies corpus-based translation studies as empirical research and research on the process of translation (Biel, 2015: 19).

In Poland, the terms 'corpus research' or 'corpus analysis' are most commonly used. However, this is a gross oversimplification. Theorists and practitioners draw attention to the fact that corpus research methodologies are heterogeneous (Biel, 2015; Grabowski, Hebal-Jezierska, 2016; McEnery, Wilson, 1996). Elena Tognini-Bonelli (2002), who created the terminology for this type of research, proposed an approach that seems to be one of the more popular and widely adopted in corpus analysis. As Hebal-Jezierska (2016) writes, the differences in corpus-based research lie in the different approaches to the status of linguistic data, the direction of analysis, and the role of translator intuition. Hebal-Jezierska points to two possibilities. These are:

1. the so-called *corpus-driven approach*, or inductive approach. The analysis of the linguistic data takes place after it has been extracted from the texts, only then is the appropriate theory selected. The raw linguistic data, i.e., word forms not framed by any theory of language, are analysed. Research hypotheses are formed on the basis of quantitative data on word usage, distribution, or sequences in the text;
2. the so-called *corpus-based approach* – a reverse deductive research approach. The researcher first selects a theory of language, then sets a research hypothesis, and only then, as a result of the research conducted, verifies it. With this method, it is possible to analyse, for example, idioms, phrases,[12] expressions, or verbo-nominal phrases (Grabowski, Hebal-Jezierska, 2016: 68).

12 A phrase is understood in this case as a single word or phrase that, when analysed using a computer, allows specific content to be retrieved.

Selecting a single method for corpus-based research is, however, difficult, as Biel (2015) also highlights, suggesting the use of methodological triangulation. This is an option where the use of several research methods in a single project should be considered (this procedure can also apply to the use of several research theories or techniques). When viewed in this way, it becomes important to note that none of the methods used is better or worse than the others,[13] and this strategy is intended to enable a broader view of the problem under investigation, to make more accurate observations, and ultimately to produce better quality research results. As Agata Stolecka-Makowska writes: 'Through methodological triangulation, it is possible to gather data to create broad, deep and contextual knowledge. Triangulation makes it possible to minimise the inadequacies and drawbacks of the individual research methods used separately and to maintain the reliability and validity of the inference, ensuring the reliability of the research results' (Stolecka-Makowska, 2016: 52).

By applying the triangulation procedure (see Tab. 1), the author of this work aimed to obtain the widest possible spectrum of information concerning the problematic corpus research conducted on the texts of civil law contracts.

Tab. 1: Research methods and techniques used and type of information obtained

Method	Information obtained
Comparative analysis of parallel texts of civil law contracts in Czech and Polish	differences and similarities between texts without any translation intention; verification of the incompatibility of legal systems; characterisation of the functioning of texts in each cultural context and legal system

(*continued*)

13 Each method has specific characteristics, thus producing a different type of data. Therefore, no one method can be regarded as better or worse than the others (Kędzior, Karcz, 2010).

Tab. 1: Continued

Method	Information obtained
Contrastive research using interactive corpus search	verifying the use of a dictionary term in a modern language (in the corpus of the language of civil law contracts); answering the question of to what extent dictionary terms are used in the reality of a given legal system and target culture
Quantitative studies (attendance lists), collocations, concordances	examination of the most frequently occurring words, verb-nominal phrases and phrases in the Czech and Polish language versions of civil law contracts; examination of the phrase environment
Terminology	excerpting specialised terminology
Email questionnaire	translation as a product – understanding the perspectives of the client, the contractor, and the end user of the text

Source: Author's own development.

As mentioned above, the aim of this work is to investigate the so-called translational universals in terms of the hypothesis put forward by Baker.[14] This issue arose when *descriptive translation studies* emerged in translation work. Research projects based on this methodology require the preparation of a parallel bilingual corpus[15] containing texts in the source language and

14 The term *translation universals* was introduced by Mona Baker. It first appeared in a 1993 article entitled *Corpus linguistics and translation studies – implications and applications*. Mona Baker has put forward the much-debated thesis that there are linguistic features that occur with greater frequency in translated texts than in texts that are not translations. The assumption is also accompanied by the condition that these features are not due to the influence of the original language on the target language, although this approach is now considered a radical version of this thesis. Mona Baker herself is considered to have pioneered corpus-based translational research in the 1990s, publishing a series of articles on the subject. The stimulus to undertake research related to corpus translation studies came from polysystems theory, Toury's translation studies, and skopos theory (Biel, 2015).

15 Corpus research, as Biel (2015: 20) says, is based on two principles formulated by Michael Stubbs: (1) the observer must not interfere with the object of observation, i.e., research must be performed on authentic texts; (2) recurring events are important – frequency and distribution play a key role.

texts in the target language. Translation universals include such phenomena as *avoidance of repetitions present in the source text*, *simplification*, *normalization*, *discourse transfer*, *distinctive distribution of lexical items*, and *explicitation* (Baker, 1993: 243; Laviosa, 2011: 306).

This work attempts to conduct contrastive research using a corpus of civil law contracts and to answer the question of whether such translation universals also exist for close, related languages. As Stubbs (2004, after: Biel, 2015: 20) points out, 'corpora show what is "central and typical, normal and expected" in the use of language, they also demonstrate that language provides us with numerous "prefabrications". The focus is not on words, but on repeated units (lexical-grammatical patterns)'.

Verbo-nominal phrases were also studied in accordance with the methodology developed in the German-speaking area of linguistics by, among others, Alain Kamber, Janusz Taborek, and Elżbieta Dziurewicz.[16] Firstly, the characteristic verbo-nominal phrases were identified from the dictionary, and then, based on corpus research, their use and usage were verified. During the study, the Lewandowska-Tomaszczyk matrix (Tab. 2) was used and adapted as appropriate to the units studied.[17]

Tab. 2: Example of a matrix for the term 'termination'

Domena	Prawo
Subdomena	prawo zobowiązaniowe
Język	Polski
Termin	wypowiedzenie (umowy o pracę)
Kategoria gramatyczna	rzeczownik
Definicja	jednostronne oświadczenie woli pracownika lub pracodawcy, które ma na celu rozwiązanie umowy o pracę wraz z upływem wypowiedzenia
Synonim	–
Kolokacja	–

(*continued*)

16 Based on the methodology of these researchers, a pilot study was carried out, as presented in a paper by Lukasz Piątkowski (2018: 134).

17 The matrix is taken from the book *Podstawy językoznawstwa korpusowego* by Barbara Lewandowska-Tomaszczyk.

Tab. 2: Continued

	czasownik: (kontekst lewostronny): powiadomić o ~, wystąpić z ~ (kontekst prawostronny): ~ uskutecznia się, ~ wymaga, ~ może nastąpić
	rzeczownik: (kontekst lewostronny) okres ~, początek ~, termin ~, złożenie ~, w przypadku ~, pod rygorem ~, dokonanie ~, (kontekst prawostronny) ~ umowy, ~ zlecenia
	przymiotnik: (jedno/trzy) miesięczne ~, jednostronne ~, wcześniejsze ~
	przyimek: za ~
Przykłady użycia terminu z korpusu	okres wypowiedzenia umowy pożyczki wynosi 14 dni; Przyjmujący zobowiązuje się powiadomić Składającego z jednomiesięcznym wypowiedzeniem
Terminy pokrewne	odstąpienie

Source: Lewandowska-Tomaszczyk, 2005: 193.

The final stage of the research is the analysis of email questionnaires addressed to principals, contractors, and target recipients of the translations.

1.3. Corpus analysis and its tools

1.3.1. The corpus and its types

Several definitions of the term 'corpus' have emerged in corpus linguistics.[18] Lewandowska-Tomaszczyk (2005b: 26) takes as a corpus a collection of

18 The term 'corpus' was already known in antiquity, as discussed by Łukasz Grabowski and Milena Hebal-Jezierska in their paper. Originally, the term referred to non-linguistic collections of texts. One of the earliest corpora was the 'Corpus Iuris Civilis' dating from the 6th century, created on the initiative of Emperor Justinian I the Great. It was a collection of early Roman law with examples and an interpretation of the new law. By the 18th century, on the other hand, the term 'corpus' was already identified with a linguistic collection of texts. 'The Latin Corpus Glossary' can serve as an example. The development

written texts or records of spoken language. However, a corpus framed in linguistic terms (a linguistic corpus) requires some refinement. To be able to distinguish a simple set of texts from a linguistic corpus, several conditions are required. The first description of such conditions was formulated in 1996 by John Sinclair. He believed that a corpus could be defined as a collection of linguistic creations organised and selected according to specific criteria, which include: quantity (the corpus should contain a significant number of words), quality (the collected data should be characterised by authenticity), simplicity (in Sinclair's time it was a matter of encoding in pure ASCII computer format, today Unicode formatting is in force), and documentation (the collected linguistic data in a corpus should be fully and accurately documented, preferably in the form of a separate database) (Lewandowska-Tomaszczyk, 2005b: 27).

A different set of criteria was proposed by Lancaster University researchers Tony McEnery and Andrew Wilson. A collection of texts called a language corpus should have attributes such as representativeness (the corpus should be as representative as possible of the language area of interest), finite size (precise word count),[19] electronic format (computer processing of text data), and reference to a standard variety of the language in question (the corpus should be representative of the language area in question). Ewa Kraskowska defines electronic language corpora as huge collections of digitised texts – language utterances – or samples thereof selected according to specific criteria. These can be scope, form, or temporal reference. Such collections are, according to this definition, used to analyse various linguistic phenomena (Kraskowska, 2018: 87). A linguistic corpus, on the other hand, as understood by Piątkowski, is not only a collection of texts but also metadata containing information on the author, date of publication, and place of appearance of the analysed textual unit, as well as linguistic annotations

---

of corpus linguistics was brought about by English research from the 18th century (Grabowski, Hebal-Jezierska, 2016: 65–85).

19 Lewandowska-Tomaszczyk comments on this aspect as controversial, pointing out that there are two distinct approaches to this issue. Researchers from the Birmingham centre favour a view that pays homage to the idea of an open corpus, i.e., a monitoring corpus, in contrast to the Lancaster researchers who advocate the idea of a closed corpus, i.e., a reference corpus, referring to a given period (Lewandowska-Tomaszczyk, 2005b: 29).

(grammatical qualifiers), e.g., distinguishing parts of speech, identifying the side or aspect of a verb, or the singular or plural of a noun (Lemnitzer, 2015; Piątkowski, 2018). Corpora are designed to enable researchers to observe how modern language functions. Depending on the type of research conducted,[20] several types of corpora can be distinguished, as presented in the graphic below (Fig. 1).

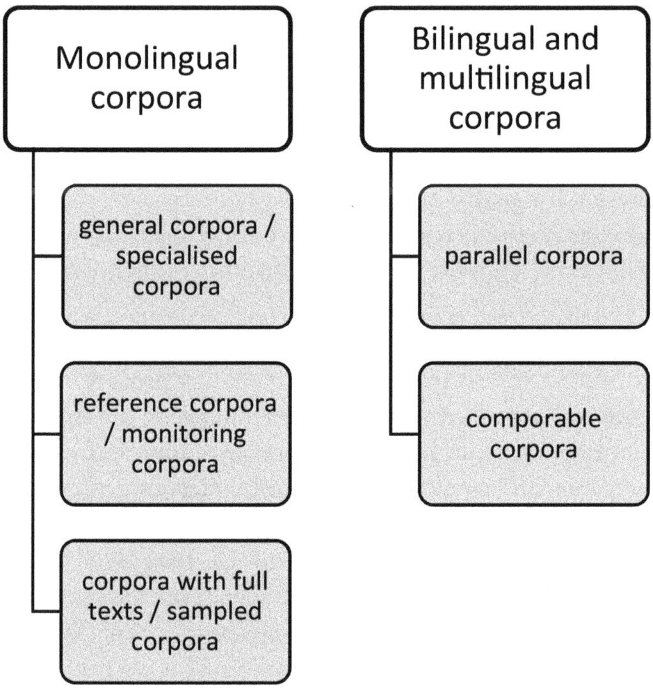

Fig. 1: Classification of corpora
Source: Own development based on: Waliński, 2005: 27–41.

20 The work of Łukasz Grabowski and Milena Hebal-Jezierska, already referred to, also presents an interpretation of the notion of corpus in the context of linguistic research, which treats corpora as an experimental base, enabling them to verify existing linguistic theories or develop new research hypotheses, while corpus linguists focus on statistical research, on the frequency of occurrence of linguistic units and classes. In order to confirm or reject a given hypothesis, researchers use authentic texts produced in real communication situations (Grabowski, Hebal-Jezierska, 2016).

Regarding the number of languages in the corpus, a distinction is made between monolingual corpora (which contain untranslated texts in one language, for example, the 'National Corpus of Polish' or the 'Czech National Corpus'),[21] and bilingual and multilingual corpora (which contain texts in two or more languages). This classification is presented in Fig. 1. Among monolingual corpora, we can distinguish between general or specialised corpora, reference or monitoring corpora, and corpora with full texts or sampled corpora. The category of multilingual corpora includes parallel corpora and comparative corpora. A general corpus accommodates texts in a commonly used language familiar to the ordinary, average user. The corpus maps the language at a basic level and does not include jargon, dialects, or specialised texts (Walinski, 2005). In contrast to a general corpus, a specialised corpus includes texts specific to a particular branch or field, and specific specialised terminology – these may be legal, technical, or medical texts, etc. The purpose of a specialised corpus is to present the language functioning in a particular field or industry. A specialised corpus is characterised by an appropriately selected collection of texts that may be typical of a particular field or a specific type of text. Selection criteria can also include the author or the date of the text. A specialised corpus may also be separated from a general corpus, according to the criteria chosen, and thus constitute a subcorpus.

A reference corpus is a closed corpus. It presents the use of language in a given period, as opposed to a monitoring corpus, which is constantly updated and changed. Corpora may contain full texts (for example, the full wording of contracts or legal acts) or only representative extracts (for example, only data protection clauses, interview excerpts, or excerpts from books).

Among multilingual corpora, we distinguish between parallel corpora *(parallel corpus, translation corpus)*, which contain texts in the source language and texts in the target language (translated texts), and comparable corpora, which contain untranslated texts. Parallel corpora are also known as translation corpora. The texts in such a corpus are linked at the

---

21 A typology of corpora has been developed by, among others, Jacek Waliński (2005) and Lucia Biel (2015).

sentence level – a sentence in the source language is matched to a sentence in the target language. Comparable corpora are several corpora (at least two) of similar size that contain texts that can be compared with each other and are therefore prepared and selected based on analogous criteria. Biel (2015) further distinguishes the category of a comparative-parallel corpus, comprising at least three categories of texts: translations, source texts, and untranslated texts in the target language.

For the purpose of carrying out the research in this work, the author attempted to prepare a parallel corpus containing texts written in Czech and translated into Polish. It is the intention of the author to create a specialised corpus covering the texts of civil law contracts. The reference corpus consists of the 'National Corpus of Polish' and the 'Czech National Corpus', as well as the EUR-Lex database of EU texts. The corpus was prepared using the Sketch Engine tool.

The question of the importance of corpora in the translator's work should be asked at this point. Corpora are a very valuable tool. By being able to study the functioning of phraseological compounds, syntax, and verbo-nominal units in the modern target language, the translator can prepare a high-quality translation with the standards of the target language. He or she can also observe how a particular expression functions in the language of translation, thus demonstrating not only experience in translation but also linguistic erudition. Obtaining knowledge of how an expression works in a given context and linguistic setting is very time-consuming and often difficult, and looking up expressions in dictionaries does not always guarantee that a given interpretation is correct in the context of the text being translated. Furthermore, corpora – unlike dictionaries – contain up-to-date data. It should be noted that, unfortunately, there are still few translators using these tools, and translators are sometimes unaware of their existence and availability. Translators working on so-called CATs (CAT – *computer-assisted translation*) can additionally prepare a corpus containing a rich and already tested terminology database, which can be quickly browsed and searched.[22] Corpora offer a range of possibilities that are not a closed circle,

22 The author uses the Trados Studio tool in her professional work. By being able to create terminology databases, so-called translation memories, as appropriate to the translations in question, she was able to create her own parallel corpus.

but continue to expand the field for research, exploration, and practical application in the translation process.

1.3.2. Corpus analysis software

There are several programmes available to carry out corpus research, search linguistic databases, or create new corpora.[23] The author of this work chose to use a paid programme called Sketch Engine.[24] The creator of the programme is the late linguist, Adam Kilgarriff. The programme was established in 2003 and is being developed by an English-Czech team of researchers. Sketch Engine (SE) supports more than 90 languages, has tools for working with parallel corpora, and, more importantly, by using Trados Studio for translators, for example, you can very quickly and efficiently prepare your own corpus. Thanks to the fact that SE supports work in both Czech and Polish, it was possible, for the purposes of this study, to prepare a corpus of more than 1 million words. The corpus was created based on the translation memory held and developed by the author from the Trados Studio programme, with which she has been carrying out translation assignments for more than seven years. SE's developers claim that it is a unique tool for exploring the mechanisms of language. SE algorithms analyse authentic texts. This database has more than one trillion words. The programme shows what is typical of the language and what is peculiar, what is unusual and what language mechanisms have been used in new ways. As a tool for linguists, translators, or lexicographers, SE was designed to analyse text as well as conduct text research. In advertising their services, the software developers suggest that SE is the first-choice tool for publishers, universities,[25] translation agencies, and national language institutes worldwide. SE contains 500 ready-to-use corpora in more than 90 languages. Each corpus holds 30 trillion words, so it can

---

Corpus building is a very interesting experience. It opens the translator to new possibilities and teaches them how to draw additional knowledge from completed translation projects.

23 A summary of software for analysing monolingual corpora is presented in tabular form by Lucja Biel (2015) in her paper 'Corpus Translation Studies'.

24 www.sketchengine.eu

25 In Poland, the University of Warsaw, for example, uses the software.

reliably demonstrate how a language works. At the word level, the SE can present typical word combinations and collocations, indicate synonyms, compare a word with other words, give an example of usage, as well as find the translation of a word into another language. At the phrase level, the SE can show typical combinations and example uses of the phrase in context. At the text level, SE can, for example, generate monolingual and bilingual terminology, neologisms, and statistical data. It should be noted that the programme developers have also taken care of their customers – a great many training presentations of several minutes have been uploaded to YouTube. The mechanics of the corpus tool are presented in an accessible and understandable way. As a result, even a newcomer to the field can assimilate the knowledge contained in the training courses in a relatively short period of time and prepare his or her own body of work. The support of the SE team is an added advantage – queries handled by email are treated as a priority, and responses and feedback are provided very reliably and in a timely manner. Below is a presentation of the basic methods and tools provided by SE that are required for corpus research.

Tab. 3: Research methods used in corpus analysis

Research method	Description of research method options
Interactive search	Ability to search for words, sequences of characters, and phrases. The system searches for information according to the query, which is displayed on the screen in the form of lists/tables. The very clear layout of the site makes the tool a pleasure to use, and it is quick to work through the material collected.
Hashing (lemmatisation)	Hashing, otherwise known as lemmatisation, is the connection of different inflectional forms of the same word to its basic form (lemma, lexeme). A lexeme is, for example, the infinitive for a verb, or the nominative for a noun. Such an action serves to make the presentation of attendance lists more reliable and of better quality.

(*continued*)

Tab. 3: Continued

Research method	Description of research method options
Frequency lists	Frequency lists are one of the basic tools in quantitative research. They show the frequency with which words, phrases, and word forms are used. This allows, for example, a foreign language learner to see which words and phrases are most commonly used in a modern language.
Keywords	This option allows the retrieval of keywords/terminology specific to the subject matter of the corpus. Keywords distinguish the corpus from the reference corpus by showing the corpus' domain, and what terminology is dominant in the corpus. The Keywords function applies to both words alone and multi-word combinations.
Word sketch	This function allows the presentation of word collocations and the observation of the behaviour of other lexical units in the vicinity of a given collocation.[a]
Concordance	The tool has a range of search options and allows searching for words, phrases, tags,[b] documents, text types, or corpus structures, presenting the results in context, in the form of concordances. The results can be sorted and filtered so that further research can be conducted as efficiently as possible.[c]
Collocations	This is one of the most interesting features in terms of the translator's work, as it shows the most common word combinations in the language. These are, for example, idiomatic phrases or expressions, or such combinations of words that have become established in a particular language. These connections are shown as occurring in specific contexts (see also: Lewandowska-Tomaszczyk, 2005: 39).

(*continued*)

Tab. 3: Continued

Research method	Description of research method options
Thesaurus	This option allows the automatic generation of a list of synonyms or words belonging to the same category (semantic field). The list is created based on the context in which the word occurs in the selected corpus. Most corpora only support nouns, adjectives, verbs, and adverbs.

Source: Author's own development.

a Biel (2015) describes this function as 'automatically creating "maps" of the grammatical and collocational behaviour of words'.

b Tags that provide information about the structure of the text, unusual or incorrect words and constructions, and characterise the authors and participants in the conversation. Source: based on the description of the corpus structure after: SJP, 2020.

c Tomaszczyk-Lewandowska (2005: 118), citing Sinclair's work, explains that 'a concordance is a collection of examples of the use of a given word form, each presented in its own textual environment'. It is considered to be one of the most important and basic tools for corpus analysis, as it contains certain patterns of word usage.

Thanks to the abundant information on the SE website and the instructional videos on YouTube, the above methods become very accessible and positive results can be achieved in a relatively short period of time. An undoubted advantage of SE is that it supports Trados Studio files so that the specialist text translator can create effective tools on an ongoing basis for specific assignments.

1.3.3. National Corpus of Polish Language

The 'National Corpus of Polish Language' (hereafter NKJP) was created as a joint initiative of the Institute of Computer Science at the Polish Academy of Sciences (acting as the project coordinator), the Institute of Polish Language at the Polish Academy of Sciences, the Polish Scientific Publishers PWN, and the Department of Computational and Corpus Linguistics at the University of Łódź. This is a research and development project of the Ministry of Science and Higher Education. The project team consists of: Mirosław Bańko, Rafał L. Górski, Barbara Lewandowska-Tomaszczyk, Marek Łaziński, Piotr Pęzik, Adam Przepiórkowski, and the teams for administration, programming work, linguistic work, text acquisition, and support. Thanks to this initiative, alongside the British, Czechs, Germans, Russians and many other nations, the Poles can also boast their own language corpus. The NKJP is a reference corpus of more than one and a half billion words. Corpora for inflectional languages require more complex and specialised tools. NKJP has tools that make it possible to search resources in such a way as to include the inflexion of Polish words or even to analyse the construction of Polish sentences[26]. As you can read on the project website, the corpus contains texts from the classics of Polish literature, the daily press, and the specialist press, as well as internet texts and recordings of interviews.

Tab. 4: Typology of NKJP texts

Text type
Fiction (poetry, prose, drama)
Non-fiction
Quasi-speech texts
Non-fiction books not classified
Letters
Spoken conversational texts
Spoken media texts
Scientific and didactic type
Informative and advisory type
Other written texts (clerical type, persuasive texts, advertisements, political propaganda, short instructional texts)
Publicity and short press releases
Internet (a) interactive websites, forums, chat rooms (b) static web pages

Source: Own compilation based on information on the NKJP website.

The project's website provides a full summary of the books and press texts included in the corpus. NKJP also constitutes the material base for the new *Great Dictionary of the Polish Language*, which is being developed at the Institute of Polish Language at the Polish Academy of Sciences, while

26 All information on the NKJP was taken from www.nkjp.pl.

researchers use some of the corpus texts in their work on the Polish-Russian Corpus project, affiliated with the Faculty of Polish Studies at the UW in cooperation with the Pedagogical University of Ufa and the Russian National Corpus.[27] The most important feature of the corpus, however, in addition to its wealth of sources and resources, is its free availability to all users. Work on the corpus has been ongoing since 2007, when the project received a funding grant. They are run by the PELCRA team in the Department of English Language and Applied Linguistics at the University of Łódź. In the introduction to the collective work on the NKJP, one can read that the 1960s brought an increased interest among linguists in studies devoted to the frequency of use of different linguistic forms and the probability of their occurrence in different varieties of language (Przepiórkowski et al., 2012: 11). A language corpus is defined as 'a computerised collection of authentic linguistic texts, spoken and written, representing different varieties, styles and types of texts' (ibid.). The first commonly used language corpus was a million-word corpus. It was created in the 1960s by Henry Kučera and Nelson Francis and focused on American English. The corpus now comprises hundreds of millions or even billions of units. In Poland, the first corpus-based dictionary of the Polish language was the attendance lists of different varieties of Polish from the 1960s.

Tab. 5: Application of corpora materials

Place of application
Quantification of dialectological/sociolinguistic research
Development of dictionaries
In studies
Development of teaching materials
In cultural studies
In translations
Language research on different user groups
In literary studies
In computational linguistics for natural language processing using machine learning methods

Source: Compiled from information contained in the NKJP publication.

27 The NKJP website also contains an extensive bibliography of literature on NKJP.

Piotr Pęzik, co-author of the NKJP, describes the corpus of Polish as a reference corpus. This corpus represents not only the general register of the language. It is intended to represent the use of very different registers and functional types of language (Pęzik, 2012). The researcher draws attention to the role a corpus can play in the work of a translator (ibid.: 301–310). He emphasises that the quality of a translation depends first and foremost on the understanding of the source text and only later on the linguistic competence of the translator.[28] In the translator's work, the primary corpus tool is the parallel corpus, which allows direct comparison between units in the source language and in the target language that are related to each other. However, the reference corpus[29] is also a very valuable tool for the translator, as it possesses many features that an informed and experienced translator can use to ensure that the text is not only translated efficiently, but that it acquires additional qualities.

28 Pęzik (2012) refers to the old Latin maxim *Rem tene, verba sequentur.*

29 Pęzik (2012) defines a reference corpus as 'a large, bibliographically, structurally and linguistically annotated, diverse collection of written and spoken texts'.

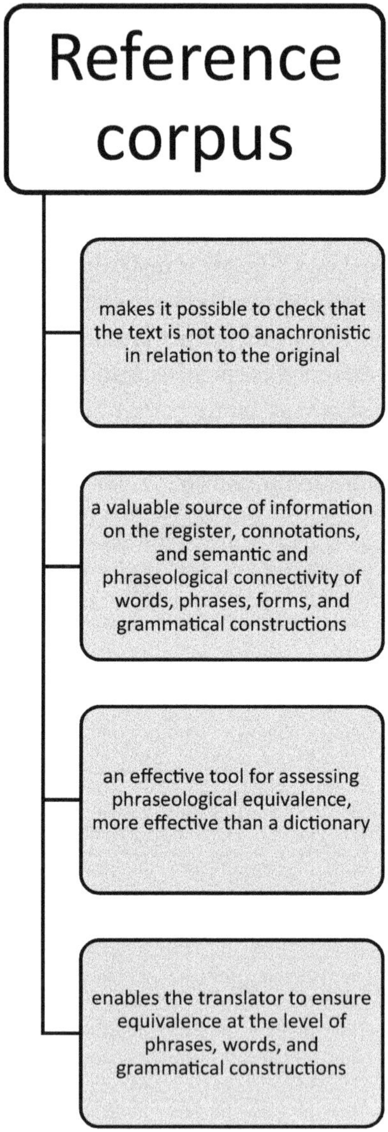

Fig. 2: The reference corpus and its advantages
Source: Own compilation based on information in the 2012 NKJP publication.

Pęzik emphasises that the reference corpus significantly influences the quality of translation work. It enables verification of the correctness and phraseological and lexical-grammatical equivalence of translations. Dictionaries, unfortunately, cannot provide such a multi-faceted verification of the translation, with such a wide range of information in terms of collocations, terms, multi-word nouns, and idioms. It is at this level that the translator should strive to maintain a balance between the original and the translation (Pęzik, 2012: 303). The corpus can be an ideal supplement to dictionaries when proofreading and verifying a translation. In addition, it can also serve as an effective means of making the translation 'not only more faithful to the original, but also more grammatically correct and accessible to the reader' (ibid.: 310).

1.3.4. Czech National Corpus

The 'Czech National Corpus' (*Český národní korpus*, hereafter ČNK)[30] is an academic project launched in 1994 and run at FF UK.[31] The corpus is administered by the *Ústav Českého národního korpusu*. The purpose of the corpus is to map the Czech language and other languages against the Czech language. As in Poland, access to the corpus is free of charge, although prior registration is required. The ČNK website defines a corpus as an electronic collection of authentic texts (written or spoken) in which relevant linguistic phenomena can be easily searched for, and their functioning in a given context can be observed.

The ČNK is a much older project than the NKJP, moreover, it is constantly being developed and supplemented by the research team. The data is continuously being updated, and there are more and more tools and applications that enable increasingly broad and detailed use of the corpora. From the translator's point of view, the ČNK's very extensive parallel corpus, InterCorp, is certainly worthy of attention. The primary tool for working with these corpora is the KonText application, which, by

30 www.korpus.cz.

31 FF UK – *Filozofická fakulta Univerzity Karlovy*, Faculty of Arts, Charles University, Prague.

entering simple queries into a search engine, can produce attendance and quality data. The SyD application, on the other hand, makes it possible to study variants, e.g., how often a particular variant is used today and in the history of the Czech language. The Morfio application allows for the search of word relationships.

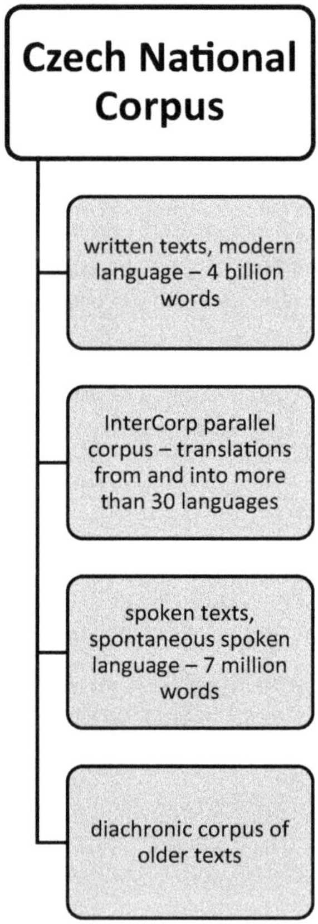

Fig. 3: Czech National Corpus – typology of texts
Source: Own compilation based on information at www.korpus.cz.

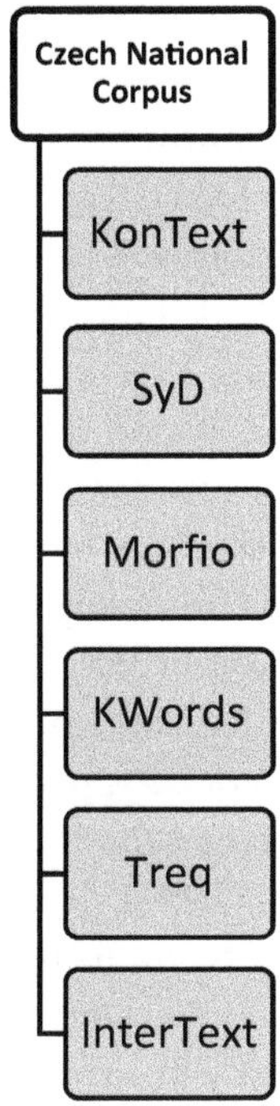

Fig. 4: Czech National Corpus–- some of the resource applications
Source: Own compilation based on information at www.korpus.cz.

It is worth mentioning the numerous manuals and extensive training and support for ČNK users. ČNK websites are enriched with fresh information and new data, webinars are organised, and implementation programmes are frequent. The ČNK is a very reliable source of knowledge for linguists, but, as with the NKJP, it is, primarily thanks to InterCorp, a great tool for translators.

1.4. Criteria for the selection of source material

In analysing the translation studies carried out so far, the author of this work has drawn on both the literature on the study of Czech and Polish texts, as well as on materials constituting a study of the translation of specialist texts in German and English. Research from the Anglo-Saxon area should certainly be considered more comprehensive and broader than for the Slavic languages, as well as more advanced. These materials inspired the analyses in this work. In this work, the author draws primarily on the corpus research publications *Corpora in Translation Studies* by Mona Baker (1995) and *Corpus Linguistics at Work* by Elena Tognini-Bonelli (2001). On the other hand, from the area of Polish literature on the subject, the author refers to the works of Barbara Tomaszczyk-Lewandowska and Łucja Biel, as well as to such publications by Danuta Kierzkowska as *Tłumaczenie prawnicze* (2002) and *Dokumenty polskie. Wybór dla tłumaczy sądowych* (2007), as well as to Anna Jopek-Bosiacka's *Przekład prawny i sądowy* (2006). As far as Czech authors who address the issue of legal and juridical translation in their research are concerned, the following works are worth noting: Michal Tomášek, *Překlad v právní praxi* (1998), *Antologie odborného překladu* (2007), Tomáš Duběda, David Mraček, and Vanda Obdržálková, *Překlad do nemateřského jazyka. Fakta, otázky, perspektivy* (2018); Edvard Lotko, *Čeština a polština v překladatelské a tlumočnické praxi* (1986), *Synchronní konfrontace češtiny a polštiny* (1997). In addressing the issue of equivalence in translation, the author refers to the publication *Ekwiwalencja w tłumaczeniu tekstów prawnych i prawniczych* by Anna Kizińska (2015). Literature on examinations for sworn translators, both in Poland and the Czech Republic, was also helpful. Artur Dariusz Kubacki devotes considerable attention to the quality of certified translations and parallel texts in his noteworthy works such as *Tłumaczenie poświadczone: status, kształcenie, warsztat i odpowiedzialność* (2012), *Teksty paralelne jako narzędzie pomocnicze przy sporządzaniu tłumaczeń (specjalistycznych)* (2001). In turn, the publication *Jak czytać, rozumieć i tłumaczyć dokumenty prawnicze i gospodarcze* by Leszek Berezowski (2018) provided a better insight into the issues of reading and understanding specialised texts properly.

This work is devoted to the study of the language of civil law contracts, therefore, the source material for the analysis is the text of such contracts. The observations were carried out using several research methods and techniques. The analysis included civil law contracts in Czech and in Polish. The agreements were not translations but were created to function in the Czech and Polish legal systems respectively. Drawing on parallel texts,[32]

32 Parallel texts and their role in the translator's work will be discussed later in the paper.

the work author sought to characterise their function in each legal system. The content of the documents without any intention of translation was obtained from Czech and Polish law offices, and the texts of contracts that the author received as an entrepreneur running her company were also used. The study considered contractual agreements, namely:

- donation agreement;
- work contract;
- service agreement;
- cooperation agreement;
- sales contract;
- lease agreement.

Only civil law contracts of obligation were selected for the new corpus. The parallel texts are model contracts (they do not contain data on addresses, company names, or the parties' representatives), the condition being that they were not translations but authentic examples of documents operating in the legal system in question.

Next, excerpts from the contracts were analysed, constituting the so-called *translation memory* (a translation memory, a terminological base, was created based on translations carried out over seven years of work). Contracts included in the corpus of civil law contracts were examined using the Sketch Engine tool. The corpus included the source texts and their translations made by a group of translators. The contracts were included in the corpus after having been anonymised, but it is worth noting that the Sketch Engine tool prevents outsiders from accessing the data contained in the corpus.[33] Only the creator of the corpus can make it available. The corpus on which the research was carried out has approximately 1.5 million words, and therefore represents a relatively terminologically rich resource for conducting research and analysing linguistic phenomena.

33 The contracts included in the created corpus have been anonymised, but no outsider has access to the data contained therein without the consent of the corpus author. This is an important aspect of the research, as the analysis only covers language mechanisms, while sensitive data has been removed. Only terminology bases were examined.

1.5. Email questionnaire

The email questionnaire drawn up for this study is not a typical survey. It is more like an environmental study. The respondents were recipients and creators of translations. The responses were intended to illuminate the problem of receiving translation and working with translation as a product, and creating translation as a text in the target language, taking into account the target culture or the target legal system. A questionnaire consisting of six questions was sent by email to the respondents, who were sworn translators of different language combinations, notaries, lawyers, translation agencies, and businesses using translation services. Forty-eight respondents took part in the survey. The findings will be presented in the research section of the work.

The aim of the study is to present the role of translation as a product functioning for the recipient as a tool to realise their plans and intentions. As Douglas Robinson (1997) and Anthony Pym (1993) write, for the translator, translation is a process, while for the client, it is a product, a 'thing' that is used to achieve their own goals and objectives. The questionnaire aims to show the role of aspects such as quality, timeliness, translator experience and competence, knowledge of terminology, and precision. Respondents also answered the question of how important they consider the translator's experience in translating specialised texts to be.

2 The process of translating specialised texts

2.1. Translation of specialised texts: Dilemmas and challenges

2.1.1. Translation process

Translation is a complex and multi-faceted issue. Numerous researchers have tried to define the translation process, interpreting it in their own way. Each approach essentially assumes that translation is the transfer of a text from the source language to the target language. The aim of the process is to create equivalents in the target language and culture in such a way that the recipient can best understand them. The definitions created by the researchers indicate the essence of the different elements. Some place a stronger emphasis on the meaning of the source text, while others emphasise the search for equivalence or the purpose of translation. Table 6 provides a summary of what the author considers to be the most interesting approaches to translation.

The approach of Karl Dedecius, who argues that translation is not only the transfer of content from the source language to the target language, but also the only way to extinguish all interpersonal conflicts, seems extremely important and an interesting approach to the issue of translation these days.

Karl Dedecius, in describing the process of translation, used a certain geometrical comparison, which is presented in Fig. 5.

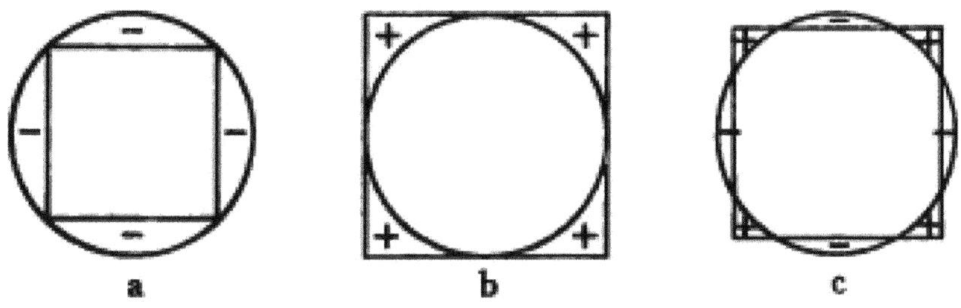

Fig. 5: The squaring of the circle according to Karl Dedecius. The square symbolises the translation, the circle symbolises the original
Source: Dedecius, 1988: 76.

Tab. 6: Translation as interpreted by researchers

Researcher	Perception of translation
Roman Jakobson	Three basic types of translation: – interlingual translation – involves translating the signs of one language into the signs of a second language; – intralinguistic translation – involves the translation of signs into other signs within one language; – intersemiotic translation – involves translating from one sign system into another sign system (Pisarska, Tomaszkiewicz, 1996).
Eugene Nida	Translation as the reproduction in the language of the recipient of the closest natural equivalent of the content conveyed in the source language, first in terms of meaning, then in terms of style (Nida, 1964).
Wolfram Wilss, Werner Koller (School of *Übersetzungswissenschaft*)	Translation being a search for equivalence (Pisarska, Tomaszkiewicz, 1996).
Hans J. Vermeer (co-inventor of the skopos theory)	Translation understood as intercultural transfer (Pisarska, Tomaszkiewicz, 1996).
Maurice Pergnier (The French School)	Understood in the context of the communicative situation, translation places particular emphasis on the analysis of the meaning of the text (Pisarska, Tomaszkiewicz, 1996).
Peter Newmark	Good translation = literal translation. The question of what literal translation actually is subject to discussion here, as defining it proves extremely difficult in the field of translation studies (Pisarska, Tomaszkiewicz, 1996).
Jiří Levý	Translation is a process of communication aimed at conveying the content of the original to a foreign reader. Translation as decision-making (Levý, 1967).

Tab. 6: Continued

Researcher	Perception of translation
Karl Dedecius	Translation seen as 'giving a name to alien beings, hitherto nameless. Interpreters create the praxis for this coexistence. They make the unfamiliar familiar and comprehensible at the same time.' Translation is the only means of extinguishing interpersonal conflicts, a means of achieving understanding (Dedecius, 1988: 30).

Source: Author's own development.

As Karl Dedecius (1988: 76) says, 'language systems relate to each other like different figures, e.g., circles and squares. Here a little too little (a), there a little too much (b), or the plus and minus values balance out evenly (c).' Figure 5 illustrates how ambiguous the situation can be for a translator faced with the challenge of translating a text where the linguistic systems of the source culture and the target culture do not match.

Dedecius then goes on to present a 'realistic and flexible' (Dedecius, 1988: 76) approach to translation issues.

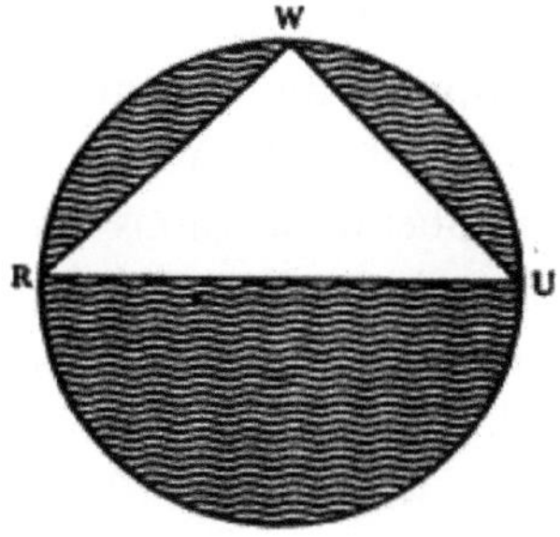

Fig. 6: Squaring the circle according to Karl Dedecius (Fig. 2)

A	B	C
1. dictionary	literality	verbal fidelity
2. syntactically	conformity of opinion	stylistic fidelity
3. phraseologically	conformity of meaning	fidelity of meaning
4. artistically	artistic consistency	fidelity of form

Source: Dedecius, 1988: 77.

Figure 6 depicts 'the forces at work (and thus both author and translator), which are subject to a subjective force of attraction in addition to objective reality' (Dedecius, 1988: 76). The letter symbols R, W, U in the figure stand for reason, will, and feeling respectively – 'arranged into a figure, a fact, a fate' (ibid.: 76). They form a triangle suspended in a 'concrete atmosphere', a triangle 'not floating disorderly in the air, but "alive" ' (ibid.: 76). The atmosphere referred to by the researcher abounds with more or less anonymous activities. 'In works of art, positions and places (priorities) are determined primarily by the manner of representation, conditioned by the nature of the imagery. So too, in the art of translation. He who translates "a" takes "b" into account in the first line and reaches "c" ' (ibid.: 77). This symbolically presented approach to translation captures its complexity and multifaceted nature. The translator faces numerous challenges in rendering content in the target language. Content transfer takes place on several levels, the available options and possibilities are never the only ones allowed, and the translator must make a choice every time. When translating, he or she makes a number of decisions that affect the final reception of the message in the target culture.

When considering the issue of specialised translation, it is possible to consider the extent to which the above definitions also apply to non-literary translations. Krzysztof Hejwowski (2012: 10) rightly argues that, in principle, the problems of specialist translation are no different from those of literary translation – in the latter case, it is simply that the density of their occurrence is much greater. Of course, each translation has its own peculiarities, and characteristic problematic issues, however, the issue always boils down to one premise, namely the most perfect rendering of the content in the target language.

Norman Davies, in his introduction to Elżbieta Tabakowska's book *O przekładzie na przykładzie. Rozprawa tłumacza z Europą Normana Daviesa* challenges the words of an English writer of the Elizabethan era, quoted in numerous works on translation, that translation is like 'the left side of a Turkish carpet'. Davies believes that 'no translation is an integral part of the original'. In his view, the translation is a new and individual creative work, modelled on the original, but at the same time distinct and full of subtle differences (Davies, 1999: 7). Instead, he offers his definition, set in the world of music:

> I think that translation is like a melody played on a different instrument and in a different key. Bach's *G-string aria*, composed for violin, can be recognised if you hear it played on a trombone in the key of B major. Some arrangements can turn out to be almost as good as Bac"s original arrangement. None, however, will sound exactly the same (Davies, 1999: 7).

The eminent Polish translator Professor Elżbieta Tabakowska, cited above, in her book *O przekładzie na przykładzie. Rozprawa tłumacza z Europą Normana Daviesa* reflects on what translation is and leans not only towards Davies' definition but also towards the interpretation of the concept of translation proposed by his wife, who believes:

> [...] translating a text is like remaking it from your grandfather's old coat. Each such alteration has to be carried out according to some one unique strategy, which in detail depends, for example, on where in the overcoat halves the grandfather burned a hole with hot pipe ash. In other words, there is no ready-made recipe for translation. All sewing courses only teach how to sew from new. By now, every dressmaker has to learn how to do this herself (Tabakowska, 1999: 24).

One should also recall the thought of Norman Shapiro, who compares a good translation to a pane of glass, which is only visible when it has cracks and blemishes – an ideal translation should be free of these, just as an ideal translation should be free of errors and imperfections (Hejwowski, 2012: 21). The sheer number of attempts at defining the translation process confirms that the translator is always faced with a challenge – he or she must know what translation is, how to translate the text, what strategy to adopt, and what techniques and tools to use so that the client receives a product that meets his or her expectations and can be used to achieve his or her goals.

The next chapter presents the expectations of the client and the expectations facing the interpreter.

2.1.2. External perspective *(user's view)*

Translation can be viewed in two ways: taking an internal perspective, from inside the process, or taking an external perspective, treating it as a product commissioned by the client. An advocate of just such an approach to translation is Douglas Robinson,[34] an American translation scholar and theorist. He argues that translation means different things to different groups of people. For creators of translation, it is identical to an action, to a certain creative process, the result of which is a translated text. For those who are not translators and are not professionally involved in translating texts, translation is simply a text, a product, or even a tool to achieve their goals (Robinson, 2003). Australian translation scholar Anthony Pym (1993)[35] argues that translation is a text from the perspective of *external knowledge* and an action (whose purpose is to produce a text) from the perspective of *internal knowledge*. According to this concept, the interpreter represents an internal perspective. He or she is in the middle of the translation process and sees the nuances and problems posed by commissioning a text to be translated. The interpreter has the capacity to understand the translation process while being aware of the limitations of the commissioned text. He or she must constantly choose from a range of possibilities, constantly make translatological decisions in the knowledge that the translation will never be as perfect as the source text. Unlike the translator, the recipient

---

34 Douglas Robinson is an acclaimed American translation scholar and theorist, as well as a practitioner – he has done many translations from Finnish. He has worked in China for more than six years, where he is Professor of Translation Studies at the Chinese University of Hong Kong. He is the author of numerous works on literary studies, translation, and rhetoric. On Professor Anthony Pym's YouTube channel (https://www.youtube.com/user/AnthonyPym), there is an interview with Douglas Robinson from six years ago on the issue of translation and Robinson's work.

35 Anthony Pym is originally from Australia and works at universities in Spain and South Africa. From 2010 to 2016, he headed the *European Society for Translation Studies*. He is active on social media, promoting translation research. He is himself a long-time practising translator.

of the text – the person commissioning the translation of the text – has no knowledge of the frailties of the translation process and the challenges faced by the translator. He or she is usually the consumer, the orderer, the entity that finances the translation, but does not speak the target language. The recipient views the translation process 'from the outside', and cares about the outcome of the process – the translated text.

Tab. 7: Translator's perspective

Translator's perspective – internal perspective – Translation as a process The most important thing is action
1. The path to translation competence
2. Acquisition and development of orders
3. Conducting research and searches
4. Cooperation in the translation environment
5. Translation of words, expressions, and registers
6. Editing and proofreading of the translated text
7. Handing over the completed order to the customer
8. Issuing an invoice and receiving payment

Source: Own development based on: Robinson, 1997.

The text has an important function in the above chain of activities, but the translation process is not limited to the text itself. For a translator, running his or her own company involves many activities: obtaining the right to practise, promoting and advertising the company, establishing relationships with potential clients and developing a network of contacts, and finally, winning and fulfilling orders. The translator receives a salary, but as an entrepreneur, he or she incurs business costs, not only in the form of office fees, utilities, or consumables, but also, for example, specialised translation software, licences, training, or participation in industry conferences.

From an external perspective, the text has a product function and plays a key role. Robinson emphasises that translation studies to date have largely focused on the translator's perspective. From a user perspective, three main priorities can be highlighted: *reliability*, often equated with *equivalence* or *fidelity*, but also *timeliness* and *translation costs*.

Tab. 8: **Customer perspective**

Customer perspective – external perspective – **Translation as a product** **The translated text is the most important**
1. Reliability of the text (reliability, equivalence, fidelity)
2. Timeliness
3. The translator's reliability
4. Cost

Source: Own development based on: Robinson, 1997.

A client who does not know the ins and outs of the art of translation sees translation in terms of understanding a foreign-language text. *Textual reliability*, as described by Douglas Robinson, means from the client's point of view that the translation can be read on par with the original. The user of the translation, and therefore the translator's client, undertakes his or her intended actions on the assumption that the translation is equivalent to the original. Most often, the client's efforts to obtain a text in the desired target language are limited to finding a translator or translation agency, sending – usually by e-mail – a file to be translated, and setting expectations regarding the deadline (or delegating these activities to someone else in the company; often assistants, receptionists, or employees in the company's department trained to do so). The client does not think about the difficulties of transferring content from one language to another, while the translator often finds it difficult to discuss with the client the details of the other party's expectations. Practice shows that such a conversation at the beginning of an assignment is usually lacking, although it would dispel several potential problems when handing over the finished text to the client. More often than not, problems start with a completely mundane issue, such as the readability and completeness of the documents sent.[36] Sometimes, before they reach the person who orders the translation, they

36 Łukasz Zarzycki also writes about informative translation strategies in his book *Dylematy tłumacza. Zastosowanie pięciu typów ekwiwalencji Kollera oraz modelu bezpośredniego i pośredniego Vinay i Darbelnet w tłumaczeniu terminologii medycznej z języka angielskiego na polski.* He has created a chart of questions that an interpreter should answer before undertaking an assignment. Among these are issues such as the ability to complete the assignment on

are sent from hand to hand without any verification. At the end of the chain is the translator, who must first verify the format of the files, the complete number of pages, the editability of the figures and tables, as well as the legibility of the graphics, figures, and drawings.

From the client's perspective, the matter is obvious and simple – the sent file is to be translated. The translator often must decide, in a sense, 'for the client', what the final translation should look like, considering the purpose of the text. After all, as a tool in the hands of the client, the text has a function, and the client will only judge the translation positively if it plays that role. The customer needs fully functional and working tools, not a few pieces that he has to put together himself. He, therefore, expects a comprehensive translation, a text that is equivalent not only in terms of content, but also fulfils stylistic, terminological, and even graphical requirements (the target text must include descriptions of drawings in the target language or dictionaries for them, as well as tables, diagrams, and figures – all these elements are treated as integral elements of the order and must be included in the final translation file).

The most difficult challenge for the translator is when he or she is trying to contact the client in order to clarify details (e.g., on specialised terminology, machine design, or confirmation of the functionality of a component in the overall machine, usually when there are several possibilities for using different terms for a given word in the source language), and on the other side, his or her conversation partner turns out to be a completely uninformed person who is merely an intermediary (an assistant, a delegated employee, or even a translation agency employee who does not have the right relationship with the client). In Robinson's view, an experienced and wise interpreter has this uncanny ability to 'read' the client's expectations. He or she is able not only to take in and read the source text with understanding but also to imagine in some way what function the translated text will have for the client and his or her needs in the target culture. A translator will take a different approach when translating a children's textbook, another when translating a marketing text, and yet another when translating tender

time, knowledge of the field being translated, readability, and completeness of the text.

documentation. The translation of a text of an advertising or marketing nature will require considerable creativity on the part of the translator, an understanding of the target culture, and even the ability to predict how a client in the target culture will perceive messages of this nature.[37] It may be that an advertising slogan will sound quite different from what the literal translation would indicate, but adaptation to market conditions requires that such a text be adapted accordingly. In such a situation, it is important to consider what the customer cares about – the literalness of the translation or the effectiveness of the impact of the advertising slogan, which is intended to result in the sale of the advertised product. The translation of a children's textbook must take into account the capabilities of the recipient – a pre-schooler, early childhood, or high school student. The aim of a publisher launching a new textbook is for students to be able to realistically use and apply the information contained in the book. A literal translation may be very abstract or so culturally distant in its reception that the young reader will not understand the essential content of the message. Translating extensive tender documentation for a client who is about to take part in a tender process will require some thought and the right translation strategy. If the translation is labour-intensive, the deadline for bidding is very short and urgent, and the documentation contains many details, you need to think about prioritising. As in the previous two examples, the most important

37 In his work *Becoming a Translator*, Douglas Robinson lists the different *types of text fidelity (types of text reliability)*. These are: *literalism* – the translation is a virtually *literal* rendering of the original content, the syntactic structures of the source text are very much in evidence; *foreignness* – the text is very 'fluid' in its reception, with only locally visible '*foreign*' elements that diverge from the target culture; *fluency* – the translation reads as if the text had originally been written in the target language and it is difficult for the recipient to realise that the text they are reading is in fact a translation; *summary* – the translation includes a summary of the main points in the source text; *commentary* – the translation contains explanatory notes and comments on content not explicitly stated in the source text; a combination of summary and commentary – the text summarises the main points of the original, while at the same time containing passages that further explain content not explicitly stated in the source document; *encryption* – the translation encodes certain content for a certain audience who know the right 'key' to read it (Robinson, 2003: 10).

thing in such a situation is to talk to the client. Perhaps consideration should be given to the possibility of summarising certain parts of the tender documentation and concentrating as much as possible on details such as figures, dimensions, weights, and colours (for example, tender documentation for fire engines, a fleet of buses, or the supply of ambulances), as their correct description in the bid submitted by the client will be crucial to his or her business situation.

Precision and timeliness are key elements in the work of a translator undertaking assignments for specialised texts. There are many times when the translator would like to discuss translation strategies and techniques with the client, but this turns out to be impossible. Sometimes the translator simply has to decide on his or her own how he or she will, let's say, translate an advertising text or a banking contract. The translator is often forced to appeal to his or her professional intuition and to act according to what it prompts, as well as to experience, while being aware of the full responsibility he or she bears for these choices and translational actions. Ultimately, it is the satisfied client who will pay the invoice for the job and may recommend the interpreter to the next person or use their services again in the future. For the client, a good translation is one that is a functional tool for achieving the goals they have set.

In addition to textual fidelity, the fidelity of the translator is also expected. Robinson discusses what is meant by this term, pointing out what he believes are the two most important characteristics of a translation contractor: *correctness* and a professional approach to the work *(professionalism)*. These are just two qualities named explicitly, but underneath these terms are many other qualities of a translator, such as accuracy, reliability, diligence, punctuality, or discretion. A professional translator is characterised by the ability to read the client's needs and expectations for the translation so that the text fulfils its role in the client's business plans. In addition, the wise and experienced translator pays attention to collocation and contextual nuances *(attention to detail)*, listens to the client, talks to the client, and follows the client's instructions and guidelines *(sensitivity to user's needs)*, and searches for textual and cultural parallels, consults specialists, researches online sources, books, and databases in order to fulfil the job in the most reliable way possible *(research)*. Any questionable issues are corrected before the completed order is handed over to the client *(checking)*. In addition to professionalism in the translation itself, professionalism in behaviour towards the client is also expected. A translator can be a very *versatile* person *(versatility)*, however, he or she should be able to honestly admit that a particular specialisation is beyond his or her capabilities and turn down an assignment because he or she lacks the necessary competence and knowledge. Such fairness to the client is extremely important, especially in the case of highly specialised texts, where the translator's misapplication of terminology or misunderstanding of business processes (e.g., production or technology) can prove disastrous. Accountability is also required when the interpreter makes certain *promises* to the client *(promises)*. The translator, knowing his or her craft and time constraints, should realistically confirm the deadline for the translation and, in case of delays, inform the client well in advance, setting an alternative time. A client, surprised at not receiving an assignment on the agreed date, not only will not come back to the translator with another job, but may potentially even provide negative publicity for the translator. The business consequences resulting from such an action by the translator may turn out to be irreversible (inability to submit a tender offer, failure to fulfil the contract on time, or inability to sign an attractive business contract). In addition, *confidentiality* and *friendliness* are highly valued nowadays, although they may seem natural and obvious for business development. When commissioning the translation of a lucrative contract, the client expects that the content will not fall into the wrong hands. The translator's professionalism and serious approach to his or her work is also underlined by his or her professional technological background *(hardware and software)*. Douglas Robinson's work was published at the end of the 1990s, and in it, he emphasises such elements of the professional translator's workshop as a good computer, legitimate software, a functioning e-mail, and a fax machine, which we take for granted today. It should be emphasised that skilful self-management in time and organisation of work are also valuable qualities for an interpreter.

However, there are two sides to every coin. Good translation requires an experienced translator who has spent an appropriate amount of time on education and continues to work on his or her craft, enhances his or her own competencies, reads professional literature, and devotes time to professional development.[38] There must be adequate remuneration for a professionally produced translation. A translator is not a computer that will do the translation quickly and automatically. Although machine translation and the rapid development of artificial intelligence in the translation industry may compete with the painstaking work of a translator, nothing can replace the human factor in the translation process, which requires accuracy, constant refinement, and correction of content, editing, and proofreading.[39] A machine can translate a text quickly, but it will never understand the meaning of the translated content.

---

38 Magdalena Fitas-Dukaczewska, a conference interpreter in Russian and translator of diplomats and politicians, including Prime Minister Donald Tusk, interviewed for *Diuna Language Services* in August 2020, cited some of the most essential qualities of a good interpreter, listing among them accuracy, precision, courage and literacy, knowledge of the industry, the ability to maintain discretion, as well as the ability to keep confidential the facts and data learned by the interpreter during the assignment (PRZEtłumacze, 2020).

39 Market research on the translation industry has been carried out since 2013. The project is called the *European Language Survey* and is an initiative of six professional organisations – in 2020 these were Elia, EMT, EUATC, FIT EUROPE, GALA, and LIND. The Translation Market Report has been prepared in the form of a survey continuously since 2013 and focuses on translation service providers and clients, freelancers, training companies, and private and public entities specialising in translation. The study investigates numerous aspects of the market, such as expectations and assumptions of the translation market, challenges and threats, as well as observed changes in business practices. Competition in the translation market, as in other sectors, is fierce, and the pressure of time and money does not make things easy for translators, although the competition may have an impact on the need for translators to keep learning, developing their skills and the quality of their work.

2.1.3. *Translator's view*

Translators carry out assignments because it is their paid work and a way of life. While the external perspective described above puts the needs of the client first, the translator should also be able to find his or her place among these needs. The text, the client, and the translator are all closely intertwined elements in the translation process.

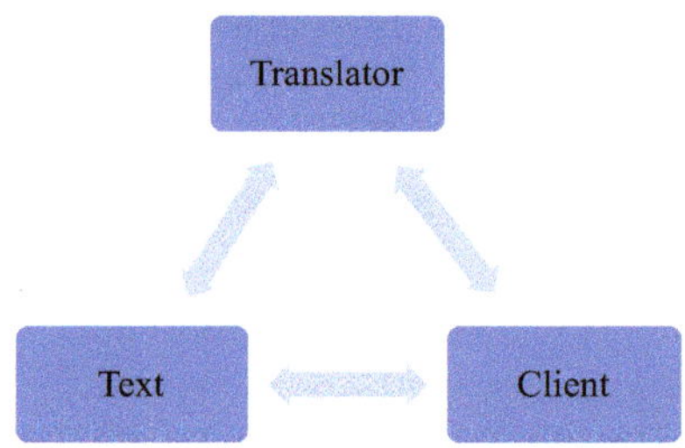

Fig. 7: Elements of the translation process that must work together
Source: Author's own development.

In order to deliver credible translated texts with professionalism and timeliness, the translator should develop a high level of service quality, diligence, and the ability to manage him or herself and the project in time, setting a realistic schedule to meet the deadlines offered and confirmed to the client. If the interpreter does not ensure that he or she finds his or her work enjoyable and a source of satisfaction, symptoms of burnout can very quickly set in. Both Anthony Pym and Douglas Robinson reflect on the predisposition and competence of those who become interpreters.

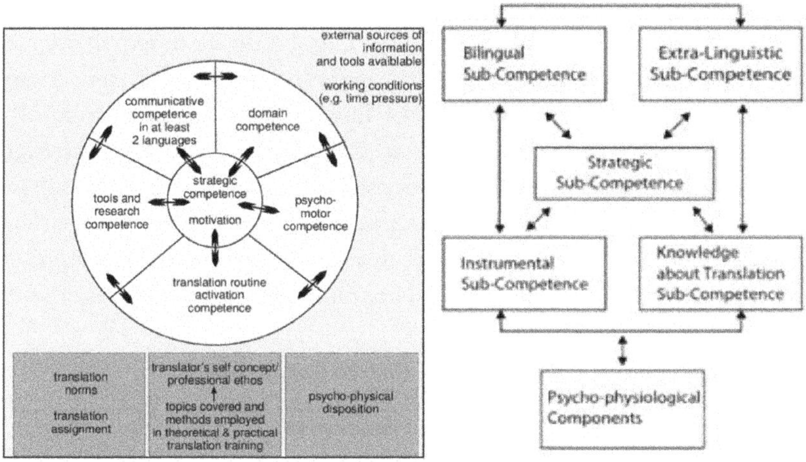

Fig. 8: Competence of future interpreters according to Anthony Pym
Source: Pym, 2021.[40]

Some people give up after a short adventure in translation. Some people very quickly experience discouragement or professional burnout as a result of time pressure, but also the pressure of money. Financial uncertainty is an integral part of the work of a self-employed translator. There is also a certain group of people who pursue translation purely out of a passion for translation. They do the translations in the afternoons or at weekends, treating these activities as an additional occupation. It is, therefore, important to consider what it is that determines a person's ability to dedicate themselves completely to the art of translation and to make a living from translation, while also being a sought-after professional in this field. Douglas Robinson (2003: 34) compares translators with talented actors who become doctors, lawyers, builders, tradesmen, etc., for the duration of the translation. Among the interpreter's traits, he sees the following: the ability to remember words after hearing them once, eloquence, sometimes even the

40 The Anthony Pym material used in this work has been made available with the express permission of the author.

ability to read four books at the same time (and in different languages), a love of travelling and exploring the world, and a desire to experience and discover new things, places, and cultures. Translation is also very often a second-choice profession – people who have previously taken up a job in another profession become translators. Indeed, it is often the case that a degree in philological studies alone does not guarantee the ability to produce good translations,[41] as it becomes necessary to have work experience in a certain industry, to know a field, production processes, and company customs in order to have a deeper understanding of the translated content.[42]

Tab. 9: The interpreter's perspective – an internal perspective

The interpreter's perspective – the internal perspective – What is most important to the interpreter
1. *Professional pride*
2. *Income*
3. *Enjoyment*

Source: Own development based on: Robinson, 1997.

For an interpreter, it is important that the work they do is appreciated by the recipient. Sometimes, a lower fee and a satisfied client are worth more to the translator than a high translation fee for an unsatisfactory

41 In August 2020, Anthony Pym's website (2021) published a presentation on why most translatology students do not work as translators.

42 This topic was also discussed at the TIFO 2019 conference. An interesting discussion ensued with Chris Durban, a Paris-based French translator of specialised texts in the financial industry, where hypotheses were made about the potential career path of a translator who does not start as a translator after graduation, but works for several years in another industry, learning not only the specialised language and terminology, but also the processes, expectations, and perspectives of the client. He then goes on to further his training as a translator, gaining additional qualifications and practice working with translation agencies, and at the very end, he just starts his career as an independent translator. The discussion revolved around the notion of the specific maturity needed to practise as a translator.

job. The translator needs to feel that his or her work is good, important, needed, and valued. It should be stressed that he or she is not always able to meet the client's expectations, not only in terms of the rate for translation or the deadline for the job but also for ethical reasons. Krzysztof Hejwowski (2012: 27) argues that 'the good work of a translator can be judged by an expert (a translator, a critic, a literary scholar, a sophisticated reader) – only after comparing the translation with the original', but most often the greatest critic of one's own work is the translator himself. According to Douglas, the concept of an interpreter's *professional pride* consists of elements such as *reliability*, *involvement in the profession,* and *ethics*. The client's expectations are limited to receiving a reliable translation delivered within the agreed deadline for a set price. On the other side is the translator, who is not always able to meet the client's expectations. Sometimes the deadline proposed by the client is beyond the interpreter's real capacity. The tight deadlines and volume range of translations can disorganise a translator's private life. A client's suggested method of translation may also be unethical in the eyes of the translator. Translation fees, on the other hand, can be the driving wheel of a machine that traps translators – the illusory belief that a low rate and a large number of assignments will ensure their financial stability very often leads not only to a significant deterioration in the quality of the services provided but also to the failure to meet agreed deadlines. Problems cascade in the form of numerous complaints, dissatisfied clients who are just bad publicity, and very often interpreter fatigue as a result of the heavy workload for which they are unsatisfactorily remunerated. An experienced and wise translator looks at his profession from a broad perspective. He is aware that he cannot have everything at once and at the same time. Developing a stable position in the translation market requires hours of diligent work, earning the trust and loyalty of clients. Long-term relationships with clients satisfied with translations require considerable effort. Such activities also involve the interpreter's personal dedication to the work they do and the professional environment they are in. The translator should be involved in translator organisations and attend industry events to improve his or her knowledge and have the opportunity to exchange experiences with other translators.

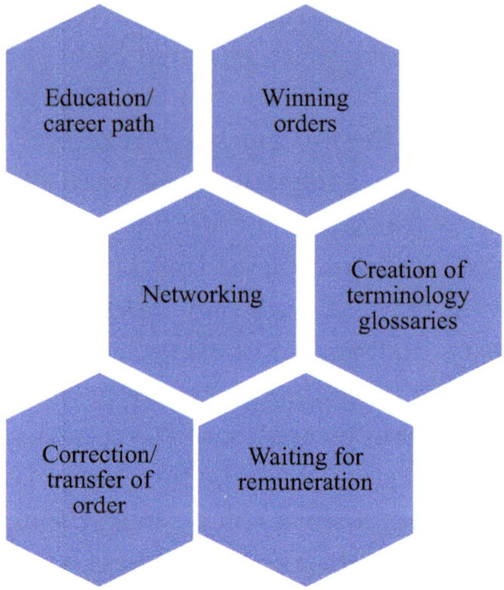

Fig. 9: Some aspects of the translator's work
Source: Author's own development.

Such activities provide the interpreter with an incentive to develop his or her skills, and the sense of belonging to unions and professional associations provides support in situations where concerns arise. Networking and being active in an industry environment are a kind of lifeline in a tedious and sometimes very tedious job. Translators must support and assist each other and offer each other advice – these are recommendations found in many translation organisations' statutes.

The issue of ethics is also raised very frequently in the translation community. It used to be accepted that it is unethical in the translation process to distort and misrepresent the content of the source text. Of course, such a definition of the concept of ethics in the work of a translator seems a significant simplification. In many situations, the translator must opt for a translation technique that involves a kind of 'distortion' of the content of the source text. This is, of course, done within a certain framework, such as the adaptation of a text to the needs of the target audience or, for example, the new composition of an advertising slogan for an advertising campaign in the target culture. For the translator, the question of professional ethics is a much more complex issue. He is sometimes faced with questions such as: whether to undertake the translation of an offensive text, what to do when professional ethics conflict with the expectations of the client who is paying for the translation, whether a translator should undertake the translation of a text that is sexist, whether to translate racist content, whether to undertake the translation of a text that is an advertisement for a company that supports unethical production and exploitation of people at work. In the opinion of Douglas Robinson (2003: 26), looking at translation from an external perspective, such questions cannot and should not occur. The translator undertakes the assignment irrespective of his or her views and beliefs, and carries out the translation with due care, appropriate to the client's needs and expectations. He should not get personally involved in the content of the text. However, an insider's perspective, speaking as a researcher and translator, dictates otherwise. An interpreter is not a machine but a human being who has views, feelings, and the ability to assess reality. There are interpreters for whom it becomes impossible to fulfil certain assignments because of their beliefs and views. They can opt out of doing the translation precisely because of ethics. Still, the question can be raised: to what extent are moral principles able to determine the interpreter's decisions? Professional translators pursue their profession because they enjoy translating, and take pride in their work, but also because it brings them income opportunities. Interpreters tend to feel that their remuneration is not commensurate with the effort they put in, and they often have to fight for remuneration. However, it is not an isolated industry in this respect, and, as entrepreneurs, they simply need to find their way in the language services market and develop their own strategy.

In conclusion, the translator is not a machine and will never perform translation as an automated process. He always needs the right amount of time to complete an assignment, even if he uses programmes and tools that streamline and facilitate his work. There will always be a human factor behind the translation process, creating a potential risk of error, but also meaning that the translation was done by a thinking, educated human being with a range of competencies necessary to understand the meaning of the text, which for machines and artificial intelligence still remains elusive.

2.2. Tools in the work of a professional translator

2.2.1. Parallel texts

The President of the Polish Society of Sworn and Specialised Translators (TEPIS), Danuta Kierzkowska, in her work *Tłumaczenie prawnicze*, seeks to answer the question of how to translate legal and juridical texts. In seeking an answer to this question, she points to aspects of the communicative situation 'whose elements are the institutional status and intentions of the author of the original legal or juridical text, i.e., the primary author; the institutional status and goals of the translator, i.e., the author of the text translation and at the same time the secondary sender; the characteristics of the primary recipient and the final recipient' (Kierzkowska, 2008: 15). The communicative situation in question concerns the transfer of a text from the source language to the target language. Renata Świgońska,[43] a sworn translator of English and German, experienced lawyer, and organiser of mentoring courses for future sworn translators, recommends that the translation process, which is the transformation of a text from one language to another, involve three (main) stages.

At the first stage, the source text must be studied very carefully – in the case of a specialised text, it is even necessary to read the text with comprehension several times before starting the translation, as failure to understand the source text is often the cause of very serious translation errors. As a second step, the lawyer and translator points to the search for the correct specialised terminology and phraseology, recommending looking for it in parallel texts. The context determines the appropriate understanding of the word, the specialised terminology, and the phraseological compounds used – in this case, dictionaries alone prove to be an insufficient tool for the translator. The third stage is the final transformation of the source text,

43 Renata Świgońska was one of the first people in Poland to undertake a series of social media and online activities to educate candidates for sworn interpreters. A lawyer and sworn translator with many years of experience, she runs a blog on legal translation issues and organises courses to prepare for the sworn translator examination. She also addressed an open letter to the Minister of Justice in Poland to allow the possibility of taking exams using computers (Legal and Judicial Translation Blog 2020).

where translation strategies and techniques, the incompatibility of legal systems, or different types of equivalence play the most important role.

Dariusz Kubacki, a Germanist and a member of the examination board during the examination for a sworn translator in Poland, points out in his scientific work the importance of parallel texts in the translation process. A parallel text, according to Kubacki's definition, is a text of the same type, on the same topic, and one that has been produced in the same communicative situation.[44] Parallel texts are primarily used to translate specialist texts; as Kubacki points out, it is difficult to speak of parallel texts in the case of literature or poetry. Thus, parallel texts can be spoken of primarily in the case of specialist translations. Danuta Kierzkowska also emphasises that parallel texts are an invaluable aid for translators. The researcher argues that they are a source of correct phraseology and stylistic devices, as well as correct terminology, which in turn is helpful when translating into a language specific to another legal system (Kierzkowska, 2008: 56). Kubacki points out that parallel texts have a great many advantages over dictionaries, because, in addition to being an excellent terminological source, they also provide a suitable basis for imitation in other respects – namely strictly linguistic and stylistic issues and the fact that these texts are excellent authentic textual models. Dictionaries age over time, and language is constantly evolving. According to the researcher, parallel texts fulfil three basic functions. Firstly, they help the translator to better understand the source text and thus make a more reliable translation. Secondly, they enable the translator to familiarise themselves with different textual genres, not only from a global perspective, but also from a macro and micro approach. Thirdly, parallel texts lend themselves to imitation and use up-to-date terminology, often absent from dictionaries. Table 10 presents a summary of interpretations of the concept of parallel texts by various researchers.[45]

44 The conclusions are based on the content of a teleconference with Prof. Dariusz Kubacki during a course for sworn translators.
45 Data taken from training materials provided by Renata Świgońska.

Tab. 10: Parallel texts as interpreted by researchers.

Author	What is a parallel text?
Delisle	A parallel text is a text in the target language belonging to the same genre as the source text and/or treating the same subject matter, from which the translator can extract the terms and expressions he or she needs to do the translation (Delisle, 1999).
Krzysztoforska-Weisswasser	Parallel texts are texts of the same type, on the same topic, which were produced in the same communicative situation (Krzysztoforska-Weisswasser, 1995: 18; Kubacki, 2013: 145).
S. Šarčević	Parallel texts are equal language versions of normative texts (1997: 104; Weigt, 2012: 135).
Göpferich	Parallel texts are texts in different languages, each produced in the mother tongue – preferably by a competent native speaker, which are not mutual translations, but which deal with the same topic and are compatible with each other in terms of communicative function, i.e., belonging to the same text genre (Göpferich, 2005: 184; Kubacki, 2013: 145)
Spillner	Parallel texts are original texts, produced in a specific language, which belong to the same text genre as the original text, deal with the same topic, and fulfil the same function (Spillner, 1981: 241; Kubacki, 2013: 145).
Wilss	Parallel texts are texts in different languages that coincide thematically, stylistically and situationally (Wilss, 1996: 160; Kubacki, 2013: 145).
Fabricius-Hansen	Parallel texts are original texts in different languages, but which are functionally and possibly thematically comparable, i.e., texts which, according to relevant non-textual factors such as communicative function, circumstances of production, rhetorical structure, and medium, can be assigned to the same genre or the same text genre, or at least considered to have significant similarities (Fabricius-Hansen, 2007: 323; Kubacki, 2013: 145).

Source: Own development based on the content of a teleconference with Prof. Dariusz Kubacki during a course for sworn translators and the post-conference materials provided.

In addition to parallel texts, there are also so-called authentic texts, and these are not identical concepts. Authentic texts are most often identified with the original texts in relation to their translations. 'The availability of parallel texts enables translators to emulate to some extent the relevant register and conventions of a particular legal or juridical language' (Kierzkowska, 2008: 56), and thus the translator, with a prepared translation workshop in the form of collected parallel texts, has a tool available to prepare a high-quality translation. The question to ask is: how do we look for parallel texts, and how do we use them when working on a translation? In this respect, the internet offers the translator a great many opportunities these days. It should be noted, however, that working with parallel texts is time-consuming and requires painstaking research, while collecting texts is an investment that, in the long term, allows one to accumulate very valuable material that pays off over the years. In addition to online sources, Danuta Kierzkowska points to the following:

> When translating from foreign languages into Polish, the parallel legislative texts are Polish legal acts published in such promulgation journals as: *Dziennik Ustaw Rzeczypospolitej Polskiej*, *Monitor Polski* and official journals of individual ministries. Similarly, when translating Polish legislative acts into other languages, the parallel texts will be those of foreign-language acts on similar subjects and of similar rank (Kierzkowska, 2008: 56).

Applying the above to contractual agreements, the translator, when undertaking their translation, should obtain material in the form of contracts analogous to those he or she received as a translation order. He should then familiarise himself with their content, paying attention to the terminology, as well as the stylistic and phraseological devices used, developing the workshop needed to complete the assignment. However, the fact of the incompatibility of legal systems must be considered when using parallel texts, as Danuta Kierzkowska (2008) points out: 'The usefulness of parallel texts as a source of inspiration also in the creation of terminology cannot, therefore, be denied, but only assuming full awareness and knowledge of the incompatibility of legal systems and the resulting limitations in the free transfer of names of often inadequate concepts' (Kierzkowska, 2008: 57). Thus, the use of parallel texts must not be mindless copying, but a thoughtful, analytical exercise with an understanding of aspects such as non-equivalent terms or the incompatibility of legal systems.

2.2.2. Translation strategies and techniques: Equivalence

By considering the status of a specialist translator, the ins and outs of his or her work, and the dilemmas he or she is confronted with on a daily basis, the author of this work seeks to answer the question of how the translation process should be carried out in order to satisfy the recipient and, on the other hand, to preserve the faithfulness of the message contained in the source text.[46] As mentioned earlier, a translator, when undertaking a translation, is faced with many choices and decisions that he or she must make in order to produce a quality text for the audience. In order to be able to do his or her job well, the translator should be fully aware of how the translation process works, what his or her role in the process is, and what action he or she should take at each stage. The starting point for considering translation strategies and techniques in the search for equivalents in this work is the translation system proposed by Franciszek Grucza in 1981 (Fig. 10).

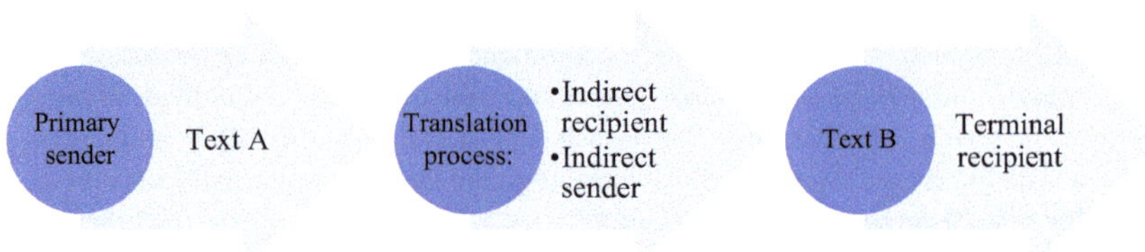

Fig. 10: Translational system according to Grucza
Source: Own development based on available literature (cf. Grucza, 1981; Kierzkowska, 2008).

The primary sender in Grucza's translational arrangement refers to the author of the source text, and the terminal receiver refers to the target recipient. The original text, i.e., the text in the original language, is text A, and the text translated into a language understood by the terminal recipient is text B. Text A and text B mark the beginning and end of the translation process, the product of which is intended for a terminal audience (cf. Kierzkowska, 2008: 26). The translational arrangement according

46 The criteria for good translation have also been addressed by Alicja Pisarska and Teresa Tomaszkiewicz (cf. Pisarska, Tomaszkiewicz, 1996: 155).

to Grucza has not lost its relevance. Its essentials were also retained in a 1999 study edited by Jean Delisle.[47] In the work in question, Delisle proposed a slightly different nomenclature, as the equivalent of the translation system in this work is a diagram entitled *Stages of translation* (Delisle, 1999: 204). For Delisle, the counterpart of text A is the source text, the counterpart of text B is the target text, and the terminal recipient is the target recipient. Delisle's depiction of the translation process emphasises the stage where the translator must decide on the essential intention of the translation, i.e., he must choose between '*source-oriented* translation'[48] and '*target-oriented* translation'.[49] Why should the interpreter make this decision? There are numerous constraints on the translation process, and these arise from 'the conditions created by the audience, the accepted textual conventions, the "*universe of discourse*", i.e., the boundaries of the so-called "*shared knowledge of the world*", and the structure and specificity of both languages of translation and directly from the source text' (Kierzkowska, 2008: 26). The next stage according to Delisle is the choice of translation strategy, understood as the choice of the type of translation (Fig. 11), followed by translation techniques, understood as the principles of translation (Fig. 12).

---

47 We are referring to a collective work published in 1999 under the auspices of the International Federation of Translators (FIT) and the International Standing Conference of University Institutes of Translators and Interpreters (CIUTI) entitled *Translation Terminology*.

48 The term 'source-oriented translation' is understood as text- and *source-language-oriented* translation, while 'target-oriented translation' is understood as text- and *target-language-oriented* translation.

49 The terms '*source-like translation*' and '*foreign-like translation*' are neologisms proposed by Danuta Kierzkowska. The author of this work adopts these definitions to guide her reflections on the process and on translation strategies and techniques.

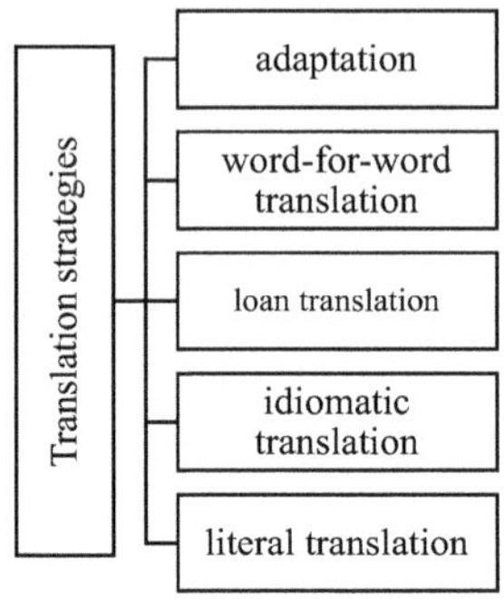

Fig. 11: Translation strategies according to Delisle
Source: Own elaboration (cf. Delisle, 1999: 204; Kierzkowska, 2008: 27).

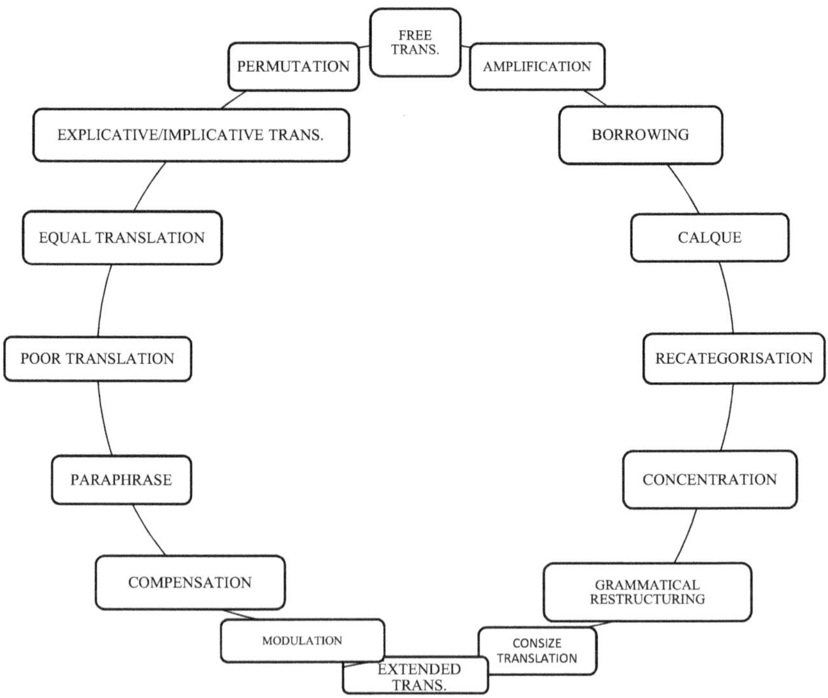

Fig. 12: Translation techniques according to Delisle
Source: Own elaboration (cf. Delisle, 1999: 204; Kierzkowska, 2008: 27).

The final stage in the translation process, according to Delisle, is for the translator to take into account the constraints imposed by the peculiarities of the original language and the target language – primarily grammatical, stylistic, and phraseological rules. The translator should also select the type of equivalence appropriate to the text, considering all the previous parameters of the translation process (Delisle, 1999: 205; Kierzkowska, 2008: 27). Both the translation system, according to Grucza and the translation stages according to Delisle, provide a definition of the translation process in this work.

This work adopts Lukszyn's definition of the term 'translation strategy' (in addition to Delisle's interpretation of the stages of translation), which states that it is 'the translator's way of proceeding in the translation process, which is subordinated to a specific translational model' (Lukszyn, 1993: 300), while translation technique 'is a way of handling specific translation situations in order to achieve equivalence between the source and target texts' (ibid.: 326).

Basically, two main translation strategies can be distinguished in translation studies: translation faithful to the original text and free translation. Below is a summary of strategies according to Magdalena Łomzik (2020: 94), a scholar of German-language translations:

- strategies of translation bringing the reader closer to the author and translation bringing the author closer to the reader – Schleiermacher's concept ([1813] 2010: 16);
- translation strategies based on formal adequacy and translation based on dynamic equivalence – Nida's concept ([1964] 2009: 56);
- strategies of *domestication* and *foreignization* – Venuti's concept (1995: 18);
- strategies of *overt translation* and *covert translation* – House's concept (1997: 66);
- functional translation and syntagmatic translation strategies – Hejwowski's concept (2004: 78);
- source-like and foreign-like translation strategies – Kierzkowska's concept (2011a: 129);
- translation strategies by equivalents and by references – Radziszewska's concept (2012: 138).

Other definitions of translation strategies and techniques, along with their types as interpreted by the cited researchers (Hejwowski, Piotrowska, Vinay and Darbelnet, Pieńkos, Kierzkowska), also appear later in the chapter. In their work, every translator strives to render the equivalent content (in terms of meaning, style, grammar, or even graphics) of the original message in the target language.

Olgierd Wojtasiewicz (1957: 15), the doyen of Polish translation, believed that 'the operation of translation consists in formulating in a certain language the equivalent of a statement previously formulated in another language'.[50] Equivalence[51] became a topic of heated discussion among translation scholars. Barbara Kielar believes that:

> The text of a translation should be equivalent to the original, i.e., it should fulfil certain requirements in terms of content, form, style, function, etc. This means, on the one hand, that the aim is to preserve the existing ties with the source text, i.e., 'faithfulness' to its content, while taking into account – on the other hand – the existence of specific conventions of the language of translation (Kielar, 1991: 133).

In her reflections on the process and quality of specialist translation, Kielar seeks to show how to create a translation that meets the expectations of secondary audiences in terms of communication and that can function in the context of their culture alongside texts of a similar kind (Kielar, 1991: 134). However, further on, referring to the translation of specialised texts, she stresses that 'when translating specialised texts, equivalent professional

50 One has to give credit to Krzysztof Hejwowski, who repeatedly emphasised that 'when writing his book, Wojtasiewicz did not have at his disposal all the complex conceptual apparatus developed in the following decades by translation studies and other fields of the humanities. He did not – for understandable reasons – use concepts such as equivalence, polyphonicity, intertextuality or globalisation. Instead, he had knowledge of several languages, a working knowledge of translation, an extraordinary insight of mind and a great deal of common sense. This was enough to come to the right conclusions on many translation issues; often conclusions that others only came to after several decades' (Hejwowski, 2011: 7).

51 The creator of the term 'equivalence' is Roman Jakobson. The term first appeared in his article entitled 'On Linguistic Aspects of Translation' in 1959 (cf. Pisarska, Tomaszewska, 1996: 158). However, he did not formulate a definition of the term.

terms play an important role, as they provide points of support around which the translator develops his version of the translation, translating in a "through content" manner' (ibid.: 135). Marta Chromá, who specialises in legal and juridical translation research, highlights the complexity of the translation process:

> Proces překládání sám o sobě je způsob rozkrývání vztahů mezi jazyky (tj. srovnávací analýza, *comparative analysis*), nalézání rozdílů (tj. kontrastivní analýza, *contrastive analysis*), zjišťování kulturních rozdílů mezi prostředím výchozího a cílového jazyka (tj. mezikulturní pragmatika, *cross-cultural pragmatics*), přičemž všechny postupy mají zásadní vliv na vytvoření cílového textu tak, aby tento text dával smysl konečnému příjemci (Chromá, 2014: 4).

Chromá emphasises the importance of preparing the text properly for the final audience. In the translation of legal and jurisprudential texts, precision and care are crucial, but the basis is a proper understanding of the source text, and that the translator has adequate knowledge of the legal system of the target language culture.[52]

The concept of equivalence, as well as the interpretation of concepts such as strategy, technique, or method in translation, has been the subject of numerous studies and a number of papers.[53] Interpretations of the techniques and strategies, as seen by various researchers, are presented below.

---

52 Target culture refers to the culture of the language of translation, while source culture refers to the culture of the source language (cf. Jopek-Bosiacka, 2021: 243). It is important to emphasise here the complexity of this problem, due to the different legal systems and cultures in the country of the source language and the country of the target language. Jerzy Pieńkos (1999: 158) writes: 'the semantic uncertainty that characterises legal vocabulary is due to the fact that no two legal systems in the world are identical, even within the same political or ideological community', which can be applied in a similar way to the translation of any specialised text, where there are cultural differences (including business culture).

53 In her work, Maria Piotrowska asks whether knowledge of techniques and strategies is necessary in every translator's workshop. She made a concise resource analysis of definitions from various sources of terms such as 'strategy', 'procedure', and 'technique'. The analysis showed that their terminological status is negligible, while 'in most of the contexts analysed they are used interchangeably or do not appear as separate headwords at all' (Piotrowska, 2006: 219).

2.2.2.1. *Position of Krzysztof Hejwowski*[54]

Krzysztof Hejwowski uses terms such as 'method', 'procedure', 'technique', and 'strategy' in his work. He considers that they encompass qualitatively different concepts:

> Strategy, understood as the translator's preferred (consciously or not) way of proceeding throughout the text or its significant parts, secondly technique, understood as the choice of a certain solution to a specific problem encountered during the translation process and finally the translation solution itself, which can be directly evaluated in the translation text (Hejwowski, 2012: 76).

Thus, when speaking of translation strategies, methods, or procedures, one can assume, following Hejwowski, that in this case, they would refer to both the way of proceeding during the translation process and specific translation solutions. Essentially, a recurring issue in equivalence studies is whether the translated text is to be closer to the sender (closer to the source culture) or closer to the receiver (more adapted to the needs of the receiver and the requirements of the target culture) (cf. Kizinska, 2015; Kierzkowska, 2020), as well as what methods, strategies, and techniques the translator should use in order to achieve the intended result, i.e., produce a high-quality translation. Hejwowski (2012: 76) recognises that domestication and foreignisation (in the sense of Venuti's concept of translation closer to the recipient – domestication, or closer to the source text – foreignisation)[55] are strategies, as is the strategy of syntagmatic or functional translation.[56] As part of the strategy, the translator uses translation techniques. For example, the domestication strategy is

---

54 The author cites some of Krzysztof Hejwowski's work because he is an extremely well-known researcher in the field of translation in Poland, who worked for many years at the Institute of Applied Linguistics at the University of Warsaw, overseeing the master's and doctoral theses of numerous contemporary scholars (e.g., Anna Kizinska, a researcher of English non-adaptive terms, cited above).

55 Friedriech Schleiermacher's work *Über die verschiedenen Methoden des Übersetzens* (1813) distinguished *alienation* and *naturalisation* of translation for the first time. Lawrence Venuti developed this idea in his work *The Translator's Invisiblity – The History of Translation* (1995), introducing the terms 'exoticisation' and 'domestication' to denote a translation closer to the source text or the target audience.

56 In Hejwowski's case, techniques are all the methods, procedures, and strategies mentioned in Vinay and Darbelnet, Newmark, and Chesterman (cf. Kizinska, 2015).

characterised by the frequent use of techniques such as the use of functional and descriptive equivalents or the omission of parts of the sentence (ibid.). He also proposes his own classification of translation techniques (Tab. 11).

Tab. 11: Classification of translation techniques according to Krzysztof Hejwowski

1. Reproduction without explanation
   → the use in translation of a word/expression used in the target language that is not assimilated in the source text; this technique may or may not involve some orthographic retouching or transliteration (in the case of different alphabets) (Hejwowski, 2012: 76–77)
2. Reproduction with explanation
   → a technique that enables the reader to reconstruct relevant patterns, scenarios, and scenes (ibid.: 77–78)
3. Syntagmatic translation without explanation
   → a technique involving the literal translation of the greater part of a sentence; it carries the risk of clumsiness or concealing the correct message 'hidden' in the content (ibid.)
4. Syntagmatic translation with explanation
   → a technique requiring the use of an explanatory note or commentary; a technique also not without its drawbacks; the explanation should be concise, clear, and truthful for the technique to be effective (ibid.)
5. Recognised equivalent
   → A technique used most often when translating the names of institutions, organisations, and some geographical names, sometimes also when translating the names of famous people (ibid.: 78–80)
6. Functional equivalent
   → the technique of replacing the name of a phenomenon better known in the output culture with the name of a phenomenon better known in the target culture (Hejwowski adopts what Newmark referred to as functional equivalence and cultural equivalence) (ibid.: 81)
7. Hyperonym
   → a technique involving reference to a more general entity; Hejwowski gives as examples: 'Chevrolet' – 'car', 'A-Levels' – 'exams' (ibid.: 82)
8. Descriptive equivalent
   → a technique used when an element appears once in a text and does not play a significant role in it; it involves substituting a description or definition for the term (ibid.: 82)
9. Leaving
   → a technique which is a last resort solution, involving the omission of a cultural element in the translation (ibid.: 83)

Source: Own elaboration based on: Hejwowski, 2012.

2.2.2.2. *Position of Maria Piotrowska*

Maria Piotrowska (2006: 223) classifies translation strategies,[57] taking into account aspects such as the linguistic structure of the text, the stage of the translation process, the pragmatic knowledge of the translator, and the cultural element of foreignness in the text. Piotrowska distinguishes four types of strategy (ibid.: 223–225):

- structural strategies (she includes strategies in structural terms, citing Nida, Newmark, Baker, and Pieńkos as representative researchers);
- psycholinguistic strategies (psycholinguistic research on translation plays a key role; Piotrowska points to names such as Gerloff, Krings, and Sequinot);
- pragmatic-cognitive strategies (there is a strong connection with mental schemas and the levelling of world knowledge, matching intellectual experience with the extent of pragmatic knowledge, which is different in the recipient of the original and the recipient of the translation);
- cultural strategies (a cultural element is considered an important factor in the formation of awareness and knowledge as a determinant of strategic translation; concepts coined by Venuti: 'exoticisation' and 'domestication').

According to Piotrowska (2006: 227), 'the strategy is global (encompasses the holistic translation task), antecedent (procedures are used as a result), textual and macro-contextual (concerns the entire translation task, e.g., the written text), abstract (deals with concepts), general (the aim is to perform the translation task) and dominant (overridingly determines the choice of technique)'. In contrast, she considers techniques to be 'local, unitary (deals with individual translation units), consequential (results from the strategy adopted), problem and micro-contextual (used to solve a specific problem), concrete (deals with specific solutions), purposive (aimed at achieving the intended goal) and subordinate (subject to the chosen strategy)' (ibid.).

---

57 For classifications of translation strategies (cf. Kwieciński, 2001; Nerlicki, 2003).

2.2.2.3. *Position of Vinay and Darbelnet*

In 1958, Jean-Paul Vinay and Jean Darbelnet published a paper entitled *Stylistique comparée du français et de l'anglais*, in which they outlined their idea of translation. These researchers distinguish between *translation methods* and *translation procedures*. According to the approach of these linguists, the translator has two options: to translate literally or freely.[58] Literal translation methods/strategies (literal methods in Hejwowski's terminology / direct translation methods in Zarzycki's terminology) include procedures such as borrowing, word-for-word, and literal translation. In the case of free translation (circular method in Hejwowski's terminology / indirect translation in Zarzycki's terminology), there are procedures such as transposition, modulation, equivalence, and adaptation.

Tab. 12: Classification of translation methods according to Vinay and Darbelnet

Literal translation methods	Free translation methods
Borrowing	Transposition
Word-for-word (calque)	Modulation
Literal translation	Equivalence
	Adaptation

Source: Own elaboration based on the literature.

Borrowing is used when the target language lacks the equivalent of a given unit of the source text in order to achieve a *stylistic effect* (Hejwowski, 2012: 74).[59] It can be done in translation by introducing an element of the

58 Literal translation is called *direct/literal*, while free translation is *oblique/free*. The first type of translation is literal, but grammatically and idiomatically adapted to the target language. Free translation is referred to when it is up to the translator to achieve equivalence between the source text and the target text (cf. Chromá, 2014: 4). Hejwowski (2012: 74) uses the term 'circular methods' to refer to the free translation of Vinay and Darbelnet, while Zarzycki (2016: 132) uses the terms 'direct translation' and 'indirect translation' in the context of these linguists' methods.

59 Chromá (2014: 4) in his work on the translation of legal and juridical texts, gives as an example of borrowing the word *apostilla*, which has entered current usage in both Czech and Polish and which comes from French.

source language culture into the translation in the form of a foreign word (Kizinska, 2015: 33). A specific type of borrowing is *calque*, treated as 'a literal translation of elements of the borrowed expression' (Hejwowski, 2012: 74). Vinay and Darbelnet ([1958] 2003: 85) distinguish between lexical calques and structural calques. Vinay and Darbelnet define *word-for-word* translation as 'the direct transformation of an output text into a target text while maintaining the rules of the target language, especially grammatical and idiomatic correctness' (Hejwowski, 2012: 75). *Transposition* occurs when a word of one class is replaced by a word of another class while preserving the meaning of the utterance (Hejwowski, 2012: 75; Chromá, 2014: 4).[60] *Modulation* means changing the form of speech in such a way that the perspective and lexis in the target language are modified.[61] *Equivalence*, as defined by Vinay and Darbelnet, is 'the replacement of the phraseologism of the original text by its functional equivalent, which need not be stylistically or structurally similar to it' (Hejwowski, 2012: 75). Chromá (2014: 4) instead states that such equivalence occurs at the level of terminology, larger sentence fragments, or parts of the text and depends on the context. *Adaptation* is a method used when the phenomena/events that are expressed in the source language do not exist in the target language (ibid.). Hejwowski emphasises that in such a situation, 'the interpreter creates a situation that can be considered equivalent' (2012: 75).

2.2.2.4. *Eugene Nida's position in the context of translation strategies and techniques*

A different point of view on equivalence and translation strategies and techniques was presented by Eugene Nida in 1964. The author of *Toward a Science of Translating* focuses his attention on the recipient of translation and his perception of translation, linking it closely to equivalence. Nida is the creator of concepts such as 'formal equivalence' *(formal, gloss)* and 'dynamic equivalence' *(dynamic)*. Translation using dynamic equivalence,

60 Chromá (2014: 4) in turn mentions an example of making necessary grammatical changes as a result of the incompatibility of the legal systems of the source language and the target language.

61 Hejwowski (2012: 75) gives as an example of modulation the replacement of the expression 'never doubted' with 'always was sure'.

as understood by Nida, is characterised by the fact that the culture of the target language country, rather than the culture of the source language country, was the most important factor for the translator. The focus is on the recipient's comfort with the translation; the translation is close to him, not to the source text. In order to achieve this type of equivalence, it is necessary to create the type of relationship between the transmitted information and the recipient of the translated text as the one that exists between the message and the recipient in the original language (Pisarska, Tomaszkiewicz, 1996: 160). In contrast to dynamic equivalence, for translation using formal equivalence, the culture of the source language comes first. With the use of the translator's footnotes *(glosses)*, the recipient of the translation has the chance to familiarise himself with the secrets of the source culture, with elements that are foreign and exotic to him (cf. Chromá, 2014: 5).

2.2.2.5. Position of Peter Newmark

Peter Newmark, writing about the translation process, distinguishes between *literal* translation and *free* translation. Newmark's techniques are called procedures. Free translation in Newmark's sense is very close to Nida's notion of dynamic equivalence, for, as in Nida's case, the key emphasis is on the culture of the target language and the reception of the translation by the end recipient (Chromá, 2014: 5).

Tab. 13: Classification of translation procedures according to Newmark

Translation procedure
1. Literal translation[a]
2. Transfer[b]
3. Naturalisation[c]
4. Cultural equivalent
5. Functional equivalent
6. Descriptive equivalent
7. Synonymy
8. Calque[d]
9. Transposition[e]
10. Modulation[f]
11. Recognised translation (official)

Tab. 13: Continued

12.	Compensation
13.	Constituent analysis
14.	Reduction/extension
15.	Translation doublet[g]
16.	Footnotes
17.	Appendices and explanatory notes

Source: Own elaboration based on: Newmark, 1988: 81–92; Hejwowski, 2012: 75.

a As with Vinay and Darbelnet.
b The equivalent of borrowing for Vinay and Darbelnet.
c The application of this procedure is characterised by the fact that the borrowed word is adapted to the pronunciation and spelling rules of the target language (compare Hejwowski, 2012: 75; Newmark, 1988: 82).
d As with Vinay and Darbelnet.
e As with Vinay and Darbelnet.
f As with Vinay and Darbelnet.
g This procedure means applying two procedures simultaneously.

2.2.2.6. The position of Danuta Kierzkowska

When looking for the best recipe for understanding and applying equivalence in the case of specialist texts,[62] it is worth referring to the work of Danuta Kierzkowska, who, in her work on specialist translation, more specifically legal translation, created a division of recipients into types, taking

62 This work presents just a few lines of interpretation of the equivalence phenomenon. There are many more researchers who have dealt with the issue of equivalence. It is worth noting the work of: James Catford (1965), creator of the concept of textual equivalence, Otto Kade (1968), who identified different levels of lexical adequacy, Wolfram Wilss (1977), author of a study of textual equivalence in which he emphasised the aspect of the translator, the text, and the recipient, Gideon Toury (1980), whose approach to the concept of equivalence was defined by the presentation of relationships in translation, the criteria for establishing them, and the fields of translation studies that deal with them (compare Pisarska, Tomaszkiewicz, 1996: 166), Anthony Pym (1992), who refers to equivalence as follows: 'Equivalence can be everything to any researcher. Equivalence is unidirectional, purposeless and without a perpetrator. The equivalence is asymmetrical. Equivalence is an economic term. Equivalence does not express the natural relationship between systems. Equivalence has become unfashionable'. An opponent of the introduction of equivalence into translation studies is Mary Snell-Hornby (1988), who considers it irrelevant and impossible to define precisely (cf. Kujawska-Lis, 2008: 124).

into account their characteristics. In doing so, she identified the needs of the recipients and their perception of translation.

Tab. 14: Recipient imperative

Recipient type	Recipient characteristics	Example
Close recipient	familiar with j1 culture or motivated to learn it	businessman, lawyer, student, translator
Distant recipient	not familiar with j1 culture, not intending to learn it	tourist, lay reader abroad
Self-determined recipient	using its own terminology as a 'principal's usus'	publishing house, translation agency, industrial plant

Source: Kierzkowska, 2008: 88.

By identifying the recipients and their needs, the translator can undertake the right strategy and use appropriate translation techniques.

'Close recipient' and 'distant recipient' are conventional terms used by Kierzkowska to distinguish between two different types of translation recipients. Close recipients are people who, due to their scientific or business activities, should be and are interested in learning and exploring the realities described in the source language (Kierzkowska, 2008: 88). In contrast, the distant recipient is not interested in exploring the ins and outs of the culture or legal system of the source language country. This refers to the kind of person for whom a general approximation of the content in the target language is sufficient, without having to go into detail about the realities of the source culture (ibid.: 89). The last group of recipients are the so-called self-identified recipients, i.e., institutions or individuals using 'prescriptive terminology[63] defined as the "usus of the principal" ' (ibid.). The purpose of

63 Under the concept of prescriptive terminology, Kierzkowska (2008: 90) understands the terminology 'inflicted' on the interpreter in this case. The translator should apply it because of its use and application in the client's previous translations. The phenomenon of 'imposing' terminology is particularly common in legal, juridical, and specialist texts. The standardised terminology is intended to facilitate the understanding and reception of texts with the same subject matter and similar purpose. The terminology used in the translation of European Union legislation can serve as an example of such a procedure.

the source texts and their translations from the perspective of the principal is important in this case. Once used in earlier translations, the terminology should also be retained for subsequent assignments. Determining the final recipients of translations is, according to Kierzkowska (2011b: 13), a practical application of Vermeer's skopos theory[64] on pragmatic translation. Regarding translation strategies and the notion of equivalence in translation, Kierzkowska refers to the division into so-called frame references proposed by Koller.

Tab. 15: Translation strategy

Type of equivalence principle adopted	Recipient type	Type of texts
Denotational equivalence	close recipient	legislative texts
Connotational equivalence	distant recipient	legal texts
Pragmatic equivalence	self-defined recipient	legal texts, legislative texts
Text-normative equivalence	all recipients	all texts

Source: Kierzkowska, 2008: 95.

Under the concept of denotational equivalence, Kierzkowska (2008: 95) understands 'the principle of relating the translation text to extra-linguistic denotatives'.[65] The concept of connotational equivalence is understood as 'the principle of relating the terms and the concepts they denote of the source text to the connotations (associations) of the target language culture, i.e., to the concepts associated by the recipient of the translation' (ibid.).

64 Skopos theory, so-called *Skopostheorie*, is a theory formulated by the German translation scholar Hans Vermeer in the second half of the 20th century. According to this theory, translation is a purposeful action, the most important thing in the process of translation becomes the goal, or *skopos*, and the translation is subordinated to that goal (cf. Vermeer, 1996).

65 Speaking of specialist, legal, and jurisprudential texts, the author has in mind 'references to the source text and the concepts (institutions) of the legal system relevant to it' (Kierzkowska, 2008: 95).

A particular type of equivalence from the perspective of the translation of specialised texts is pragmatic equivalence. Its purpose is 'to meet the special needs of the recipient of the translation who, for reasons known to himself, demands the use of a particular kind of equivalence which he himself defines and imposes on the translator' (ibid.). The translation of specialised texts may, in some ways, involve a limitation of the translator's possibilities as a result of interference from the client, who determines, for example, the use of certain equivalents.

2.2.2.7. Position of Jerzy Pieńkos

Jerzy Pieńkos, another Polish scholar specialising in the study of translation of legal and juridical texts, argues that the tools for achieving equivalence are appropriate strategies and techniques. At the same time, it adopts a definition of equivalence as a relationship occurring between the translation text (or a fragment thereof) and the corresponding source text (or a fragment thereof) (Pieńkos, 1993: 165). He also considers that 'equivalence should be called a fixed, equivalent conformity, as a rule independent of context' (ibid.: 166). He argues that it is up to the translator to render what was said in the original, as well as to decide how the transmission should be done (ibid.: 168). In his view, 'for the process of translation, it is extremely important to distinguish between the semantic equivalence of a word out of context and the equivalence of its contextual sense' (ibid.). This finding is important to the extent that it impinges on the work and the way translation tools are selected and used in the translation process. Like Kielar and Kierzkowska, cited earlier, Pieńkos also argues that dictionaries alone are insufficient to achieve equivalence in translation. The behaviour of a particular term in a given context must be analysed – again, the role of parallel texts as a tool for achieving equivalence must be emphasised here. Pieńkos makes a clear distinction between translation work based solely on dictionary and lexicographical resources and analytical work during the translation process, stating:

> Those who limit themselves to the dictionary in their translation work and who look for the equivalents given in lexicographical works at any cost confuse the concept of the dictionary meaning of a word with its contextual sense. Where the meaning of a text needs to be extracted, a dictionary can never replace the exegesis that the translator must make. This exegesis is the analytical and synthetic reasoning inherent in

any work of translation. A dictionary will not resolve all the difficulties of translation, so it certainly cannot be the greatest authority (Pieńkos, 1993: 169).

Pieńkos also distinguishes between two levels of equivalence, as presented in Tab. 16.

Tab. 16: Equivalence, according to Jerzy Pieńkos

Semantic equivalence		Pragmatic equivalence
meaningful	situational	➜ equivalence at translator level ➜ equivalence of the response of the recipient of the translation compared to the response of the recipient of the original ➜ equivalence of communicative intent

Source: Own elaboration based on: Pieńkos, 1993: 169.

Referring to the problem of achieving equivalence in translations of specialised texts, Pieńkos points out that the cognitive function of the text is a key element during such translations. According to him, formal equivalence, a literal translation technique, is far more frequently used in texts of this nature, because 'in specialist texts, the most important elements of translation are the concepts conveyed by the terms' (Pieńkos, 1993: 272). The researcher also argues that the search for equivalents should result in 'either the selection of a disposable equivalent or, if there is an absolute necessity, the creation of a neologism' (ibid.: 275). This raises another issue, namely whether every term has an equivalent, whether every concept can be translated, whether there is a phenomenon of non-translatability, and what the translator should do when so-called non-equivalent terms appear.

2.2.2.8. Position of Mona Baker

The statement of another translation scholar, Mona Baker, is interesting in this context. Taking a stance towards the phenomenon of equivalence, she draws attention to translation problems that already exist at the word level, defined by her as follows: 'a lack of equivalence at the word level means that there is no direct equivalent in the target language of a word that occurs in the source text' (Baker, 2006: 20, after: Kizinska, 2015: 24).

Tab. 17: Sources of lack of equivalence according to Mona Baker[66] (lack of equivalence at the word level)

Source of lack of equivalence at word level	Proposed strategies
Occurrence of concepts closely related to culture	use of a hyperonym, use of a more neutral/less expressive word, use of a cultural substitute, use of borrowing, use of borrowing with explanation, translation by paraphrase with a related word, translation by paraphrase with a word that is not related, translation by omission, translation by illustration
Occurrence of concepts from the source language that are not lexicalised in the target language	
Occurrence of semantically complex source language concepts	
Existence of other distinctions in the source and target languages in terms of meaning	
Absence of hyperonyms in the target language	
No hyponym in the target language	
Existence of differences in physical and interpersonal perspectives	
Differences in the expressive meaning of the word	
Differences in the form of expression	
Differences in frequency and purpose of using a particular form of expression	
Use of borrowings not found in the target language in the source text	

Source: Own elaboration based on the work of Anna Kizinska (2015: 24–26) and Mona Baker (2006: 26–42).

Baker also distinguishes equivalence at a higher level than at the word level. This is equivalence in terms of collocations, idioms, and established expressions and phrases.

66 Mona Baker's current articles on translation studies are also available on her author website www.monabaker.org.

Tab. 18: Sources of lack of equivalence, according to Mona Baker[67] (lack of equivalence at the level of collocations, idioms, and established expressions and phrases)

Source of lack of equivalence at the level of collocations, idioms, and established expressions and phrases	Proposed strategies
Excessive repetition of source text patterns when there is no semantically similar collocation in the target language	use of an idiom with a similar meaning and form, use of an idiom with a similar meaning but different form, use of paraphrase, translation by omission
Lack of understanding of collocation occurring in the source text	
The need to choose between accuracy and naturalness	
Occurrence of collocations closely related to the culture of the source language	
Occurrence in the source text of superlative collocations (new and unnatural collocations denoting new phenomena and concepts)	
Difficulty in correctly identifying idioms in the source text	
No equivalent idiom/phrase/expression in the target language	
Different connotations for similar expressions	
Occurrence of an idiom that can be used both literally and idiomatically	

Source: Own elaboration based on the work of Anna Kizinska (2015: 24–26) and Mona Baker (2006: 26–42).

According to Baker, equivalence should be achieved at the level of the text, not at the level of the word or phrase (Kizinska, 2015: 26). The translator's aspiration in his translation work is to obtain a text in the target language that the recipient would recognise as the original (Baker, 2006: 111, after: Kizinska, 2015: 36).

67 Mona Baker's current articles on translation studies are also available on her author website www.monabaker.org.

2.2.2.9. *Non-equivalent terms in specialist translations*

This raises the question of whether everything can be translated and what happens when the translator encounters a so-called non-equivalent term. Are there any limits to translatability? Researchers such as Danuta Kierzkowska (2007), Olgierd Wojtasiewicz (1958), and Barbara Kielar (1988) draw attention to this problem in their work.

Taking a position from the perspective of a translator of legal texts, Danuta Kierzkowska points out that:

> Any guidance on the choice of translation strategy, i.e., the choice of denotational equivalence, oriented towards the source language (source-similar translation), or connotational equivalence, oriented towards the target language (connotative translation), can be helpful in situations where there is a possibility of comparison, i.e., only when similar concepts exist in the two legal systems being compared, and the translator only has to decide on the degree of this similarity and the possibility of applying the appropriate type of equivalence. The question arises, however, what the translator should or can do in a situation where it is known that the legal system of the target language lacks the concept referred to in the source text (Kierzkowska, 2008: 113).

Kierzkowska suggests the use of various techniques to create non-equivalent terms[68] (Tab. 19).

---

68 Danuta Kierzkowska draws attention to the problem of the expression 'non-equivalent term' itself. In her view, it is understood to mean 'the absence of a concept in the legal system of the target language'. However, even such a precise definition of the term's meaning may prove somewhat relative, as 'it can always be contrasted with a rough equivalent' (Kierzkowska, 2007: 114). Barbara Kielar (1988: 89), analysing the limits of translatability, considers that 'the translator reaches the limits of translatability when he has exhausted all the means available in the language of translation, but still has not achieved functional equivalence between the original text and the translated text'. This researcher, in describing an inequivalent expression, characterises this phenomenon as 'the absence in the language of translation of a pre-lexicalised and commonly accepted conventional equivalent of a given term' (ibid.: 92). Olgierd Wojtasiewicz (1957: 30), writing in the 1960s, pointed out the obstacles standing in the way of formulating content in the language of translation, such as: '1. the language into which we intend to translate does not dispose of the structural means existing in the original language; 2. in the language into which we intend to translate it is not possible to render certain concepts expressible in the original language'. Krzysztof Hejwowski (2012: 71) sees the source of relative non-translatability, as does Olgierd Wojtasiewicz (1957: 30), in cultural differences and in language differences.

Tab. 19: Techniques for creating non-equivalent terms

Equivalent name	Description of the equivalent
Natural (functional) equivalent distant	Unlike the linguistic equivalent of a term, it is the equivalent that the recipient associates more naturally. In the case of legal and juridical texts, it is a term familiar to the recipient from the legal system of the target language (Kierzkowska, 2007: 118).
Natural (functional) equivalent close to	It is an equivalence that defines the basic function inherent in the definition of a concept; such equivalences are also commonly used for similar concepts in other legal systems (e.g., judge, court) (Kierzkowska, 2007: 119).
Seminatural equivalent	It is a type of equivalent that is a modification of the natural equivalent. It combines the features of the natural equivalent with those of the term in the source language (Kierzkowska, 2007: 120).
Lexical word calque	It is an equivalence in which 'a word or expression is formed using native language elements according to the semantic pattern of the foreign language' (Polański, 1999: 284, after: Kierzkowska, 2007: 120).
Simple borrowing	It is 'a translation technique that involves leaving a word or phrase from the original language unchanged in the translated text' (Lukszyn, 1993: 99, after: Kierzkowska, 2007: 121).
Naturalized borrowing	It is a technique that involves adapting ('naturalising') to the phonetic requirements of a term from the source language, which facilitates the pronunciation of the concept in question.
Descriptive equivalent	Similar to Krzysztof Hejwowski's use of this term (see above) – this technique is used when the translator does not want or sees no basis for using a foreign-sounding borrowing or natural equivalent for a given concept in the text (Kierzkowska, 2007: 122).

Tab. 19: Continued

Equivalent name	Description of the equivalent
Phraseological equivalent	In legal and jurisprudential texts, the technique of phraseological equivalence is widely used and desired by the audience. Verb phrases used in texts of this nature require the translator to be familiar with the conventions of the target language 'in terms of the inter-word relationships adopted for each of them (phrases), the so-called collocations. Collocations in any language allow for connections between different parts of speech in a well-defined way […]' (Kierzkowska, 2007: 123).

Source: Own elaboration based on the work of Danuta Kierzkowska (2007: 113–123).

Following Krzysztof Hejwowski (2012: 83), it should be emphasised that the selection of the appropriate translation strategy and techniques largely depends on the type of text. Some techniques and strategies will prevail for literary texts, where aesthetic value plays an important role, and others for specialised texts, where the semantic side of the text plays a key role.

Barbara Kielar (1988: 86) stresses that 'the differences in customs, beliefs, views, legal and state institutions of European societies make it necessary to use appropriate translation strategies and to seek optimal solutions when translating texts'. The translator, therefore, needs to be aware of and knowledgeable about the available translation strategies and techniques that he or she can use in their work. He or she must also have knowledge of the sources of potential translation problems in order to be able to correctly identify them and then assess and take appropriate measures to create the correct equivalent in the target language. A lack of such competencies means a significantly poorer translator's workshop and a lack of self-development and self-education in translation work. Lack of knowledge of the sources of potential errors causes the translator to work 'in the dark', often making even trivial mistakes that, unfortunately, affect the credibility and value of his or her work. It is worth emphasising that theory and practice meet at a tangent point, so that a translator with the necessary experience can draw on the resources of his or her theoretical knowledge to achieve a satisfactory result in the form of a high level of translation.

2.2.3. Glossary

According to the definition given in the PWN dictionary of the Polish language, a glossary is 'a dictionary explaining unknown words in an ancient or foreign-language text' (SJP, 2021). In the past, glossaries were created by manuscript copyists; they explained the meaning of more difficult words or terms found in the text and did so in the margins of the page. It used to be that the glossary was an indispensable tool in the work of a translator of specialised texts, his 'private' terminological base and, therefore, the foundation of his work. For the purposes of this work, the author adopted the definition of the word 'term' taken from Franciszek Grucza, stating that a term is 'a word or word combination with a clearly defined meaning' (Grucza, 1991b: 16). Grucza points out that the terms currently cause many problems for language users.

> [...] the role of terms has been growing enormously for some time now. The number of people for whom terms are a source of increasing inconvenience has been growing rapidly, the number of language users is rapidly increasing, and the number of language users who are increasingly obliged to deal with terms creatively – to create and process them – should now include all specialists in all fields, both practical-productive and cognitive-creative. Their unification, ordering, etc., but they should also be aware that both the creation of terms and their use need to be rationalised, and that if this is to be done, one must first consider, among other things, what terms are and what functions they fulfil (Grucza, 1991b: 17).

When writing this text thirty years ago, Franciszek Grucza accurately predicted the development of specialist terminology, while at the same time somewhat foreshadowing the negative impact of poor-quality language, which is happening today under the influence of the development of the internet. When looking for a definition for the word 'term' in the context of specialist translation, the author of this work also reached for a definition from the *Thesaurus of Translation Terminology*, where the concept of a term was defined as 'a strictly defined word or word combination as a verbal unit of a specialist vocabulary' (Lukszyn, 1993: 342). Legal and jurisprudential texts are characterised by terminology that is closely related to the context. In addition, the fact of the incompatibility of the legal systems of the countries of the translated language pair[69]

69 By language pair, this work understands the two languages involved in the translation process – the source language and the target language.

and the phenomenon of homonymy make the translation of these texts difficult. Danuta Kierzkowska's work addresses the problem of the incompatibility of legal systems and its impact on the difficulty of legal and juridical translation. Recalling Falber's words that a name should, as far as possible, be assigned to only one concept and that all homonymy and synonymy should be excluded (Felber et al., 1994: 152, after: Kierzkowska, 2008: 21), Kierzkowska stresses that the principle of avoiding these two phenomena when creating a secondary terminological system is of vital importance (Kierzkowska, 2008: 21). In her decalogue of the principles of legal translation, Kierzkowska (2020: 175) includes 'the principle of one equivalent for the same concept'. Once used for a given term, the equivalent should be used consistently throughout the translation[70] (in this respect, CAT tools that use translation memories are extremely helpful, so that consistent terminology is maintained throughout the translation). Another principle – the 'principle of priority of recommended terminology'[71] – states that the translator should use the recommended, unified terminology adopted by the client. This makes things much easier for the translator, and the translation of European Union legislation can serve as an example of how this can be applied. Glossaries of standardised terminology are regularly developed and published by the Translation Service of the European Community Commission (Kierzkowska, 2020: 178). This allows a large team of translators to undertake one large project together while being confident that the same terms will not be translated in different ways by each of the translators participating in the project.

70 In accordance with the Decree of the President of the Council of Ministers of 20 June 2002 on the 'Principles of Legislative Techniques', the principle of single equivalence is applied in Polish legislation. In accordance with par. 147 'if the meaning of a term is established in a law or other normative act by way of definition, a term with a different meaning must not be used within that act' (after: Kierzkowska, 2020: 176).

71 Recommended terminology is understood as official terminology and authoritative terminology (Kierzkowska, 2020: 178).

Tab. 20: Glossary of selected examples of Czech-Polish homonyms from specialist translations

Polish language system		Czech language system	
Meaning	**Form**	**Form**	**Importance**
ustawa	*zákon*	*zakon*	organizacja/ zrzeszenie o charakterze religijnym
kodeks	*zakoník*	*zakonnik*	mnich
gniazdo (tech.)	*lože*	*łoże*	duże łóżko
maszyna	*stroj*	*strój*	ubranie
karta, dokument (tech.)	*list*	*list*	korespondencja
pozew	*žaloba*	*żałoba*	przeżywanie straty po śmierci bliskiej osoby
mandat	*pokuta*	*pokuta*	rodzaj praktyki religijnej

Source: Own study modelled on the glossary of Polish-Finnish homonyms compiled by Katarzyna Wojan (Wojan, 2017: 56).

Tab. 21: Example glossary of terminology related to the European Court of Human Rights

Original version	Translation proposal	Name of text
Europejski Trybunał Praw Człowieka	Evropský soud pro lidská práva	Europejski Trybunał Praw Człowieka
Europejska konwencja o ochronie praw człowieka i podstawowych wolności	Evropská úmluva o ochraně lidských práv a základních svobod	Europejski Trybunał Praw Człowieka
Kasacja	kasační stížnost, mimořadný opravný prostředek	Europejski Trybunał Praw Człowieka
Konstytucja	Ústava	Europejski Trybunał Praw Człowieka
niezgodność przepisu	nesoulad ustanovení	Europejski Trybunał Praw Człowieka

Tab. 21: Continued

Original version	Translation proposal	Name of text
przepis niezgodny z konstytucją	ústanovení protiústavní	Europejski Trybunał Praw Człowieka
postępowanie sądowo-administracyjne	soudní řízení správní	Europejski Trybunał Praw Człowieka
prawo do rzetelnego procesu sądowego	práva na spravedlivý proces	Europejski Trybunał Praw Człowieka
prawo do skutecznego środka odwoławczego	právo na účinný opravný prostředek	Europejski Trybunał Praw Człowieka
prawo do zawarcia małżeństwa	právo na uzavření manželství	Europejski Trybunał Praw Człowieka
prawo do wolności i bezpieczeństwa osobistego	právo na svobodu a osobní bezpečnost	Europejski Trybunał Praw Człowieka
prawa obywatelskie	občanská práva	Europejski Trybunał Praw Człowieka
prawo do życia	právo na život	Europejski Trybunał Praw Człowieka
skarga na naruszenie prawa strony do rozpoznania sprawy w postępowaniu sądowym bez nieuzasadnionej zwłoki	porušení práva žalobce na projednání věci u soudního řízení bez zbytečné prodlevy	Europejski Trybunał Praw Człowieka
stałeś się ofiarą naruszenia przez państwo praw zawartych w Konwencji…	stal jste se obětí porušení statem práv přiznaných Úmluvou	Europejski Trybunał Praw Człowieka
wolność zgromadzania się i stowarzyszania się	svoboda shromažďování a sdružování	Europejski Trybunał Praw Człowieka
wnieść skargę do Trybunału	předložit věc Soudnímu dvoru	Europejski Trybunał Praw Człowieka

Source: Own study modelled on the glossary of law and legal terms compiled by Marek Kuźniak (Kuźniak, 2015).

Awareness of the importance of glossaries and terminology databases has increased in the translation community with the development of CAT tools, which enable the automatic creation of terminology databases and dictionaries based on translations made using translation memories. Such databases are very often developed by translators or translation agencies during long-term cooperation with a particular client or when they specialise in translations for a specific industry or branch. They help to maintain uniform terminology used in translations (e.g., for a given client by several translators). The glossary may contain individual words and terms as well as their explanations. Such a database can take the form of a bilingual or monolingual dictionary (in which case it provides an aid to understanding the meaning of a term in context), and the production of a good industry terminology database requires accuracy and precision during creation (the best glossaries are produced when industry specialists can be consulted at every stage of the creation of such a dictionary). Glossaries allow translators to have a sense of consistency in terminology at every stage of the job, while the client can be confident that once an equivalent term is used, it will be used consistently over the following months or even years of collaboration with the translator. It is worth adding that the importance of the glossary increases if the client commissions translations into several languages simultaneously. Although glossaries require considerable care and a lot of work, they are worth developing and learning to work with when completing assignments. Each translator certainly has his or her own idea and individual method of creating glossaries. In Tab. 22, the author has included examples of glossaries made by hand by translators. The relatively accessible and even easy technique of creating glossaries is still not a frequently practised element in the work of translators. Those who are just starting out[72] with translations rarely create a glossary at the outset, which, after all, naturally becomes a better and more necessary tool with each successive assignment.

72 The author of this work, when teaching specialised translation classes, always takes up the topic of glossaries with her students. Few consciously create dictionaries and terminology databases at the very beginning of their work. It often helps to direct them, show them how to do it and use it in practice.

Tab. 22: Example of a Polish-Czech glossary of law and legal terms

Term/expression in Polish	Proposal for equivalence in Czech	Type of text
A		
alimenty	výživné	Family law
akt notarialny	notářský zapis	Akt notarialny
akapit	Pododstavec	Akt notarialny
B		
bez uszczerbku dla przepisów art. 4 rozporządzenia Rady	aniž je dotčen článek 4 nařízení Rady	UE
bezskuteczny	Neučinný	UE
banknot	Bankovka	UE
biegły z zakresu weterynarii	veterinární znalec	Sąd
biegły rewident	nezávislý revizor	Sąd
C		
całkowite przysposobienie	plné osvojení	Adopcja
cyberprzestępczość	počítačová kriminalita	Sąd
D		
do czasu powtórnych oględzin	do doby opakované prohlídky	Gdy zostaniesz poszkodowany
domniemane naruszenie	domnělé protiprávní jednání	Gdy zostaniesz poszkodowany

Source: Own elaboration modelled on the glossary of legal and jurisprudential terms compiled by Marek Kuźniak (Kuźniak, 2015).

Naturally, in addition to manually preparing glossaries themselves, which can seem tedious and labour-intensive, translators also have a range of modern technological solutions at their disposal. The so-called CATs, which are specialised programmes that support the translator during his or her work, enable not only a more efficient execution of the translation itself but also the creation of terminology databases. One of the most commonly used tools by translators is Trados Studio. Among other things, it has two options for creating a kind of glossary – a terminology database. The first and most well-known terminology base is the so-called *translation memory*. When completing an assignment, the translator can save a special file (sort of like a specialised dictionary on a shelf in a library) in which terminology will be collected during the translation. It can be created based on an industry (e.g., a dictionary for metallurgy or machining only), a customer (a dictionary with a terminology base specifically for one customer), or some other field of human activity (a dictionary designed for sport, covering all disciplines). This file enables the translator to complete the next job faster, as the word equivalents already entered are automatically substituted in the next text. Of course, such a solution also has its drawbacks, as a wrongly introduced equivalent will consistently appear in subsequent texts. The translator may have dozens of such terminology databases and may also pass them on to another translator with whom he or she undertakes a co-delivery job – in this way, it is possible to ensure uniform terminology regardless of the number of translators working on a given project. This is important because, for example, in the case of EU translations, many people work on the same project, and each of them should use the same range of terminology. In addition to translation memories, CAT programmes such as Trados Studio have their own tools for managing terminology databases. SDL MultiTerm allows, for example, a graphic or picture to be attached to a word (it is then easier for the translator to find the right equivalent because he or she sees a picture or drawing of, for example, a piece of machinery or equipment). This tool allows the management, completion, and modification of the terminology database. By using a self-made corpus (or reference corpus) in their daily work, translators can also develop their own terminology base as appropriate to the context. By working on the translation and, at the same time, compiling a glossary, the translator not only consolidates his or her knowledge of specialised vocabulary but also better understands the context in which the term functions and remembers it more quickly. Corpora created with Sketch Engine, for example, allows the terminology base to be automatically downloaded and exported to a separate file as a bilingual dictionary. There are many possibilities for the creation of glossaries, but the most important issue remains the translat'rs' willingness to develop glossaries in a reliable and systematic way.

There is another aspect of the creation of terminology bases by specialist translators, which Franciszek Grucza draws attention to in his work. Language today changes rapidly, leading to a 'quantitative proliferation of terms used in various fields of human activity, both cognitive, above all scientific, and practical – productive, economic, as well as social and public' (Grucza, 1991a: 7). Because of the emergence of a huge and growing number of new terms in different areas of life, it is becoming increasingly difficult to master new terminology in both a passive and active sense (ibid.). This process is unlikely to slow down in the coming years, given the development of new technologies, which in turn is showing an impact on economic and business development. Printed dictionaries are not always able to keep up with current developments in specialised terminology, while online databases are sometimes not reliable and dependable sources of knowledge. The professional translator in such a situation should develop his or her own dictionary databases on an ongoing basis, including those on specialised terminology, taking into account the different contexts in which the concepts and terms are used.

Franciszek Grucza, however, points to another important issue related to rapid economic development affecting vocabulary. He rightly argues that 'the rapid proliferation of terms, their uncontrolled production and borrowing threatens not only the "purity" of the native language, but significantly disrupts and sometimes completely blocks the functioning of not only purely communicative (informational), but also various productive, economic, political, etc. systems' (Grucza, 1991a: 15). Terminology and its development can have a positive impact on cognitive and practical, social and economic progress provided that the terminology's quality is maintained at an appropriate level, otherwise terminology can have a negative impact on progress. Maria Piotrowska (2007: 116), on the other hand, calls for the inclusion of general skills in translator training, such as recognising translation problems, adopting appropriate strategies when carrying out a translation assignment, acquiring information and, at the same time, using databases, and terminology management. 'Effective search terms and the systematic creation of one's own databases are the cornerstones of a translator's terminology workshop' (Perdek, 2016: 100). Creating terminology databases and glossaries is not just about creating a bilingual table of words and phrases. This is a much more demanding and time-consuming undertaking. This is because it generates the need for a proper understanding of the term in the source language according to the context, which often also requires environmental consultations, and analyses of parallel texts and internet sources. As Magdalena Perdek rightly points out, 'No matter where one finds a translation of a term, it should be verified either in another reliable source or with a specialist in the field' (ibid.). Ongoing reading and the collection of parallel texts (i.e., the use of case-law databases, the archiving of contract texts, or the preservation of relevant sources of specialised terminology) provide a basis for searching and exploring perceived linguistic nuances, and thus offer the possibility of developing a valuable and reliable tool for the translator of specialised texts.

2.3. Professional texts

2.3.1. Problems of translation of specialised texts

When addressing the issue of translation of specialised texts, it is important to define what a specialised text and a specialised language are. Numerous Polish researchers have addressed this topic in the literature (Pisarska, Tomaszkiewicz, 1996; Pieńkos, 1993; Lewandowska-Tomaszczyk, 2005b; Kielar, 1991; Grucza, 1991a; Jopek-Bosiacka, 2019; Kierzkowska, 2020 et al.). In the work of Alicja Pisarska and Teresa Tomaszkiewicz, specialised translation is identical to applied translation. They applied the criterion of the purpose of specialised translation described below:

> The translator most often translates specialised texts to a given order and they are immediately used for some specific social purpose: they help to understand the functioning of some machine, they become a legal act in a particular situation, they make it possible to treat, for example, a patient whose medical history has been translated; these translations are most often supported by the rapid flow of information (Pisarska, Tomaszkiewicz, 1996: 182).[73]

Jerzy Pieńkos (1993) and Barbara Lewandowska-Tomaszczyk (2005b) accept the definition by Aleksander Szulc, who states that:

> Specialised (expert) language is a particular form of general language adapted to describe a specific branch of knowledge or technology as precisely as possible. It differs from the supra-dialectal language primarily in its professional vocabulary, often containing many internationalisms, and in its syntax, as well as in the frequency of use of certain grammatical forms (e.g., *passivum* in German technical language) (Szulc, 1984: 106–107).

---

73 In the context of specialised/utilitarian translation, Pisarska and Tomaszkiewicz emphasise the fact that different categories of texts function in different areas of

In addition, Barbara Lewandowska-Tomaszczyk emphasises the difficulty in the conception of a specialised language, citing different positions, e.g., Pieńkos, who believes that 'it is almost impossible to indicate a clear boundary between a specialised language and a general language', and Rey and Mounin, who question 'the existence of a specialised language as a subsystem functioning in the system of language as a whole' (Lewandowska-Tomaszczyk, 2005b: 175).[74]

In this context, the notion of sublinguality emerges, which Barbara Kielar (1991: 134) understands as 'a variety of natural language, distinguished according to sociological correlates and formal features'. Various sublanguages can therefore be distinguished, such as legal language, technical language, or medical language (Kierzkowska, 2020: 173). This division is also dictated by terminology, for as Barbara Kielar writes in her work on the problems of translating specialised texts:

> In the sub-languages distinguished, specialist terms usually come to the fore, with which specialists attempt to organise and systematise their section of extra-linguistic reality as unambiguously as possible. The term[75] in the specialty/field should mean a well-defined concept, i.e., a generalised mental content that captures the properties and interrelationships between objects. A given concept is usually related to other concepts, e.g., of an overarching or subordinate nature, thus entering into a certain conceptual system. Analogously, name systems are linked (Kielar, 1991: 134).

This is a very valuable thought, as it underlines the importance of translating a specialised text considering the wider context. At this point, it is also important to recall the definition of legal and juridical language, understood as a sub-language, which will appear in the context of specialised translation. The Polish literature accepts the definition by Bronisław Wróblewski,

---

the economy, e.g., in the field of economics there are texts on trade, accounting, or banking (Pisarska, Tomaszkiewicz, 1996: 183). In their work, they addressed the issues of technical translation and legal translation understood as specialised translation.

74 These researchers postulated the existence of only a specialist vocabulary, not a language (Lewandowska-Tomaszczyk, 2005b: 175).

75 Franciszek Grucza (1991a) writes about the status and meaning of terminology in his work, issues in the field of terminology are also described by Małgorzata Tryuk (1991), while issues related to the standardisation of Polish technical terminology are addressed by Halina Rybicka-Nowacka (1991).

which understands legal language to be the language of the legislator – it is the language of legal acts, and its source is legal regulations. The language used by lawyers, on the other hand, is Maciej Zieliński language, which is a metalanguage related to legal language (Wroblewski, 1948: 56; compare Jopek-Bosiacka, 2021: 12; Zieliński, 1999: 50–72; Kierzkowska, 2008: 14–18). Maciej Zieliński created the contemporary categorisation of legal and juridical languages, which is also referred to by Anna Jopek-Bosiacka, a researcher of legal and judicial translation.[76] The division into legal and juridical languages, according to Zieliński, is reproduced below (Figs. 13 and 14).

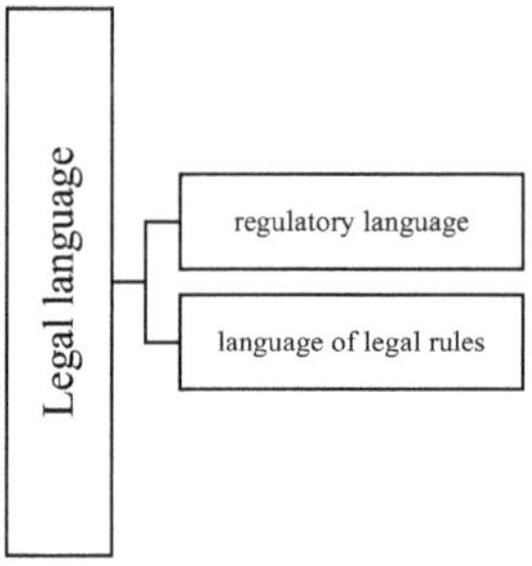

Fig. 13: Legal language according to Maciej Zieliński's categorisation
Source: Own elaboration based on: Zieliński, 1999; Wróblewski, 1948; Jopek-Bosiacka, 2021.

76 It should be mentioned that the Polish term 'legal translation' was coined by practising translators, as mentioned by Danuta Kierzkowska (2008: 55), in collaboration with such translation theorists as Olgierd A. Wojtasiewicz, Jerzy Pieńkos, and Barbara Z. Kielar. It refers to a concept that covers the translation of all types of texts in both legal and juridical language. It is assumed to be an umbrella term over the term 'translation of legal texts', i.e., texts written in legal language, and includes legal texts (Kierzkowska, 2008: 55). This is also the interpretation of the above terms in this trial.

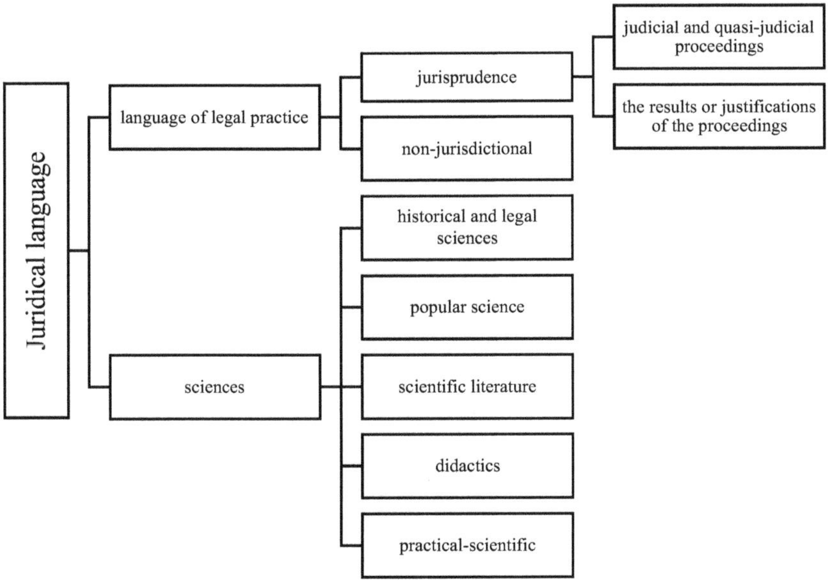

Fig. 14: Juridical language according to Maciej Zieliński's categorisation
Source: Own elaboration based on: Zielińskim 1999; Wróblewski, 1948; Jopek-Bosiacka, 2021.

The terms 'law language' and 'legal language' in this work are used in accordance with the definition created by Bogusław Wróblewski and in accordance with Maciej Zieliński's categorisation.

In studies on specialised translation, translators are recommended to use parallel texts rather than just monolingual dictionaries. Using such materials, the translator acquires proficiency in the use of textual constructions, so that later, intuitively, he or she will use and imitate them (Voellnagel, 2014; Kielar, 1991). When translating a specialised text, the translator is faced with choices related to problems around adapting to the textual conventions of the language of translation (Kielar, 1991: 137), for 'the text is translated as a coherent whole and not its detached elements' (ibid.: 138).[77] Jerzy

77 In her work on the problems of translating specialist texts, Barbara Kielar also draws attention to the phenomenon of intertextuality, which, she says takes on a particular form in the case of translation. 'The translated text enters into intertextual relations with parallel original texts in the target language. The

Pieńkos, in his search for a definition of specialised language, turns to an approach that talks about specialised vocabulary. Indeed, he recognises that the primary functions of specialised language include the cognitive function and the communicative function. Specialised language is intended for learning about and conveying the specialised content of a linguistic message (Pieńkos, 1993: 268). Pieńkos also notes that an important part of the specialist vocabulary is nouns. At the same time, he stresses that a specialist language term cannot be detached from its social function or the environment in which it functions (Pieńkos, 1993: 271).

The author of this work, when considering the issue of specialist translation, leans towards the approach of Anna Jopek-Bosiacka, who has devoted her research to the problems of legal and judicial translation. Namely, she emphasises the strong relationship that exists between expertise and the language of texts used in specialist communication (Jopek-Bosiacka, 2008: 10). This approach makes it possible for the three basic elements, namely language, knowledge, and text, to interact within specialised communication, which includes, in her view, specialised language. Such an approach takes into account an important aspect of the difference in understanding of expertise between specialists and lay people (ibid.). This differentiation of knowledge (Bosiacka refers to Sager's words) defines specialised languages in a certain way. The specialised texts themselves play an important role manifested 'in achieving the communicative goals defined by the specialised communication framework' (ibid.).

Danuta Kierzkowska, writing her book *Legal Translation* a dozen years ago, was already drawing attention to the increasing demand for specialist translators. The nature of the work of specialist translators changed fundamentally as a result of the political and economic events that took place around the world in the early 2000s, when '[...] increased processes of disintegration of old systems and integration of new ones resulted in a sharp

---

translator is thus faced with double intertextual relationships. It has the task of "assimilating" the J1 (source language) text for an audience belonging to the J2 (target language) community. It thus seeks to adapt the translation text being produced to the conventions of J2, but, acting on the basis of a ready-made textual creation in the source language, it is unable to detach itself completely from its original intertextuality' (Kielar, 1991: 138).

increase in the demand for the work of specialist translators in general and legal translators in particular' (Kierzkowska, 2008: 58). This has consequently increased the interest of specialist translators in self-education and the improvement of their working practices. The range of translation services has also expanded to include new possibilities, such as dubbing lists, localisation, or translations of interfaces for mobile devices.[78] Similarly, Maria Piotrowska, in her work on the translator's decision-making process, points to global changes that have affected the way translators work:

> In the age of globalisation, localisation and migration, it has taken on a new dimension. The creation of the interpreter's attitude and the social dimension of his/her role is in constant flux, and the creation of his/her image through the pragmatic and professional context is dynamic and subject to various conditions. The manufactouristic nature of his workshop is transforming into a networked, technological system of text processing, and the globalisation of translation markets is leading to a shortening of the production cycle of translated texts. The flow of information and knowledge, which is nowadays already possible on a global scale, and the growing importance of economics mean that the requirements of principals are increasing (Piotrowska, 2007: 7).

The modern translator of specialised texts faces several challenges arising not only from the level of difficulty of the texts to be translated, but also from market needs and expectations. Now that a significant part of the

78 It seems a very interesting experience today to read the work of Olgierd Wojtasiewicz (1958) in the context of the changes that have taken place in the world as a result of globalisation and internationalisation, also in relation to language. Wojtasiewicz wrote his paper more than sixty years ago, almost prophetically predicting what followed fifty years later: 'It is also conceivable that – at a much slower rate – intensive international and intercultural contacts will lead to a blurring of many differences in language structures. In fact, we are already seeing this in the form of the adoption of idioms in commercial, technical and scientific texts, which to some extent implies a commodification of syntax, and in the form of a fairly widespread simplification of forms of address to second persons. […] These predictions, moreover, do not have much practical significance for us at the moment, but serve only to indicate how some – and in the very distant future perhaps even all – theoretical problems of translation will automatically find a solution, at least as far as newly emerging texts unencumbered by the tradition of cultural and linguistic differences are concerned' (Wojtasiewicz, 1975: 107). One can only wonder whether there is really a chance that the new texts will be free of this cultural and linguistic burden.

commercial activity of both Polish and foreign companies has moved to the internet, the demand for translations of websites and webshop interfaces has increased significantly. A simple translation of such pages is nowadays insufficient not only from a utilitarian point of view (the content may sound artificial to the reader), but also from a business point of view (the products will not sell). Adequate textual adaptation to the needs and requirements of the recipient has become a prerequisite in modern translation services.[79] Localisation, as it is referred to in the dictionary, is 'making a translation with adaptation to local conditions'.[80] A localisation service consists of preparing the translation of content from the source language in such a way that the recipient gets the impression that they are dealing with something that has been skilfully adapted to their cultural patterns (the cultural patterns of the target language), often without realising that the original is of foreign origin (Puławska, 2005: 91). This is also known as textual matching or naturalness of translation (Biel, 2011). Elżbieta Puławska defines product localisation as adapting a product to the cultural and legal context of another country, in areas such as:

- graphic localisation (graphic elements that appear in the text need to be adapted to the target culture, to the standards of the culture and language concerned);
- audio localisation (a type of localisation often used in the creation of material for websites or in the preparation of electronic publications; audio material necessitates appropriate preparation not only in terms of the translation itself, but also in terms of sound, and it is necessary to use the appropriate technical facilities necessary for sound production);

79 Sometimes a trader, anticipating that his product will be sold abroad, removes cultural elements in the content of the website or elements of the product descriptions in the online shop. 'Associated with the localisation process is "internationalisation" in a new sense of the word. An internationalised product is one that has been designed in such a way that it can be easily received in different countries and cultural environments without any redesign' (Pulawska, 2005: 92).

80 Definition based on the *New Dictionary of the Kosciuszko Foundation* (after: Puławska, 2005: 90).

- cultural adaptation (for example, the preparation of website content – the message contained on websites must be prepared 'in the spirit' of the country in question, this is particularly true of today's popular online shops, where translation and localisation are key to selling a product in another country);
- localisation of specific elements (a service related to adapting the content of, for example, textbooks or advertising content to the target culture; any jokes, anecdotes, sayings, and examples need to be appropriately adapted to the audience's culture).[81]

Localisation also poses a number of problems for the translator[82] – these include linguistic problems, dilemmas arising from the content of the text and cultural phenomena,[83] as well as problems of a technical nature (Puławska, 2005). Such translations require a great deal of experience and familiarity with the various types of source texts and the cultures in which these texts were produced – the skills and competence of a web translator are very evident. Machine translation is unlikely to be applicable to this type of translation (machine translation of web pages is usually of very poor quality), although it cannot be denied that if the content is uncomplicated, most often allowing the recipient to successfully complete a simple online purchase, CAT tools work well to assist the translator with content with a high number of repetitions, numbers, or highly unified and formalised texts. Often such a translation also requires the proper adaptation of very different elements, for example, icons, graphic elements, the accounting system, the metric and currency system, and even the proper adaptation of polite forms (referring to somebody with the American-style 'you' will

81 Currently, localisation is a type of service/product that is on offer from translation agencies, e.g., www.skrivanek.pl, www.skrivanek.cz, www.zelenka.cz.

82 It is worth keeping an eye on the website of the Warsaw Translators' Conference (www.konferencja-tlumaczy.pl), which includes lectures on web localisation, showing the new challenges facing translators, as well as a range of modern solutions and opportunities.

83 Also, Olgierd Wojtasiewicz (1957: 105) points out that, in fact, translation problems are primarily issues arising from cultural differences, and not only linguistic problems or problems relating to underlying structural differences between languages.

not always work in the Polish business reality, for example).[84] 'Successful localisation (translation) requires an in-depth knowledge of the source and target civilizational and cultural conditions' (Puławska, 2005: 93), the translation, therefore, requires a high degree of precision and therefore also the cooperation of a proofreader, preferably speaking the language of the target culture at the level of the mother tongue. The issue of the character system of the target culture's language is also not insignificant – the two-bit character systems in Far Eastern languages result in the need for more space for text, software changes, and source code (Puławska, 2005: 93).[85] The popularity of phone apps provides a field of action for modern translators who, more than dictionary knowledge of the language, need to have the skills to operate mobile devices in foreign markets. Operating menus, commands, or even banking applications requires knowledge of how the application works in the target culture environment. Such knowledge is not acquired at university, as it often requires experience working abroad or doing business in a different language culture.[86]

Producing specialised translation entails having the right competence, knowledge, and experience, as well as the translator being extremely responsible and aware of the importance of his or her work.

The work by Alicja Pisarska and Teresa Tomaszkiewicz (1996), mentioned at the beginning of this chapter, gives an indication of the potential problems when translating specialised texts:

1. The rich specialised terminology, used by a specific group of users familiar with the ins and outs of the field to which the translated text relates, is multidimensional in nature. Firstly, the terms are not

---

84 An interesting example of cultural adjustment is given by Olgierd Wojtasiewicz in his *Introduction to Translation Theory*. Namely, he cites the case of the translation of the *Our Father* prayer into Inuit. Due to the lack of a term in the Inuit language that corresponds to the Polish 'bread', the phrase 'daily bread' was translated as 'daily fish' (Wojtasiewicz, 1957: 24).

85 The Localization Industry Standards Association (LISA) was an organisation established in 1990 in Switzerland. It dealt with issues in the field of localization service standards, with more than 400 members from around the world.

86 Reflecting on the education system for future interpreters in this context, any international exchanges within the framework of student exchange programmes may prove to be the most relevant and effective idea. Gaining experience and language competence while abroad is invaluable for future work as a translator.

unambiguous – one term in a foreign language may correspond to several terms in Polish, for example.
2. Terminology used in everyday language can take on a completely new meaning when used in a different context in a specialised text (for example, a legal or technical text).[87] The translator must therefore be familiar with the terminology of the field to which the text he or she is translating belongs. They must understand the meaning of the translated content.[88]
3. Pisarska and Tomaszkiewicz highlight the existence of so-called doublets – these are native terms and borrowings that have the same meaning.
4. The issue of the translation of specialised texts does not concern terminology alone, but a range of linguistic phenomena, such as the occurrence of phraseologisms, word compounds, specific structures, or syntax.
5. The translator should be highly aware of the purpose of the translation – what the client needs it for and what it will be used for, and therefore who the actual recipient of the text will be, who should be able to understand the text, and for what purpose the recipient needs to understand the text. A proper understanding of the original is key to getting the translation right. The meaning of the content being conveyed is of key importance in specialist translation.
6. Technical translation requires constant monitoring of linguistic and terminological developments – dictionaries and lexicons do not always contain up-to-date information; both parallel texts and the internet can help the translator with this.[89]
7. In the case of legal translation, the difficulty lies primarily in the mutual incompatibility of legal systems and the consequent difficulty of using

---

87 Jerzy Pieńkos (1993: 269).

88 It is worth mentioning here the approach of Jerzy Pieńkos (1993: 269), who emphasised that 'the signs of specialised language strive for unambiguity (monosemy), whereas the signs of general language lexis are carriers of complex psychological and social connotations, defining the personality of the speaker; by their very nature they must be characterised by greater polysemy'. Compare also: Kierzkowska, 2020.

89 Jerzy Pieńkos (1993: 270) in this context also points to the strong development of lexis in specialised texts, thanks to the discovery of a new world through science and technology.

> the appropriate terminology for the names of institutions, procedures, or phenomena.[90] The translator must not only have knowledge of the law, but also the style of legal language. Achieving equivalence when translating legal and jurisprudential texts is an enormous challenge (Pisarska, Tomaszkiewicz, 1996: 185).[91]

Jerzy Pieńkos, who has focused his research largely on the translation of legal and juridical texts, sees two missions for the translator: 'not harming' the language (passive role) and contributing to its development (active role). It is these that constitute the primary goal of the translator's translation activity, and specialised texts require the highest level of semantic compatibility during translation (Pieńkos, 1993: 288). In order for the translator to be able to perform these missions effectively during specialised translation, he or she should choose an appropriate strategy. His task, therefore, is first to interpret the source text written in the foreign language, then to examine the source text in terms of terminology (and look at other linguistic elements), and finally to produce a text in the target language by selecting and evaluating equivalents in the target language (ibid.: 173). When it comes to specialised translations, semantic compatibility plays a key role.

Barbara Kielar, on the other hand, suggests that a broader perspective should be taken when translating:

> When translating a specialised text, it is necessary to adopt a translation system of the appropriate type as a reference point in order to situate the specific text and the elements of the communication system in question within the broader context of social experience. This concerns, in particular, the question of the translator's qualifications, the features of the source text in its intertextual links with J1 parallel texts and the target text, which should meet the communicative expectations of the new audience, enter into intertextual links with J2 parallel texts (Kielar, 1991: 139).

---

90 Anna Jopek-Bosiacka (2008: 11), who is a lawyer, a certified English translator, as well as a university lecturer, says that 'translating legal texts is not only a real challenge for the translator, but also a fascinating journey through different systems, cultures and legal discourses'. In this context, it should be emphasised that this is a journey with a very heavy burden of responsibility on the interpreter.

91 'The peculiarity of this type of translation lies in the necessity to move from one legal system to another, as well as in the nature of the normative texts that are translated, and in the resulting legal consequences' (Pisarska, Tomaszkiewicz, 1996: 191).

Reliably reading the source document, understanding it, analysing the terminology, and consulting a database of parallel texts are the tips mentioned so far that are valuable to specialist translators when translating. The translator of specialised texts encounters many challenges in his work and has to make numerous decisions in addition to his chosen strategy. In the course of his work, it is worthwhile for him to refer to the decalogue of principles created by the eminent Polish sworn translator Danuta Kierzkowska (2020). As she herself points out, these principles are the quintessence of numerous translation principles.

1. The principle of a single target language

According to this principle, the translator should decide on one target language and stick consistently to the decision made throughout the translation (if, for example, regional variations, a specific register, etc., are available, the choice, once made, should be applied consistently throughout the translation). Exceptions are interjections in a 'third' language, such as in Latin (name of a disease, a legal paremia, a legal term, or the proper name of, e.g., software or technology).

2. Principle of proper register of the target language

> This principle states the inviolability of certain linguistic conventions, which include phraseology and terminology specific to the sub-language of the chosen target language. [...] Respecting the conventions of particular registers excludes the possibility of word-for-word and literal translation of specialised texts, which at the level of the whole text always require transpositional translation (Kierzkowska, 2020: 173).[92]

In formulating the above principle, Danuta Kierzkowska cautions against changing the register of the source text to another register in translation. Such an approach entails certain risks, because, according to this principle, the translator should assume that the recipient of the text has a certain level and range of knowledge to be able to understand the text (technical, legal, or other specialised). A departure from this principle is

92 The definitions of 'literal', 'literal translation', and 'transposition' in the sense of Kierzkowska are cited later in the paper.

permissible in the case of translations of texts for so-called distant recipients (cf. Kierzkowska, 2007).

3. Principle of one equivalent for the same concept

Once adopted, the equivalent of a given concept should, according to this principle, be consistently applied throughout the translation. This procedure requires attentiveness and care on the part of the translator, while sometimes creating an impression of tedious routine and repetition in the translated text.[93]

4. Principle of different equivalents for different terms

This principle is like a mirror image of the principle of one equivalent for the same concept. Just as one term should consistently use one chosen equivalent, an equivalent should be used for a dissimilar term that distinguishes it from another similar term.[94]

5. Principle of priority of prescribed terminology

Where a unified terminology has been established for a particular type of specialised text, the translator should follow it. The official terminology of EU legislation can serve as an example. Official legal terminology in Polish is a resource derived from the texts of the constitution, laws, international agreements, regulations and acts of local law (art. 87 of the Constitution of the Republic of Poland, za: Kierzkowska, 2020: 178).

6. Principle of maximum similarity of selected equivalents

According to this principle, the translator would be guided by the degree of similarity of concepts in the source and target languages, preferably

93 By virtue of the Prime Minister's Decree of 20 June 2002 on the 'Principles of Legislative Techniques', it is precisely the principle of one equivalent that is applied. Paragraph 147 states: 'if the meaning of a term is established in a law or other normative act by means of a definition, the term must not be used in a different sense within that act' (after: Kierzkowska, 2020: 176).

94 Kierzkowska gave an example of the term 'position' for a Polish-English language pair. For a Polish-Czech language pair, the situation would be similar: *stanowisko pracy – pracoviště, stanowisko służbowe – pracovní pozice, stanowisko obejmowane – funkce.*

comparing the semantic range of a pair of potential equivalents. The translator should choose the pair of terms whose semantic ranges overlap to the greatest extent.[95]

7. Principles for creating linguistic equivalents in non-adaptive systems

In the absence of an equivalent in the target language, the translator must choose an appropriate strategy, analyse the translation problem, and then choose how to translate the non-equivalent term. The translator has options such as borrowing, linguistic calque, or creating a descriptive equivalent.

8. Principle of permanent link with the culture of the source language

The principle of a permanent link to the culture of the source language refers primarily to the preservation of the specific culture of the source language. In the case of legal texts, this rule applies to the legal system of the target language country and, therefore, to the terminology used in that system. Danuta Kierzkowska emphasises that this rule is not intended to calibrate phraseologisms, it cannot be applied within the whole text, but only to the terminology itself.

9. Recommendation to preserve language features typical of the period

The use of archaisms and the use of archaic language are among the difficult and rare skills of the translator. The application of the above principle may, for example, be required during the translation of very old legal texts.

10. Literal, word-for-word and transpositional translation

Literal translation is not the only or desirable way to produce faithful and beautiful translations. Literal translation has been defined by Danuta Kierzkowska as that type of translation which takes place at the level of lexical elements, while less emphasis is placed on the grammatical correctness of the construction created in the target language. The literal translation technique is most often used for texts with a strong contextual condition, i.e., where the 'immediate linguistic context of the text being translated, the culture of the country in which it was created, and the situation that defines the author, function, purpose and recipient of that text is visible'

95 Compare natural/functional equivalents.

(Kierzkowska, 2020: 185). Literal translation, on the other hand, takes place at the level of lexical elements, while maintaining grammatical correctness in the target language. In transpositional translation, the principle of correctness, not only grammatical, but also phraseological, idiomatic, and stylistic, prevails, as such translation takes place at the level of the whole text. This type of translation usually concerns texts containing, for example, numerous phraseological expressions or idioms.

In summary, we conclude that whether a translator performs specialised translation or interpreting, a range of competencies is required of him or her. The skills of a specialist translator are not limited to linguistic knowledge but also require knowledge of the subject matter, such as the law, machine construction and operating regulations, or specialised medical terminology. The basis for producing a high-quality translation of a specialised text is first to understand the meaning of the source text, and only then to realise the translation. Such knowledge, however, is not acquired during philological studies. Professional experience and sometimes even several years of work experience are also required. The question of how to prepare a translator for such complex and complicated translations is still in question.

2.4. Machine translation and post-editing

The use of computers in a translator's work and translation automation have been the subjects of many publications (Wojtasiewicz, 1957; Pisarska, Tomaszkiewicz, 1996; Konieczny, 2006; Bogucki, 2009; Stefaniak, 2012; Blaszkowska, 2012; Pym, 2018), and in light of the global changes taking place, computer-assisted translation is a very topical issue. Already Olgierd Wojtasiewicz, in his work written in the second half of the 1950s, considered the question of the potential use of machines for translating texts. He recognised the technical possibilities of machines, while pointing out their limitations, resting above all on the fact that translation is a strictly mental activity so that a machine will not be able to perform it (Wojtasiewicz, 1957: 103). Even then, however, he envisaged that machine translation could be used for certain texts, particularly standardised texts (ibid.). He saw the difficulty in the use of machines for translations where a decision must be made about the extent of non-translatability of a text when full translatability has to be chosen in favour of partial translatability. This is definitely a mental, decision-making process and, therefore, impossible for a machine that can neither think nor make analytical decisions on its own. He pointed out the advantages of the machines, such as the speed of the work (which is only applicable in the case of a large volume of work that is standardised in nature) and the potential applicability to non-literary translations. He was also already anticipating the need in the future to employ proofreaders to correct translations after the machine:

> There is a belief among many professionals that often – or perhaps as a rule – mechanically translated texts will pass through the scrutiny of a suitable proofreader, whose job it will be to smooth or correct the text where a machine geared to certain standard texts will produce a clumsy or erroneous translation. [...] Of course, the detailed scope of work of future translation machines and the extent of proofreader control will be determined in practice depending on the needs on the one hand and the technical efficiency of the machines on the other. (Wojtasiewicz, 1957: 105).

The history of machine translation (MT) dates back to the 1950s. The purpose of translation machines is to transfer content from the source language to the target language without human intervention (Zameo, 2019). Increasingly debated issues[96] in the translation industry are the security of the data that is processed by the machines, as well as the content fed into the translation engines (e.g., Google Translator). These issues seem relevant in light of clauses relating to GDPR or clauses relating to confidentiality rules signed with principals. There are also increasing questions about the reliability and credibility of machine translation, as well as the extent to which it can be used by translators and whether it poses a threat to the translation profession.

96 The use of machine translation and the implications associated with such a practice were the subject of a panel discussion at the 2019 Translation and Localization Conference. Similarly, at a conference organised as part of DGT's activities, a talk entitled *eTranslation: Was kann das maschinelle Übersetzungssystem der EU-Kommission?* addresses the opportunities and limitations of machine translation in the context of the provision of the EU machine translation engine, eTranslation. A recording of the conference is available on DGT's YouTube channel *(eTranslation: Was kann...*, 2021).

It is possible to use computer tools in translation in two ways. On the one hand, they can be used by professional translators in the case of so-called CAT tools. CAT tools such as Trados Studio, thanks to their terminology databases (the so-called *translation memories*), work well during specialised, technical, and highly repetitive translations (Konieczny, 2006; Witczak, 2016). These tools are used, for example, when translating European Union acts (Stefaniak, 2012). Not only do they have a significant impact on translation turnaround times, but above all, they are a guarantee of consistent terminology even when several translators are working on one large project. On the other hand, computers can be used in fully automated processes in the case of *machine translation* (hereafter MT).

So far, three types of machine translation systems have been distinguished:

1. *Rule-based systems* are among the first machine translation systems. They were developed in the 1980s.[97] They combined terminological resources with linguistic resources and grammatical rules. Rule-based systems perform best when translating specialised texts, assuming the user includes their terminology base. Like other MT systems, the result of the translation is not perfect and contains errors, but the resulting content is coherent and logical.
2. *Statistical-based systems*, whose development took place in the 1980s and 1990s, do not use any linguistic principles but use statistical data taken from corpora.[98] The software analyses different databases for each language, resulting in a relatively smooth but not always logical text.
3. *Neural algorithm-based systems* (hereafter NMT) based on neural networks are the latest development in MT. They were introduced in 2015. Translations performed using these systems are real-time and use word string probabilities. These machines use neural networks modelled on the human brain. NMT is a significant improvement in the quality of MT. Translations produced using these systems contain 50 %

97 In EU structures, research was conducted on the SYSTRAN system, but as the research continued, it became apparent that there would be no continuation due to the upcoming new and better statistical translation system (per: Andreas Eisele, speech at the conference: *eTranslation: Was kann das maschinelle Übersetzungssystem der EU-Kommission?*).

98 The EU tool based on this system was MT@EC, with which translations of EU legislation were carried out.

> fewer word order errors in the sentence, 17 % fewer lexical errors, and 19 % fewer grammatical errors (Zameo, 2019) in relation to what has been achieved to date in MT.[99] Neural networks have learnt, without human intervention, to correctly apply the type and case system in different languages. In contrast to rule-based systems and MT based on statistical methods, NMT uses neural networks using artificial intelligence, basing its operations on the principles of the human brain. NMT represents a huge advance in technology: a self-learning system using artificial intelligence, big data, and deep learning. NMT now makes it possible to obtain translations that form the basis for professional translations (Zameo, 2019).

These systems are capable of reproducibly producing reliable translations, as well as learning new languages. As a result, they can improve their capabilities and the quality of the content they deliver. In order to operate and grow effectively, these systems need human interaction to feed them with the right database resources and thus assist them in improving their translations and their quality. NMT can also be 'trained' appropriately for the specific requirements of a particular translation by adapting the relevant specialist terminology (e.g., legal, financial, or medical). Currently, NMT systems have been produced by Google (*Google Neural Machine Translation*, which supports 8 languages) and Microsoft (*Microsoft Translator* mobile app, which supports 60 languages), among others. In addition to many innovations, these systems also have some limitations. Specialist texts with a high degree of difficulty, involving complex, infrequently used vocabulary and highly specialised terminology, will always present NMT with a major challenge and will result in low-quality translations. Importantly, the source text must be unambiguous, readable, and clear (all ambiguous terms and multi-faceted expressions present significant difficulties for NMT). In addition, the data entered into the engines is saved and stored on servers, so compliance with confidentiality rules and security of data processing are virtually non-existent. It is also important to highlight the fact that the machines must be 're-trained' by a human all the time; it is the human who must assess potential errors or the correctness of the translation. The

---

99 The significant reduction in NMT errors was also confirmed by Andreas Eisele of DGT.

machine, when performing the next translation, uses what it has already 'learnt', assessing the appropriateness of the use of a given equivalent in the text being translated.

Texts with creative content will certainly require a lot of proofreading intervention. It should be emphasised that human action, in the case of machine translation, is essential. Human linguistic and translation skills, the ability to assess and make decisions, and knowledge of the processes surrounding the execution of orders are becoming necessary for machine translation to be used effectively. A companion product to MT is what is known as PEMT (*post-editing machine translation*). This is a machine translation that has been proofread/post-edited by a professional translator. Within human post-editing, there are two possibilities: so-called *light post-editing* (proofreading for grammatical errors, typos, slips of the tongue, omitted words, inappropriate content in a given place, making sense of the text, and ensuring its coherence) and *full post-editing* (during proofreading, terminological errors are removed, text structure, sentence formation, punctuation, style, and register are corrected; after proofreading, the text should be more natural and fluid in its reception).

Despite their many shortcomings and imperfections, NMT systems offer great savings overall, most notably time savings. The average translator can translate around 2–3,000 words per day, while a machine can translate large volumes of text in seconds. Despite the enormous amount of work that must go into fine-tuning a machine translation by the translator/post-editor/corrector, the machines, in collaboration with humans, are able to contribute to a high level of translation quality achieved in a short time. The process must involve people such as a translation project manager, localisation project manager, project developer, translator, proofreader, and post-editor.

In 2017, the Directorate-General for Translation of the European Union (hereafter DGT) launched its NMT tool called eTranslation.[100] The reason for making the tool available to EU citizens was the idea that the European Union aims for its citizens to be able to understand its laws in their own

100 The official launch date of the EU translation machine was 15/11/2017. The machine supports all the official languages of the European Union as well as Icelandic and Norwegian.

languages. Under European Union law, every citizen has the right to contact any EU institution in one of the 23 official languages and to expect a reply in that language. The EU translation machine has been fed with a wealth of terminology and translation memory resources from which past translations of EU legislation by translators have been made.

At DGT's conference in March on the possibilities and limitations of the tool, Dr Andreas Eisele (Chief Scientific Officer for eTranslation) and Katja Mai from DGT gave an overview of how the new tool works. ETranslation can be accessed not only by EU officials or translators but, in principle, by any EU citizen who creates an account on the translation platform website (eTranslation, 2021) and logs in. Using the tool is very intuitive and is similar to using Google Translator – enter the source text in the window so that the translated text appears in the adjacent window. There is much debate over the quality of translation and the skills of the EU machine translation service.[101] Translations resulting from the use of eTranslation may contain errors and have not been proofread before being passed on to the user. Since the priority is to approximate the general content of the translated text, such a translation cannot be regarded as perfect and fully reliable (after Andreas Eisele). Translation errors usually relate to the meaning of words (equivalent inappropriate to the context), style, or the appearance of a negative sentence in place of an affirmative sentence. The system does not work well for creative, poetic texts or those containing words with potentially multiple meanings. Andreas Eisele suggests exercising great caution when using the tool, stressing that it is intended to seek general knowledge regarding the content of the text to be translated. Katja Mai, on the other hand, emphasises that artificial intelligence in the case of translation machines is not really intelligent – it does not have the general knowledge of the world that is necessary to produce a reliable translation, it is not always able to correctly recognise the context and select the right equivalent, and it lacks linguistic knowledge and understanding of the content to

101 During the JTP St Jerome's Days 2020 event, two presentations focused on eTranslation. Pavel Pecina presented the possibilities and limitations of the tool, while Pavel Král attempted to answer the question of how best to use machine translation in the translator's work. The presentation is available on JTP's YouTube channel.

be translated. In an attempt to answer the question of whether the translation machine threatens the work of DGT's translators, statistics were given on the number of translations carried out by DGT between 2007 and 2020, and this was 2.3 million normative sites. The translations were carried out by 2,000 translators employed by DGT, while 30 % of the translations were outsourced to external translators working with DGT. This gives an overview of the scale of the demand for the work of good and experienced translators, who not only do the translations themselves, but are required to comply with all formal requirements, formatting requirements, and the graphic structure of the texts being translated.

During his presentation at the 2019 Translation and Localization Conference Conference in Warsaw, Marcin Miłkowski presented the current state of machine translation using Google Translate as an example, pointing out that current systems are limited to translating sentence length units. Google Translate does not interpret the text. It has numerous limitations, such as: inconsistency in translation (inconsistent terminology), violation of grammatical rules (especially consensus and government relationships), lack of logical consistency (especially in the case of pronouns), and lack of uniformity (and stylistic fidelity).[102] If just a few years ago, translations using Google tools raised an ironic smile on the face of many people, nowadays we know that the content provided by Google Translate is enough to, for example, make simple purchases on the internet (e.g., to buy shoes you do not need a specialised translation, usually information such as colour or size is sufficient, while the correct conjugation of a noun or verb is of secondary importance) or find a translation of a technical term. Certainly, Google Translate's algorithms cannot cope with fiction or poetry, but the speed at which the tool is progressing and developing is sometimes impressive. Post-editing[103] has become, as a consequence of the advent of machine

102 The examples are based on statements made by M. Miłkowski at the 2019 Translation and Localization Conference in Warsaw. His presentation was entitled *The Limits of Machine Translation without Understanding* [*Granice tłumaczenia (maszynowego) bez rozumienia*] and was presented on 28 September 2019.

103 Post-editing, as defined by EN ISO 17100, is the editing and proofreading of a machine translation product. It should also be noted that, according to this definition, 'the post-editor edits the product automatically generated by the

translation, quite firmly embedded in the reality of translation services. Nowadays, in addition to the translator or project manager, translation agencies are very keen to cooperate with proofreaders, revisers, and post-editors, i.e., specialists who can correct, edit, and prepare the translation not only by the translator, but also by the 'machine'. This fact also follows from the obligation to control the text in accordance with the requirements of the ISO standard, which will be discussed later in the work.

Karolina Stefaniak from the Polish Language Department at DGT in Luxembourg, who is familiar with the use of CAT systems and automated translation in EU structures, is critical of the unconditional use of computer technology in EU translations. She believes that:

> DGT's translation policy forces translation to be treated in mechanistic terms, subjectivity and individuality of translation are considered a disadvantage of the whole process, translation operations are performed on sentences,[104] and terminological issues[105] are put at the top of the list. Instead of relying on the creativity of interpreters, one succumbs to the dictatorship of equivalence. Instead of relying on the creativity of interpreters, one succumbs to the dictatorship of

---

machine translation system, however, this does not apply when the translator sees and uses the prompt proposed by the machine translation system integrated into the translation support software (CAT tool)'.

104 It should be clarified that the use of CAT tools means that the translator does not see the full layout of the text. [*Należy wyjaśnić, że stosowanie narzędzi CAT powoduje, że tłumacz nie widzi pełnego układu graficznego tekstu.*] The text is divided into so-called segments – one segment is one sentence. [*Tekst podzielony jest na tzw. segmenty – jeden segment to jedno zdanie.*] The translation memory, which has been read into the assignment, means that the translator can focus, for example, only on untranslated sentences that the translation memory resources have not been able to translate. [*Zaczytana do zlecenia pamięć tłumaczeniowa powoduje, że tłumacz może skupić się na przykład tylko i wyłącznie na zdaniach nieprzetłumaczonych, których zasoby pamięci tłumaczeniowej nie były w stanie przełożyć.*]

105 A translator working at DGT has a so-called terminologist as a support, who can provide clear feedback if the translator is in doubt about the use of the correct legal or juridical term. [*Tłumacz pracujący w DGT ma jako wsparcie tzw. terminologa, który w przypadku wątpliwości tłumacza w przedmiocie zastosowania właściwego terminu prawnego lub prawniczego jest w stanie udzielić mu jednoznacznej informacji zwrotnej.*] The task of the terminologists is to ensure that the terminology of EU legal acts is consistent. [*Zadaniem terminologów jest zapewnienie spójnej terminologii aktów prawnych UE.*]

> equivalence. Instead of exploiting the potential of language, it is reduced to the lowest common denominator. (Stefaniak, 2012: 204).

Stefaniak sheds a different light on the issue of machine translation and machine-assisted translation, forcing, as it were, a change of perspective on their assessment. Perhaps what should be considered is not whether machines are able to take away translators' jobs, but how they affect the status of translators and the understanding of their work. The likelihood is not that machines will replace translators, but translators will be forced to perform the tasks of post-editors and proofreaders instead of actual translation activities. Among the undoubted advantages of CAT tools is that they help to increase consistency between translated texts, making the task of subsequent translators easier. When terminology bases developed by their predecessors are made available to them, translators no longer have to struggle with terminology work (Stefaniak, 2012: 206). Among the disadvantages, Stefaniak sees 'a limitation of creativity and a weakening of the critical sense of the translator, who often prefers, for fear of inaccuracy, to use a term for which he or she is not convinced, but which already exists in the database, rather than to propose his or her own solution' (ibid.). It is, therefore, up to the translator not only to decide how the machines can translate (it is the translator who feeds them with databases) but also how his or her own work looks in light of the use of new technologies. Modern translation tools can make a huge contribution to reducing a translator's workload, but at the same time, have a significant impact on the perception of the translator's status in society.

2.5. Quality requirements in accordance with ISO 17100:2015

The translation industry, like other industries, has a standardisation document that regulates how translations are carried out. This document is the PN-EN ISO 17100 standard, which replaces the PN-EN 15038:2006 standard. This is an international standard, the European Standard EN ISO 17100:2015 *Translation Services – Requirements for translation services*

(17100:2015),[106] which has been translated into Polish and has the status of a Polish ISO standard. The document covers requirements for all aspects of the translation process, affecting both the quality and level of translation service provision. It sets out not only the demands on the translators themselves and the services they provide, but also on the translation service providers. Activities such as the management of core processes, the minimum competencies required, the availability of resources, how resources are managed, as well as other activities necessary for the provision of quality translation services are described. According to the standard, in addition to the recommendations and regulations contained therein, translation service providers should also follow the guidelines described in industry codes, best practice manuals, or legislation. The standard distinguishes between translation done by a translator and automated, machine translation. In terms of the standard, the product of machine translation is not covered by the guidelines contained therein. The second important point is that the normative regulations only cover translation, they do not apply to interpretation.

The standard runs to 24 pages and includes chapters such as: *Scope of the standard*, *Terms and definitions*, *Resources*, *Pre-processes and activities*, *Production process*, and *Post-translation activities*. In addition, the standard includes six annexes. These are: *Translation workflow according to ISO 17100*, *Contracts and project specifications*, *Project registration and reporting*, *Pre-translation tasks*, *Translation technologies*, and *Non-exhaustive list of added services.*[107]

---

106 This European standard, as it reads, exists in three official versions: English, French, and German. Translations of the content of the standard in other countries have the same status as their original versions, the translations having been made under the responsibility of the CEN member concerned. Members of CEN, the European Committee for Standardisation, include countries such as: Austria, Belgium, Bulgaria, Northern Macedonia, Croatia, Cyprus, Denmark, Estonia, Finland, France, Germany, Greece, Hungary, Iceland, Ireland, Italy, Latvia, Lithuania, Luxembourg, Malta, the Netherlands, Norway, Poland, Portugal, the Czech Republic, Romania, Slovakia, Slovenia, Spain, Sweden, Switzerland, Turkey, and the United Kingdom. This means that there is a translation standard in these countries.

107 The author would like to point out that all the information contained in this section has been derived solely from document PN-EN ISO 17100:2015. The content is an analysis and paraphrasing of the information contained in the standards document.

The terminology used in the standard is used in the wider translation industry, so it is worth looking at the definitions. These are summarised in the form of a table below, taking into account the translation work cycle, technology, control process or language, and content concepts (Tab. 23).

Tab. 23: Terms and definitions used in EN ISO 17100:2015

Terms and definitions used in EN ISO 17100:2015[a]	
To translate	Means to translate the content in the source language into the content in the target language in written form. The source language and the target language are understood according to the definitions set out in the standard.
Translation	Refers to a set of processes aimed at producing a written translation of a text from a source language into a text in the target language.
Translation work cycle	Refers to processes, or elements thereof, aimed at rendering a finished translation.
Process	Refers to the set of interrelated activities that are undertaken to achieve a goal.
Product	Denotes the end result of the process – it can be, for example, translated documentation, a book, as well as the intellectual property contained in the translated content, which is the subject of a contract between the author and the translator.
Translation service	Means an intangible product, which the standard defines as the result of the interaction between the translation service provider and the client.
Interpreting	Means to translate spoken or signed information from one language into another in oral / sign language form.
Terminology relating to the translation workflow and technology	
Computer-assisted translation	So-called *computer-assisted translation* (CAT). This is the part of the translator's job where specialised software is used to support their work.

Tab. 23: Continued

Terms and definitions used in EN ISO 17100:2015[a]	
Machine translation	So-called *machine translation* (MT), also known as automatic translation. It is the translation from one natural language to another using a computer system.
Product of machine translation	In other words: the outcome of the MT process.
Post-editing	Editing and proofreading of a machine translation product.
Checking	Controlling by the translator the translation he has produced.
Verification	Checking the translation by comparing the content in the source language with the content in the target language. The verification takes into account the compatibility in terms of the intended purpose of the translation (also: bilingual editing).
Editing	Monolingual checking of content in the target language. The editing process takes into account compatibility in terms of the intended purpose of the translation (also: monolingual editing).
Correction	Checking the revised content and making corrections (in the target language) before printing.
Project management	Project coordination and monitoring, project management at all stages.
Style guidelines	Instructions and guidance on editing and formatting.
Language and content terminology	
Content	Anything that expresses relevant information or knowledge.
Content in the source language	Content to be translated.
Content in the target language	Content that has been translated from the content in the source language into the target language.
Text	Content in writing.

(continued)

Tab. 23: Continued

Terms and definitions used in EN ISO 17100:2015[a]	
Source language	Content language in the source language (foreign language).
Target language	Language into which the translation is provided.
Language register	A variety of languages used for a specific purpose or in a specific social or industrial field.
Natural language	Language used by humans in oral, written, or signed form.
Textual conventions	A subset of specifications for the content of the language of translation related to the type and domain of the content, e.g., statutory texts for which there are certain formal conventions used by legislators.
Field	A discipline or branch of knowledge or activity that is characterised by its own linguistic features, social context, and specialised culture.
Local specificity	A set of features/information/conventions that address the specific conditions of the target audience (linguistic, cultural, technical, and geographical conditions are mentioned).
Terminology related to persons involved in the provision of translation services	
Language service provider	A person or organisation that provides language services.
Translation service provider	E.g., a translation company, an individual translator, or a translation department within a company.
Customer/recipient	A translation service requestor, a person or organisation that requests a translation service on a contractual basis.
Translator	A person doing the translation.
Verifier	A person who verifies the content in the target language with the content in the source language.
Editor	A person who performs content editing in the target language.

Tab. 23: Continued

Terms and definitions used in EN ISO 17100:2015[a]	
Proofreader	A person who proofreads content in the target language.
Project manager	A so-called *project manager* (PM), the person who manages the project and is responsible for the entire translation process, including all its aspects.
Competencies	Ability to apply knowledge, experience, and skills to achieve desired outcomes.
Terminology of the translation service process	
Control	In the sense of the standard, it means confirmation by the PM that all project specifications have been taken into account.
Document	Refers to information and its medium (e.g., paper, computer disk: magnetic, electronic or optical, photograph, or master sample) or a combination of these media.
Register	Means a document, a report that confirms the results achieved. It may also include a summary of the evidence of the activities carried out.
Correction	This is an action to correct an error (detected by the translator, verifier, proofreader, editor, or client) in the translation in the target language and may also mean correcting a non-conformity with respect to this standard (if such conformity was declared).
Corrective action	Identifying the cause of discrepancies or errors in the translation in order to eliminate them (these may be errors in the translation process or in the content in the target language).

Source: Own elaboration based on the standards document.

a All definitions and terms are taken from the standards document. Polish Committee for Standardisation: PN-EN ISO 17100:2015 (in Polish). Catalogue of Polish Standards [12/10/2020].

The provisions in the standard focus on the situation where a translation service provider, for example, a translation agency, contracts a translator to translate for the agency's client. According to the standard, the process of acceptance, execution, and handover of the completed order should be properly regulated and meet the standards and requirements set out in the standard. It is the responsibility of the translation agency, the translation service provider, to meet the normative requirements of the process. Translators, proofreaders, and editors are the people who, according to the standard, are responsible for carrying out the translation order. The document specifies what qualifications and competencies the translation service provider should require from these individuals.

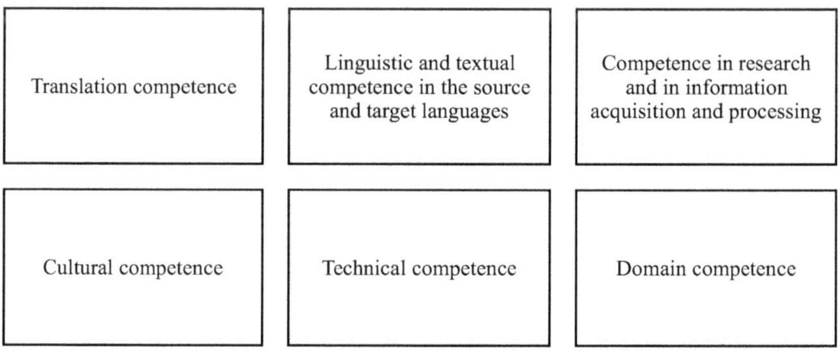

Fig. 15: Professional competence of translators and verifiers according to EN ISO 17100:2015
Source: Own elaboration based on the standards document.

Translation competence is the ability to translate according to normative requirements and the ability to solve problems of understanding and producing linguistic content. Within this competence is also the proficiency in translating content into the target language as agreed and contracted between the translation service provider and the client. The translator and proofreader must have knowledge and skills in the area of adapting their work to the specifications of the project.

Linguistic and textual competence in the source and target languages means understanding and fluency in the foreign (target) language; translators and proofreaders must also demonstrate general or specialised knowledge of textual conventions. In addition, they should be able to apply this knowledge in the process of translating or creating new content in a foreign language.

Another type of skill referred to in the standard is research competence and knowledge of information acquisition and processing. In the case of translators and proofreaders, this means the ability to effectively acquire the additional linguistic and specialised knowledge required to be able to understand the source text while producing content in the target language. Practical knowledge of research tools and experience in their use also fall within this area of competence. Proficiency in the appropriate selection and use of strategies for using available information sources also counts here.

Cultural competence is the ability of the translator and proofreader to draw on a pool of information on aspects such as behavioural norms, current nomenclature, values systems, and local specifics that characterise the culture of the source and target languages.

Technical competence is the knowledge needed to be able to perform tasks of a technical nature in the translation process. For their practical application, technical resources, tools, software, and IT systems are needed to support translation processes.

Domain competence refers to the ability to understand content in the source language and the dexterity to transfer that content into the target language using an appropriate text style and terminology. As far as the competence of editors is concerned, they are required to be specialists in their field. Both the competence of translators, proofreaders, and editors and their professional qualifications should be confirmed by appropriate diplomas and certificates. According to the standard, the translator should meet at least one of the required qualification criteria, which include a degree in translation, or a diploma in any field together with two years of full-time translation practice or five years of active translation practice. Project managers additionally play an important role in the implementation process of translation projects. They should be competent enough to support the translation process and continuously improve their skills to ensure the highest quality of service. It should be emphasised that all those involved in the translation process – from translators to proofreaders, revisers and editors to project managers – are obliged to undergo continuous training and development of their working methods. The life cycle of the translation process is presented as a diagram in Annexe A of the standard. It is divided into three main elements: pre-processes and activities, the production process, and post-delivery activities of the translation. The standard regulates each of these elements in detail so that translation quality requirements can be met at a given stage. It is worth emphasising that every translation should generally pass a triple check: the translator who produced the translation, the translator-verifier, and the editor. Such measures are aimed at eliminating potential errors during the various stages of project implementation.

The normative provisions also define the scope of additional services that a translation service provider can provide to a client. These include, for example, text adaptation services, terminology management, localisation, transcription, transliteration, or desktop publishing (DTP) – graphic design and web design. Using tools to support the translation process, the supplier is also able to prepare terminology databases, translation memories, and technical documentation for the client. The services of a translation agency can also include the production of dialogue lists for films or voiceover substitution. Interestingly, the scope of work also includes consultancy services in the area of language and cultural aspects. Every translator and person working in the translation industry should be familiar with the content of the standard. The text of the standard is available for a fee (at the cost of about PLN 100), but it provides a kind of map and guide to competent translation services.

2.6. Professional responsibility: The law on the profession of sworn translators in Poland and the Czech Republic

In both Poland and the Czech Republic[108], the profession of sworn translator is regulated by the relevant law. In Poland, this is the Act of 25 November 2004 on the profession of a sworn translator, which consists of five chapters divided into thirty-five articles. As it reads in the first article, the Act 'sets out the conditions and procedure for the acquisition and loss of the right to practice as a sworn translator, as well as the rules for the practice of this profession' (Act, 2004, art. 1). According to the Act, a sworn translator

108 While the chapter discusses the laws on the profession of a sworn translator in Poland and the Czech Republic, it is worth mentioning that there is relevant EU legislation also regulating the profession of a sworn translator in light of the right to translate in a criminal trial. The relevant act is Directive 2010/64/

in Poland may be a person who has Polish citizenship or is a citizen of one of the EU countries, has a command of the Polish language, has full capacity to perform civil acts, has no criminal record, and has a university degree.[109] The last requirement is to successfully pass the examination to become a sworn translator. It is taken in written and oral form (the examination consists of two parts; passing the written part makes it possible to take the oral part) before an examination board consisting of 11 members (four academic teachers who are philologists, three sworn translators designated by translator associations, three designated by the Minister of Justice, and one designated by the Minister responsible for labour). As the law reads, the written part of the exam consists of a translation task of four texts – two texts from Polish into a foreign language and two texts from a foreign language into Polish. The oral part involves a sight translation from a foreign language into Polish (interpretation of a read text) and consecutive interpretation from Polish into a foreign language. The cost of the examination in the amount of PLN 800[110] is to be paid by the examinee, payment of the fee is non-refundable and is a condition for taking the examination. After successfully passing the examination, the translator acquires the powers of a sworn translator, takes the oath,[111] and is entered on the list of sworn translators kept by the Minister of Justice. The Minister of Justice may also suspend a sworn translator from practising for a period of five years if the translator has not practised for more than three years, and at the request of the translator for a period of up to five years. The Minister

---

EU of the European Parliament and of the Council of 20 October 2010 on the right to interpretation and translation in criminal proceedings.

109 The legal status of court interpreters in Poland, the Czech Republic, and Slovakia is also described by Iwona Imiołо (2014). The section on the status of court interpreters in the Czech Republic is outdated in part due to the amendment of the Czech law on the profession of court interpreter in 2021, while the data for Poland and Slovakia remain relevant. In her article, Imiołо addresses the issues of becoming a sworn translator, the scope of powers, the scope of professional responsibility, and the tools of a sworn translator's job.

110 Status at the end of 2020.

111 The content of the oath also sets out a commitment to the requirements of professional responsibility and ethics: 'Aware of the importance of my words and my responsibility before the law, I solemnly swear that I will perform the tasks entrusted to me as a sworn translator conscientiously and impartially,

of Justice may also remove a translator from the list of sworn translators as a result of death, loss of Polish citizenship, or loss of legal capacity. In the event of a final sentence, it may disqualify him or her from practising his or her profession.

A sworn translator in Poland has a certain range of powers under the law. He may prepare and certify translations from Polish into a foreign language, as well as check and certify translations in this area made by others (assuming, however, full responsibility for them as if he had done them himself). He may also make certified copies of foreign language writings, check and certify copies of foreign language writings made by others, as well as – in accordance with the law – make interpretations.

The duties of a sworn translator are set out in Article 14 of the Act. According to it, the translator is obliged to exercise particular care and impartiality in the performance of his or her tasks. The interpreter also has a duty to keep confidential the facts and circumstances of which he or she becomes aware while interpreting. It is worth noting that, according to the law, the interpreter's tasks also include furthering his or her professional qualifications. The Act also sets out the rules for the transliteration and transcription of names, the possibilities for refusing an assignment, as well as the rules related to the granting of remuneration to the translator for the assignments made. The sworn translator is also obliged to keep a repertory. The law also sets out formal rules for the certification of translations (including the possibility of using an electronic signature). Supervision of the quality and reliability of the repertories is exercised by the locally competent provincial governor. Under the Act, the interpreter bears civil, criminal, and professional liability. Formally, an interpreter may be reprimanded, admonished, fined (the amount of which is determined by law), suspended, or disbarred for at least two years. Komisja Odpowiedzialności Zawodowej [The Professional Responsibility Commission – PRC] is the body which,

---

maintaining legally protected secrecy and guided in my conduct by integrity and professional ethics' (Act, 2004, art. 7 item 1). [*Mając świadomość znaczenia moich słów i odpowiedzialności przed prawem, przyrzekam uroczyście, że powierzone mi zadania tłumacza przysięgłego będę wykonywać sumiennie i bezstronnie, dochowując tajemnicy prawnie chronionej oraz kierując się w swoim postępowaniu uczciwością i etyką zawodową*].

at the request of the competent provincial governor or the Minister of Justice, may initiate and carry out professional responsibility proceedings against an interpreter. The proceedings may end with the interpreter being acquitted, a penalty being imposed, or the proceedings being discontinued. The procedure provides for a decision to be taken by means of a vote on the resolution, which is decided by a majority vote, assuming the presence of at least half of the members of the PRC.

Numerous books have been devoted to certified translations, the problems of the profession of a sworn translator, as well as to the examination for a sworn translator in Poland.[112] It is currently difficult to become a sworn translator in Poland. Before the introduction of the compulsory examination to become a sworn translator in 2004, it was sufficient to show proof of professional practice at the relevant court; since 2004, the requirements have been more precisely defined and the translator's knowledge and skills are verified by examination. Currently, the average pass rate remains at 20 % (after: Kubacki, 2012). A sensitive issue remains the training of future translators and the question of why candidates, after completing their philological studies, are unable to successfully pass the professional examination.[113] This issue is raised by Kubacki. He also raises the issue of the translation competence of certified translators who obtained their licence to practise before the introduction of the exam, pointing to inequalities not only in terms of translation knowledge and understanding of the formal rules for producing certified translations, but also

---

112 See the works of Dr. Artur Dariusz Kubacki, who is a Germanist and a member of the State Examination Commission for sworn translators. Of particular interest is his 2012 work entitled *Certified Translation. Status, training, workshop and responsibility of the sworn translator*. Another interesting publication is the 2016 book by Professor Mark Kuźniak *Examination for sworn translators in practice (an English specialist's perspective)*. Renata Świgońska, a sworn translator of English and German, owner of a law firm, and author of the blog www.tlumaczeniaprawnicze.pl, also makes a significant contribution to the education of future translators.

113 In 2008, the Commissioner for Multilingualism of the European Commission set up the Reflection Forum on Multilingualism and Interpreter Training. The unit's remit was to develop recommendations by independent experts on strategies for good translation practice and to take action to ensure better quality translator services in EU countries. The demand for court interpreters

a willingness to undergo continuing education (Kubacki, 2012).[114] A profession with such high demands and wide-ranging responsibilities should be adequately remunerated and have an appropriate status in society and state structures. Unfortunately, this is not the case. Many sworn translators struggle to be paid on time for services rendered, and often have disputes over the mode and difficulty of their assignments. It is not a profession that guarantees a well-paid contract position. The interpreter is most often self-employed, working on a piecework basis as required by state bodies, the police, the courts, or the prosecution service. Unfortunately, the status of a sworn translator also does not guarantee professional stability, with most translators treating this occupation as an additional one, alongside their regular contract of employment in another capacity. Kubacki points out this fact, emphasising that producing a certified translation requires a certain amount of work, translation competence, experience, precision, and knowledge of the terminology and issues of the translated text. Haste, time and

---

has increased as a result of globalisation, the enlargement of the borders of the European Union as a result of the accession of Member States and, consequently, more frequent breaches of the law and the consequent need for the presence of an interpreter with appropriate skills in court. Aspects such as: the profession of sworn translator as a profession requiring appropriate qualifications, the need to educate court translators of various languages, the requirement for translators to undergo continuing professional development, the requirement for translators to have and adhere to a code of ethics and professional practice in each EU country, the need to disseminate knowledge of the code of professional ethics, and the need to train judges, prosecutors, police officers, and lawyers on the rules of cooperation with court translators (see: Kierzkowska, 2009).

114 The figures cited by Kubacki seem relatively shocking. He reports, among other things, that the skills of 95 % of sworn translators in Poland have never been verified, the vast majority of them are not even familiar with the content of the The Professional Sworn Translator's Code, and they lack the desire or sense of obligation to further their education. Kubacki presented a proposal for the training of future sworn translators, covering elements such as philological training and training in the practical and theoretical aspects of the translator's work (including translation theory, the basics of the legal science of the target language country, or the translation of general and specialised texts). He also did not overlook elements of consecutive and simultaneous interpreting, the organisation of the interpreter's workshop, or the ethics of the profession.

money pressure, and responsibility are elements of a translator's job that are not only not conducive to the process of completing difficult assignments but can also contribute to potential errors, imperfections, or deficiencies in the translation. In addition to the Act, the document regulating the work of a sworn translator in Poland is the The Professional Sworn Translator's Code, which was created and adopted by a resolution on 12 January 2019 by the Polish Society of Sworn and Specialised Translators (TEPIS). It sets out the rules of professional ethics and the professional practice of a sworn translator. This document is an integral part of the work of a specialist translator. It describes not only the principles of professional ethics but also the rules of practice, together with the formal rules and regulations for the production of certified translations. It is, so to speak, a map and a signpost in the translator's work, while the lack of knowledge of this document makes it virtually impossible to produce certified translations and translations of specialised texts properly.

In the Czech Republic, the issue of legislation on sworn translators and interpreters is very topical. The new regulatory law came into force on 1 January 2021 (Law No. 354/2019, as amended by Law No. 166/2020). The law was hotly debated, and its final form caused a stir in the Czech translation community. The new regulatory acts in the Czech Republic effective from 1 January 2021 are:

- Act No. 354/2019 Coll. on sworn interpreters and translators in the wording of Act No. 166/2020 Coll., effective as of 1 January 2021 (Zákon, 2021). The long-awaited law defines what translation is, as well as who a sworn translator (hereafter TP) is, and who an interpreter is.[115] The rules on the acquisition and loss or suspension of TPs are included in the legislation. The procedure for the inclusion of an interpreter in the list of sworn interpreters is also described, together with the obligations to which he or she is subject once included in the list. The procedure for the one-off appointment of an interpreter to perform a

115 As in Poland, the interpreter also takes an oath in the Czech Republic. Following amendments to the Act, there are two oaths – for the translator: '*Slibuji, že při své překladatelské činnosti budu dodržovat právní předpisy, že překladatelskou činnost budu vykonávat podle svého nejlepšího*

service in the nature of a sworn translation has also been regulated. The law regulates precisely the rules for the performance of the interpreter's activity and how the electronic repertory is to be maintained. In addition, the legislation defines broadly the scope of a TP's liability, treated in paragraphs 21, 35, and 37–38. The penalty imposed on a TP for breaching their statutory obligations ranges from CZK 50,000 to CZK 300,000. The breaches are detailed in the paragraphs cited above and concern, for example, careless translation, inadequate maintenance of the repertory, or inappropriate use of the seal. The interpreter can also be held liable for damage caused, so – as in Poland – he or she can be liable both civilly and criminally, be suspended from his or her rights, or be deprived of the right to practice the profession. The body to which the TP is accountable, and which adjudicates on TP-related matters is the Ministry of Justice of the Czech Republic.

- Regulation No. 506/2020 Coll., on the activities of written and oral TPs, effective as of 1 January 2021 (Vyhláška, 506/2020). The regulation treating the activity of the TP regulates such elements as the application form for inclusion in the list of sworn translators, the required practice and education of the TP, qualification courses and the manner of confirming the competence necessary to practice the profession of TP, the rules for conducting the preliminary examination for the TP, issues related to the issuance of the certificate of inclusion in the list, and matters related to the issuance of the seal. It is also a regulation governing the formal rules for the production of sworn translations and how the repertory is to be kept.

---

vědomí a svědomí, nezávisle a nestranně, že budu plně využívat všech svých znalostí a dbát o jejich rozvoj a že zachovám mlčenlivost o skutečnostech, o nichž jsem se při výkonu překladatelské činnosti dozvěděl', and for the interpreter: *'Slibuji, že při své tlumočnické činnosti budu dodržovat právní předpisy, že tlumočnickou činnost budu vykonávat podle svého nejlepšího vědomí a svědomí, nezávisle a nestranně, že budu plně využívat všech svých znalostí a dbát o jejich rozvoj a že zachovám mlčenlivost o skutečnostech, o nichž jsem se při výkonu tlumočnické činnosti dozvěděl'*. Information based on: Zákon, 2021.

- Regulation No. 507/2020 Coll., on remuneration and compensation for written and oral TPs, effective from 1 January 2021 (Vyhláška, 507/2020). This regulation regulates and sets out the way in which interpreters are remunerated, including the possibility of reducing or increasing their remuneration, as well as refusing to pay an interpreter. The regulation clearly states the price range allowed for translation and interpretation.
- Regulation No. 508/2020 Coll., on remuneration and compensation for sworn translators and interpreters, effective from 1 January 2021 (Vyhláška, 508/2020). The ordinance regulates the remuneration of TPs, including the issue of offsetting cash costs incurred by TPs, as well as costs related to the remuneration of a consultant appointed in criminal proceedings.
- Regulation No. 608/2020 Coll., on the determination of the necessary level of proficiency in Czech and equivalent language examinations for the performance of sworn translators and interpreters' activities, effective from 1 January 2021 (Vyhláška, 608/2020). The shortest of all the regulations to the Act, it regulates the required level of knowledge of the Czech language.

While prior to the introduction of the amendments to the law, there were already requirements for acquiring the right to practise as a sworn translator (in addition to the formal requirements in terms of education, civil and legal capacity, lack of criminal record, or having an address in the Czech Republic, there were also compulsory postgraduate studies in the basics of law),[116] these have now been tightened and every translator is obliged to pass the so-called entrance exam. It is designed to test the examinee's knowledge of the law in relation to the areas in which he or she acts as an interpreter, as well as the formal rules for producing translations. Under the new legislation, the profession of a sworn translator has been separated into a sworn translator and a sworn interpreter. A translator may be qualified to

116 Detailed information on the requirements for obtaining the licence to practise as a sworn translator can be found on the website of the Czech Chamber of Court Interpreters and Court Translators – *Česká komora soudních tlumočníků a soudních překladatelů*, www.kstcr.cz.

do both translation and interpreting at the same time,[117] but will be obliged to use two different seals. An electronic sworn translator's repertory, recorded online on the Ministry's website, has also been introduced. It will also be possible to use a qualified electronic signature to certify translations. The transitional period for translators with regard to the amendment of the law is five years, but it is already clear today that not all the necessary infrastructure has been implemented as planned as of 1 January 2021. For example, it has not been possible to prepare an electronic repertory, the same has happened with regard to the issuing of stamps (at present, translators still have one stamp for translations), and discussions are still ongoing to refine the procedures related to the use of electronic signatures. There is also no information on when the first entrance examinations will be held (it is expected that they will be performed using computers at two examination centres, in Prague and Kroměříž, within a period of no more than six months after the candidate has applied for the examination). The uncertainty and ambiguities surrounding the law being introduced are causing much discussion in the translation community. Numerous letters are being sent to the Ministry of Justice of the Czech Republic via the Czech Chamber of Court Interpreters and Court Translators. The online platform itself,[118] which was intended to be an integral aid and support for translators, is still under development.[119]

117 It has been accepted that the term '*překladatel*' will be used to designate the sworn translator. The term '*tlumočník*' is used for an interpreter and an interpreter who is qualified to perform both written and oral types of translation.

118 www.tlumocnici.justice.cz.

119 It should be emphasised that the associations and organisations of sworn interpreters were very active in responding to the MS and were involved in the work on the law to the extent possible. During St Jerome's Days, Michal Chuchút, M.A., lawyer, KST board member, and sworn translator of the German language, spoke at the 2020 St Jerome's Days, which took place online due to the epidemic. During his speech, he talked about the changes introduced by the amended law, introducing interpreters to the ins and outs of the changes and innovations. The presentation is available on YouTube under JTP (*Jednota tlumočníků a překladatelů*).

Analysing the requirements for a translator of specialised texts, the responsibilities[120] which he or she is burdened with, and taking into account the long road he or she has to travel in order to be able to competently translate complex texts, it can be deduced that many years of training, continuous self-improvement, and practice are needed to reach this level of competence and professional proficiency. Despite this, the issue of remuneration is often surrounded by an atmosphere of struggle for punctuality and adequacy. It is difficult for translators to read in such a context the justification of one of the judgements of the Supreme Administrative Court, which describes the translation profession:

> [The translation profession] is a specialised profession, requiring particularly high qualifications. The act of becoming a sworn translator is, therefore, recognition of the candidate's high level of knowledge and professional achievement, evidence of his or her above-average translation skills and knowledge of a particular language. This, therefore, implies a real professional and ethical ennoblement of the applicant (Judgment of the Supreme Administrative Court, 1995, after: Cieślik, 2016: 6).

Compared with such public trust professions as judge, lawyer, barrister, and expert witness, the sworn translator still seems somewhat undervalued and underestimated, whereas, as the court's reasoning shows, it is an elite profession requiring a great deal of knowledge and experience.

2.7. Translation organisations and associations and their role in the work of professional translators

The activities of associations and organisations of translators are an important aspect of a translator's work. They have an impact on both the quality of the work and the enrichment of the translation workshop. They mainly provide professional support to translators and act as representatives of

120 According to the amendment of the Czech law on the profession of sworn translator, the financial penalties for an unreliable translator are in the range of CZK 500,000 – CZK 750,000, a significant difference from the previous level of CZK 50,000. In Poland, on the other hand, according to Article 233 par. 4 of the Penal Code, 'an interpreter who presents a false translation intended to serve as evidence in court proceedings faces a prison sentence of one to 10 years' (by comparison, the minimum sentence for murder is eight years).

translators before state bodies, for example, working out a common position, as happened in the case of the law on the profession of sworn translator (both in Poland and the Czech Republic). In addition, the organisations help translators with continuing education, developing their skills and workshop. They provide translators with access to periodic training and meetings and conferences. It is not uncommon for the forums of such organisations to address current industry issues, and it is possible to consult them regarding questions about the translation of particular terminology or the use of new tools.

The Association of Polish Translators and Interpreters (hereafter STP) is the oldest institution of translators in Poland. It was founded in 1981 and is based in Warsaw. As the organisation's website reads:

> STP's mission is to protect the rights of professional translators and to advocate for high standards in the translation market, translation quality, professional ethics and the protection of intellectual property. STP cares about the image of the translation profession, the integration of the community and ensuring that its interests are duly represented vis-à-vis state institutions and bodies, other organisations and associations, social partners and the public (www.stp.org.pl).

In the year 2021, STP celebrated its 40th anniversary. On this occasion, a short study was published by Wojciech Gilewski[121] on the establishment of the profession of a sworn translator in Poland and the Association's activities. The origins of the organisation date back to the 1970s, when a number of social, political, and cultural changes were taking place in Poland. At the time, sworn translators were appointed by the Minister of Justice, and later by the courts, but the rates for translations were set by the court (according to Wojciech Gilewski, always too low). These translators were not affiliated with any organisation, nor was there a manual for practising the profession, and they were very often referred to as 'trial assistants'. The situation was different for literary translators, as they were integrated into the section of translators of literature within the Polish Writers' Union (hereafter ZLP). It was an association under the auspices of the Ministry of Culture, Heritage and Sport, and the translators' section had rights (including, for example, copyright) within it. Interpreters were able to enjoy privileges

121 The publication is available on the STP website (Gilewski, 2020; Kierzkowska, 2020).

such as creative workhouses and leisure centres. On 29 January 1981, the Association of Polish Translators and Interpreters (STP) was established, following an unsuccessful attempt in the late 1970s and early 1980s, when an application to register the Association was rejected. The idea was successful thanks to the initiators and the International Federation of Translators (FIT) Congress held in the spring of 1981 in Warsaw. Andrzej Kopczyński became the first president of the Association, and after four years, his place was taken by Jerzy Pieńkos.[122] STP's greatest successes include:

- recognition by the Minister of Culture and the Arts in 1982[123] as a creative association and its members as freelance authors; for the first time, associated translators were officially recognised as authors, irrespective of the type of translation they produced;
- the granting of additional housing space by the Minister of Housing and Public Utilities for interpreters on account of their creative work;
- recognition by the Minister of Finance of the right of translators in relation to tax credits for creative work;
- the possibility for translators to benefit (during martial law) from compensation for price rises and to receive food ration cards for them and their families; in order to be able to survive the aforementioned period of martial law, STP set up a business, giving its members employment – the Agency of Authors' Translation was then established, thanks to which, for example, the issue of remuneration rates for translators was sorted out.

The 1990s and 2000s brought a lot of socio-political and technological market changes. The development of computerisation (including translation services), translation offices, and agencies has unfortunately led to a reduction in pay rates for translators and, consequently, a deterioration in working conditions. The ATA, for financial reasons, ended its activities, and

122 Many well-known personalities of the Polish translation community have served on the Association's board. Detailed information, together with a photo gallery from the Association's beginnings, is available at www.stp.org.pl.

123 On the basis of Order No. 9 of the Minister of Culture and the Arts of 30/01/1982 r.

the STP field branch structures were similarly dissolved. In its heyday, the STP had 2,200 members, and thanks to the Association, many outstanding translators have been recognised and awarded. The strongest and most active group of translators in the STP were the sworn translators (TPs). The TP Section has been very active in striving to ensure that TP status is given the right character and weight both in the professional community and among state institutions. The first set of rules for practising the TP profession – the *TP Vademecum* – was published by the Association in 1985. This group formed a new organisation in 1990 called the Polish Society of Economic, Legal and Court Translators (hereafter TEPIS),[124] with Danuta Kierzkowska as its first president. Since 2017, STP has been organising regular meetings called 'Salons', which bring together translators and those interested in translation with prominent personalities, such as writers. The aim of the meetings is to share experiences as well as to support translators in their work.

The STP's statutory objectives are:

- integration and support of the translation community;
- activities in the nature of a professional organisation;
- representing Polish translators at home and abroad and in international organisations;
- compliance with the ethics of the profession;
- protecting the rights of translators (professional, moral, and material);
- participation in the drafting of translation regulations;
- facilitating the upgrading of translators' professional qualifications;
- mentoring translators;
- conducting public benefit activities.

The Association wishes to pursue the above objectives through:

- activities of circles/forums/platforms, etc;
- interaction with relevant authorities / universities / scientific institutes / national organisations and associations;
- organisation of congresses and conferences, symposia, and lectures;

124 This is today's TEPIS society.

- offering assistance and advice to STP members;
- recognising and awarding prizes and awards.

The Polish Society of Sworn and Specialised Translators – an association of sworn translators separated from the structures of the STP – was established in 1990. It currently unites the largest number of sworn translators in Poland and has several objectives, which include deepening and spreading knowledge of the art of translation, protecting translators' copyrights, and representing translators' interests before authorities. In 2003, TEPIS became a non-profit organisation, and in 1993 it became a member of the International Federation of Translators (FIT). In 2010, TEPIS became a founding member of the European Legal Interpreters and Translators Association (EULITA). The activities of TEPIS focus primarily on organising in-service training workshops for sworn and specialised translators, conferences, retreats, laboratories, legal and specialised translation workshops, retreats for sworn and specialised translators, laboratories, and the International Forum on Legal Translation. The Translegis Publishing House, which was set up at TEPIS, additionally supports the Society in the training of translators by publishing books on the problems of legal and juridical translation and a series devoted to parallel texts in different languages. TEPIS publishes a non-periodical, specialised, point-of-view journal *Lingua Legis*, dedicated to the most important issues in translation, while society members receive the *TEPIS Bulletin*.

Another association that interacts with STP and TEPIS is the Baltic Society of Translators and Interpreters (BST). As the organisation's website (BST, 2021) states, it:

> Intends to focus mainly on regional and local issues in its activities, without, however, relinquishing participation from outside the Baltic region. Its aim is to better integrate translators, develop common standards, raise the profile of the profession and work to improve the skills of our community. (After: www.bst.org.pl)

Table 24 provides a summary of the key data for the organisations cited above.

Tab. 24: Interpreter organisations in Poland

Name	Date of establishment/ address	Statutory objectives, membership rules, key people in the organisation
Association of Polish Translators and Interpreters (STP) [*Stowarzyszenie Tłumaczy Polskich*]	1981	www.stp.org.pl Membership requires the submission of a declaration, the recommendation of two full members, proof of translation achievements, a favourable opinion from the Qualification Committee and acceptance by the STP General Board. Types of membership: honorary member, supporting member, candidate member, actual member. By being affiliated with STP, the translator is visible on the STP website to potential clients, has confirmed translator status, and has access to job opportunities.
Polish Society of Sworn and Specialised Translators (TEPIS) [*Polskie Towarzystwo Tłumaczy Przysięgłych i Specjalistycznych*]	1990	www.tepis.org.pl Membership in the Association is open to sworn translators or specialist translators with a professional record. In addition to the completed declaration, the membership fee must be paid. Membership ranks available: extraordinary member, ordinary member, expert member, supporting member, honorary member. Members are entitled, for example, to discounts on training courses organised by TEPIS for sworn translators.
Baltic Society of Translators and Interpreters (BST) [*Bałtyckie Stowarzyszenie Tłumaczy*]	2009	bst.org.pl A translator with several years of translation experience may become a member of the Society; a declaration and payment of the membership fee are required.

Source: Author's own elaboration.

As far as Czech translator associations are concerned, there are currently two main organisations: *Jednota tlumočníků a překladatelů*[125] and *Komora soudních tlumočníků.*[126]

JTP is an independent organisation which any translator who is actively translating and who wishes to support the organisation in its development can join. JTP is a trade organisation for professional translators and interpreters. The union was established in 1990. The organisation aims to protect the professional, legal, and social interests of its members, supporting them in their continuing education, and promoting them on the labour market (translation market). JTP strives to keep its members informed about career opportunities. In addition, the organisation aims to raise the prestige of the translation profession in society, educating the public about the quality of translation and interpreting. JTP is a member of the International Federation of Translators (FIT). The union also publishes a magazine for its members and organises regular training courses and seminars, as well as competitions for the best translation theses. It is also the organiser of the Czech St Jerome's Days events *(Jeronýmovy dny)*.

The Czech Chamber of Court Interpreters and Court Translators brings together only translators with the court (sworn) translation qualifications. The organisation has its own statute, is a co-author of a code of ethics for translators, and undertakes to represent the translation community before the Ministry of Justice of the Czech Republic. The Chamber's website includes an actively moderated forum where translators receive reliable information on current issues in the profession. A magazine for sworn translators entitled *Sworn Translator* [*Soudní tlumočník*] is also published twice a year. Glossaries, ready-made translations of laws, chat advice for chamber members, transcription rules for certified translations, helpful linguistic links, rulings related to translators' remuneration, tax information for translators, information on applicable membership fees, and general meetings are available to members. In addition, the Chamber provides translators with an example repertory, information relating to the most

---

125 Union of Interpreters and Translators (hereafter JTP). The organisation's website: www.jtpunion.org.

126 Chamber of Court Interpreters and Court Translators of the Czech Republic (hereafter KST). The organisation's website: www.kstcr.cz.

recent legislative developments, and a model of the translation certification clause. As the Chamber represents the interpreting community before state authorities, members also receive information regarding correspondence and communication with representatives of public authorities. The organisation's code of ethics emphasises the importance of aspects of the translator's work, such as timeliness, quality of translation, impartiality, attention to image and expression, discretion, confidentiality, and protection of entrusted data. According to the Code, the Chamber can consider a complaint against an interpreter and reprimand him or her. Complaints against interpreters are heard by a three-member disciplinary committee. The Chamber as an organisation defends the prestige of the interpreting profession, and the professional, social, and labour interests of interpreters. Members of the Chamber have access to the regulations governing the profession of sworn translators and the way in which certified translations are carried out. The Chamber supports translators in further training and continuous education and qualification (for example, by organising one-day and two-semester courses for sworn translators, as required by the Ministry of Justice). Every year, the Chamber also organises an accounting seminar for sworn translators, as well as training and seminars to improve the translators' skills in law, economics, and other fields, with the participation of specialists, such as forensic experts, auditors, lawyers, judges, or notaries. The Chamber maintains a register of interpreters on its website. The organisation also works to establish and develop contacts with other interpreter organisations at home and abroad.

Tab. 25: Czech translator and interpreter organisations

Name	Date of establishment/ address	Statutory objectives, membership rules, key people in the organisation
Union of Interpreters and Translators (JTP) [*Jednota tlumočníků a překladatelů*]	1990	www.jtpunion.org Any translator who submits a declaration and pays a membership fee may become a member of the union. Upon joining the union, the member receives access to the JTP union magazine.

Tab. 25: Continued

Name	Date of establishment/ address	Statutory objectives, membership rules, key people in the organisation
Chamber of Court Interpreters and Court Translators (KST) [*Komora soudních tlumočníků*]	1996	www.kctcr.cz Only sworn translators can become members of the Chamber, a declaration is required along with a membership fee. The member receives access to databases, glossaries, translation of laws, training, etc.

Source: Author's own elaboration.

In addition to the above-mentioned organisations, two more Czech associations are worth mentioning due to the scope of their activities and their history. The first is the Association of Conference Interpreters [*Asociace konferenčních tlumočníků*] (ASKOT) (www.askot.cz), founded in Prague in 1990. This association, like JTP and KST, only brings together active conference interpreters who have been recommended in advance by a sufficient number of other members. Members are selected not only on the number of years of professional practice but also on the basis of the quality of the services provided and the ethical standards adhered to when practising the translation profession. The aim of the organisation is to represent the common interests of conference interpreters, as well as to support continuing education and the improvement of their craft. ASKOT sent, together with JTP and KST, a letter to the Czech authorities in 2020 asking them to support the interpreting industry during the epidemic. Anyone interested in becoming a member of ASKOT, in addition to submitting an application for membership, must obtain a recommendation from two other members of the association within one year of submitting the application. In this way, the organisation seeks to maintain a high level of interpreters applying to join ASKOT, as well as to avoid random people with insufficient seniority or lack of relevant experience.

Another Czech association for translators of literature, theorists, critics, and historians involved in translation is the Czech Literary Translators' Guild [*Obec překladatelů*] (www.obecprekladatelu.cz). The organisation brings together translators, has an elaborate code of ethics, and awards an annual Josef Jungmann Prize for the best literary translation. The association's activities also include actively organising workshops and seminars for beginners and more experienced interpreters.

In addition to the organisations present in Poland and the Czech Republic, there are also thriving international organisations that work for all sworn and specialised translators worldwide. The best-known is the FIT *(Fédération Internationale des Traducteurs*), one of the oldest organisations for translators. The FIT (2020) website states that it currently includes associations and organisations of translators from various countries: more than 100 professional associations representing more than 80,000 translators from 55 countries. It aims to promote dignity, ethics, and professionalism in the work of translators. It continuously seeks to improve working conditions in the translation profession worldwide, while promoting the rights and freedom of expression of translators. This organisation is behind the creation of one of the most important acts[127] on the work and profession of translators, which has contributed to the visibility of the activities and status of the profession. It is also worth noting the historic 10th Congress in Vienna (1984), which adopted a resolution to establish uniform European standards for the training, examination, and working conditions of court interpreters (Kierzkowska, 2020: 113). This aspect is important to the extent that attitudes towards the work and qualifications of court interpreters have ultimately changed. This is because previously, it was thought that a philological education was sufficient to do legal translation. It is important to identify this belief as a misconception since producing court translations requires not only an excellent knowledge of the

127 This is the Nairobi Act of 22 November 1976. The act was entitled *Recommendation on the legal protection of Translators and Translations and the practical means to improve the status of Translator*. The document was issued by UNESCO at its General Conference in Nairobi with the participation of 145 member states. The recommendations apply not only to sworn translators, but to translators of all specialities (professional and specialised translators as well). From the translators' perspective, this act is of historical significance, having initiated a new way of looking at translators and thinking about translation (Kierzkowska, 2020: 113).

language and culture of the target language country, but also, and perhaps above all, an adequate knowledge and understanding of the legal systems[128] of the languages being translated, case law, criminal law, administrative law, and a range of other legal norms and acts.

EULITA, the European Legal Interpreters and Translators Association, was established in 2009 in Antwerp. The main focus of its activities is on the competence of court interpreters, and thus on improving the qualifications of interpreters, perfecting their skills, and preparing them adequately for work during court hearings. The incentive to do so is provided by the principle of a fair trial, according to which a suspect or accused person – in the absence of knowledge of the language of the proceedings – has the right to be assisted by a court interpreter.[129] As in the case of FIT activities, EULITA emphasises the knowledge of the law and the rules of court procedure required by sworn interpreters. Practice shows that this is not self-evident knowledge, and its absence often leads to serious consequences. Thanks to the work of EULITA, registers of sworn translators are maintained in many European countries[130] – in Poland, such a register is operated by TEPIS and in the Czech Republic by the Czech Chamber of Court Interpreters and Court Translators. EULITA continually undertakes further activities as part of its ongoing programmes to strengthen cooperation between the justice authorities and court interpreters, so it focuses not only on improving the

---

128 This fact is very often emphasised by TEPIS founder Danuta Kierzkowska in her writing or in the TEPIS-published journal *Lingua Legis*. The problem of the competence of court interpreters is pointed out by Bogusław Cieślik, Arkadiusz Kubacki, and Marek Kuźniak, members of the examination board for future court interpreters in Poland.

129 This right is enjoyed by the participant in the proceedings under the provisions of the 1950 European Convention on Human Rights, the 1965 International Covenant on Civil and Political Rights, and the 1998 Rome Statute. On 20 October 2010, in turn, Directive 2010/64/EU of the European Parliament and of the Council on the right to translation in criminal proceedings was issued. Today, this act forms the basis for extensive efforts to improve the qualifications, continuing education, and craftsmanship of the court interpreter (see also Kierzkowska, 2020: 114).

130 The effect of an actively managed register of sworn translators was achieved through the implementation of the *LIT Search*programme. It was carried out with the participation of both TEPIS and KST, as well as sworn translators' organisations from Belgium, Austria, the Netherlands, Spain or the UK.

interpreters' skills and familiarising them with the court proceedings, but also on providing them with substantive, technical, and often psychological support[131] during their work. Touching on the consequences of translation errors, it is worth citing as a warning two cases that have reverberated in both the translation community and the wider public.

1. The Melbourne case

Hiromi Nagao, president of the Japan Judicial Interpreters Association and professor at Kobe College, drew attention to the implications of the quality of court interpreting during her paper delivered in Magdeburg in November 2004 at the VII International Forum on Legal Translation. The way in which the translation is carried out can have an irreparable impact on the lives of the people involved in the legal proceedings. Take the Melbourne case as an example.

> On 15 June 1992, seven Japanese people left Japan for a tourist trip to Melbourne, Australia. Among them were men and women in their thirties and forties, one man was in his sixties at the time. On their way to Melbourne, the tour group stopped briefly in Kuala Lumpur, Malaysia, for a day tour of the city. The group's guides, who were there to pick them up, took their luggage to the minibus. As the Japanese were having lunch, one of the guides appeared in the restaurant and said that the minibus had been stolen and their luggage was lost. After waiting at the hotel for some time, the guide turned up with the information that the luggage had been found but was all shredded. He apologised to the tourists and brought them new bags. Some of them were surprised because nothing was missing from their luggage. The next day, the Japanese went to the airport for their flight to Melbourne; their luggage was carried by the guides. Meanwhile, the Australian

131 On the organisation's website www.eulita.eu news on implemented and new programmes is available. The most recently implemented project (as of March 2021) was the NETPRALA concept (2018–2020), a programme of support in pre-trial procedures that provided practice-oriented legal training. The scope and topics of the training make interpreters and bodies active in court proceedings aware that a sworn interpreter is not an empty title, but a responsible and demanding task. The current CAPISCE programme addresses the issue of the involvement of a court interpreter in proceedings involving child victims of sexual offences. Only a closer look at court hearings, pre-trial proceedings and interrogations makes both interpreters and litigants aware of the demanding task facing the court interpreter. In the case of the CAPISCE programme, court interpreters are also provided with psychological support, which seems understandable and much needed.

> Federal Police were already waiting for them at Melbourne Airport and arrested them on suspicion of drug trafficking. The drugs were hidden in double-bottomed bags. After a lengthy investigation, the case was brought before the Magistrate Court in 1992 and in February 1994 to the County Court, where it resulted in a sentence of 15 years imprisonment for the four defendants and 20 years imprisonment for the tour operator. The appeal against the judgment was dismissed. In November 2002, four parolees returned to Japan. However, they continue to claim their innocence. Lawyers in Japan consider this case to be a miscarriage of justice caused by an inadequate translation by the court interpreter (Nagao, 2005: 3).

As a result of the action taken by fifty-five lawyers from the Osaka Bar Association, the case went to the UN Human Rights Commission in 1996. The investigation led to the presentation of the interrogation procedures recorded in full (on videotape and tape). Transcripts were made recording the dialogues between the prosecutor and the interpreter in English, as well as the dialogues between the suspect and the interpreter in Japanese (excerpts from the transcripts are available in the quoted source material). The evident ineptitude of the translator, the twisting of the content, the imprecise translation, and even the modification of the meaning of the message consequently led to an irreversible change in the lives of four people who 'only' took part in the tour. One of them attempted suicide three times in prison. Upon returning to Japan, the idea of verifying the process did not catch on with the Japanese, who spent the best years of their lives in prison (Nagao, 2005: 7).

2. Another story is quoted in an article by Lucja Biel:

> According to press reports, due to blatant errors in the certified translation of several thousand pages of documentation of the criminal investigation of Andrei Żukowiec, the Bialystok District Court ordered the re-translation of all documents, which will cost the Polish taxpayer more than PLN 300 000. This Belarusian opposition figure is accused by the Belarusian authorities of defrauding him of $700,000 in loans. Żukowiec claims that he is innocent and that the evidence against him was fabricated. Following the refusal to extradite Żukowiec to Belarus, the Bialystok prosecutor's office launched an investigation based on photocopies of documents received from the Belarusian side. The translation of the documents commissioned for the secretary of the Bialystok Appellate Prosecutor's Office and her husband found significant errors to Żukowiec's disadvantage. For example, in a customs declaration, a German counterparty became a counterparty from the tax haven of the Virgin Islands; figures were confused and unsigned documents received Żukowiecs' signature in translation. After Żukowiec

notified the public prosecutor's office of the suspicion that the translators had committed a crime, the Regional Prosecutor's Office in Lublin discontinued the investigation, arguing that 'the couple was overtired' (the translators were not charged because the case was time-barred) (Biel, 2011: 13–14).

Both cases show the extreme lack of competence of the translators and interpreters. Unfortunately, no one will reimburse the victims for their lost freedom, or the years of life spent in prison.

Tab. 26: Interpreter organisations in Europe

Name	Date of establishment/ address	Statutory objectives, membership rules, key people in the organisation
International Federation of Translators FIT [*Fédération Internationale des Traducteurs*]	1953	en.fit-ift.org In addition to the declaration and membership fee, in order to join the association, you must be an organisation of qualified court, specialist, or terminology translators. Membership is not possible for universities or organisations with students in their ranks. Universities and educational institutions can apply for membership as associate members.
European Legal Interpreters and Translators Association (EULITA)	2009	www.eulita.eu Two types of membership: full member and associate member. In addition to the declaration and the payment of the membership fee, the requirements for members are defined according to the types of membership as follows: Full members – membership for national or regional associations and organisations of certified translators; Associate members – membership for national or regional associations of EU interpreters and translators, as well as researchers, trainers, and students in the translation industry.

Source: Author's own elaboration.

Tab. 27: The most important conference events for translators in Poland, the Czech Republic, and Europe

Name	Frequency	Objectives and event organisation
Translating Europe	once a year, usually in autumn, regularly since 2014	A project set up in 2014 at the initiative of the European Union Directorate-General for Translation. The project has two parts: Translating Europe Forum (a European conference on translation issues, organised in Brussels, and, during the pandemic, online) and Translating Europe Workshops (a project complementing the TEF conference in the form of translation workshops; an initiative of the Directorate-General for Translation in cooperation with universities affiliated with the European Master's in Translation Network). The initiative aims to bring together and pool the collective strengths of organisations specialising in translation, freelance translators, and translation training bodies.
Interpreters' Conference [*Konferencja Tłumaczy*]	Warsaw, once a year, in autumn, since 2016	The conference is organised on behalf of two private organisers – the translation and training agency Texem and Localize.pl. The organisers have managed to create a dynamic and interesting meeting of translators over several years, during which the most current and up-to-date issues for the translation industry are addressed. The conference hosts interesting speakers from the worlds of media, literature, culture, and art, as well as owners of translation agencies, language training centres, and language educational agencies. TEPIS actively participates in the conference by awarding its annual prize to the person most deserving in the translation industry each year.
St Jerome's Days [*Jeronymový dny*]	every year, usually on the second weekend in November, since 1994	The Czech Festival of Translation and Translators and Interpreters is held every year under the auspices of JTP. Over two days, a series of lectures, workshops, and training sessions on specialised and literary translation are held, addressing the most important issues in the field of translation and the translator's work in the domestic and foreign markets.

Source: Author's own elaboration.

Helen Keller, a deaf American writer, claimed that 'alone we can do little, together we can do so much'. There is a lot of truth in these words, and they can be applied to the translator's work. Membership in translator organisations means membership in an entity that represents the interests of the group, defending them and fighting to obtain and maintain the proper status for the translation profession. These organisations strive to win fair remuneration for translators and provide opportunities for their development and continuing education by organising numerous seminars and workshops with long-standing practitioners. The mutual exchange of experiences during the conference and workshop meetings provides an opportunity to learn from a different perspective about issues that many people in the translation services industry deal with on a daily basis. Acting in a group raises interpreters' and translators' awareness of the possibilities, but also the limitations, of the work they do. It also helps them to gain an awareness of where to seek help in the event of potential problems or questions about a translation.

3 Research section: Corpus analysis of the language of civil law contracts

3.1. Aim of the research section

This research analysis focuses on the problem of translation of Czech-Polish civil-law contract texts. As an introduction to the research, a brief characterisation and typology of civil law contracts in the hierarchy of the Czech and Polish legal systems is presented, taking into account the sources of Czech and Polish law. The main objective of the research chapter is a linguistic analysis aimed at confirming or denying the existence of translational universals in the sense of the hypothesis put forward by Mona Baker (1993: 243): 'Universals of translation are linguistic features which typically occur in translated rather than original texts and are thought to be independent of the influence of the specific language pairs involved in the process of translation'. Therefore, this research investigates whether there are linguistic features that occur with noticeably greater frequency in translated texts than in non-translated texts. These features do not result from the influence of the original language on the language of translation (Laviosa, 2011; Biel, 2015; Kraskowska, 2018). The following set of translational universals, with their definitions taken from Mona Baker, was adopted for this research:

1. *Explicitation* (E) – the expression of content that can be guessed or presumed in the source text and is expressed explicitly by the translator in the target text. This phenomenon can be seen when the translator uses, for example, lexical expressions or the addition of conjunctions.[132]
2. *Simplification* (S) – simplifying the translation, for example by simplifying syntax, removing ambiguity, or simplifying the source message itself.

132 'An overall tendency to spell things out rather than to leave them implicit in translation' (Baker, 1996: 180).

3. *Normalization* (N) – the exaggeration of typical features of the target language, the non-translation of errors appearing in the source text, in general, the adaptation of the translation to the norms of the target language.[133]
4. *Reduction* (R) – reduction or avoidance of repetitions present in the source text; stripping the text of idiosyncratic features so that translations are more similar to each other than the originals.
5. *Discourse transfer* (DT) – a procedure in which the translated utterance is constructed directly under the influence of the source text rather than in conformity with the norms of the target language. This is an instance of the so-called law of interference, formulated by Gideon Toury.

The last universal defined by Mona Baker is the *distinctive distribution of lexical items*, denoting the increased and thus perceptible frequency of certain lexemes in translated texts relative to their frequency in the corresponding source texts and in non-translated target language texts. This study abandoned an analysis of this indicator, as it would have required the collection of a very extensive body of research material, while the analysis itself lends itself more to separate research material and elaboration in a separate work. This research used a deductive research approach, the so-called *corpus-based approach*.[134]

In order to obtain a representative research sample, six different civil law contracts were analysed. The author has selected the type of texts she is most often in contact with in her daily work. To be able to observe some typical translator behaviour in the translation process and, at the same time, to obtain representative research material, each contract was translated by three different translators, each translating the same text. The volume of material commissioned for translation was 38 normative pages.[135] In an attempt to ensure that the competencies of the translators participating in the project were on a more equal footing, we selected translators who each held sworn translator status (in Poland or the Czech Republic). This

133 '[…] tendency to conform to patterns and practices which are typical of the target language, even to the point of exagerrating them' (Baker, 1996: 176–177).

134 The research approach is characterised in the first part of the work, in the chapter on research methodology.

135 A normative page is 1800 characters with spaces. Some of the contracts were shorter, others longer, but they did not deviate from market norms.

ensured that the study used material prepared by experienced translators, practitioners who deal with texts of a similar nature daily and have proven translator competencies. A total of five different translators took part in the project. The first stage of the study was to develop a brief characterisation of the contract in question, taking into account the Polish and Czech civil codes. Relevant sections of the Acts are cited to define the type of contract in question, the basic terminology used for such a contract and the nomenclature of the parties are indicated, and the features of this type of contract are defined. The material is presented in table form. The second stage of the study was the material prepared by the translators. Each text has been divided into sections to indicate the context. Adequate excerpts from the translations were then quoted (the samples were described as T1/T2/T3 to distinguish the translators; however, the samples were presented anonymously). Each passage with its translation was then analysed to identify potential translational universals. During the analysis:

- the author investigated whether and how particular translator behaviours affect translation quality;
- the presence of attestations was checked in the author's corpus, the NKJP corpus, and the InterCorp corpus;
- the translations were checked against parallel texts, an exercise aimed at verifying that the translation met the cultural norms of the target language.

Sensitive data contained in the source texts has been anonymised. The source texts are authentic contracts that have been concluded between the parties:

1. sales contract;
2. donation agreement;
3. lease agreement;
4. cooperation agreement;
5. contract of mandate;
6. work contract.

Two tables are presented at the end of each research: the first summarises the presence of universals in the translations of the contract under study, and the second presents the frequency of the universals. The analysis of each contract concludes with a graph of the phenomena observed in the chart.

The conclusions are presented after all the contracts have been analysed. The final element of the research section is a community survey carried out in the form of an email questionnaire and a free in-depth interview.

3.1.1. Sources of Czech law: Typology of civil law contracts in the Czech legal system

The Czech legal system is a continental law system based on Roman law. This system is based on written law. The most important instruments of the Czech legal system include:

- **laws** *(zákony)* – sets of rules of behaviour that regulate the main areas of the lives of people and society as a whole;
- **codes** *(zákoníky)* – laws that have a broader scope, covering an entire branch of law. The provisions contained in the codes are organised more systematically;
- **codes of procedure** *(řády)* – agreements covering the entire scope of procedural law, establishing detailed procedural rules;
- **constitutional laws** *(ústavní zákony)* – laws regulating the most important affairs of the state, the subject of which are human and civil rights. Such laws include, for example, the Ústava ČR (Constitution of the Czech Republic) and the Charter of Fundamental Rights and Freedoms.

Additional instruments supporting the aforementioned laws are the implementing regulations, which include government regulations, as well as ordinances of ministers and central government bodies and regional local government units.

International agreements ratified by the Czech Parliament are binding on the Czech Republic. They have a higher rank than national legislation (the provisions of the international agreement take precedence over national legislation, in the Czech Republic the principle of supremacy of EU law applies). As a member of the European Union, the Czech Republic is subject to European regulations.

Tab. 28: Hierarchy of sources of law in the Czech Republic

International agreements (principle of supremacy of European Union law)
Constitution and constitutional laws
Ordinary laws
Implementing provisions

Source: Own elaboration based on information at https://e-justice.europa.eu.

The issue of obligations is regulated in the Czech Republic by the Civil Code (*Občanský zakoník, OZ*), in particular, §§ 1721–3014.[136] In § 1721 (Chapter 1 of the OZ – Incurrence of an obligation and what is an obligation) we read that '*Ze závazku má věřitel vůči dlužníku právo na určité plnění jako na pohledávku a dlužník má povinnost toto právo splněním dluhu uspokojit*', while in § 1722: '*Plnění, které je předmětem závazku, musí být majetkové povahy a odpovídat zájmu věřitele, i když tento zájem není jen majetkový*'. The creation of an obligation is determined by § 1723: '*(1) Závazek vzniká ze smlouvy, z protiprávního činu, nebo z jiné právní skutečnosti, která je k tomu podle právního řádu způsobilá. (2) Ustanovení o závazcích, které vznikají ze smluv, se použijí přiměřeně i na závazky vznikající na základě jiných právních skutečností*'.

136 The Polish Civil Code is the Act of 23 April 1964 (Coll. No. 16, item 93 as amended). This law came into force on 1 January 1965 and has also undergone several modifications due to the numerous changes in the political system. The last and largest amendment took place in 1990. The Polish Civil Code is divided into four books *(Księga pierwsza. Część ogólna, Księga druga. Własność i inne prawa rzeczowe, Księga trzecia. Zobowiązania, Księga czwarta. Spadki*). The Czech Civil Code is *Občanský zákoník*, Act No. 89/2012 Coll., amended in 2014, replacing the old Czechoslovak Civil Code of 1964. The Czech Civil Code is divided into five parts: *Obecná část* (§§ 1–654), *Rodinné právo* (§§ 655–975), *Absolutní majetková práva* (§ 976–1720, includes rights in rem and inheritance law), *Relativní majetková práva* (§§ 1721–2990, includes contract law), *Ustanovení společná, přechodná a závěrečná* (§§ 2991–3081), which are divided according to the hierarchy: *část*, *hlava*, *díl*, *oddíl*. This knowledge is essential for the translator because, when translating a text in which the relevant provisions of the Civil Code are quoted or referred to, he or she should know how to translate the name of the relevant section of the Code correctly.

As for the definition of the contract itself, it is described in § 1725: '*Smlouva je uzavřena, jakmile si strany ujednaly její obsah. V mezích právního jednání je stranám ponecháno na vůli svobodně si smlouvu ujednat a určit její obsah*'.

There are several possibilities to divide and classify contracts depending on the aspect being considered. Making a more general, theoretical division, considering the types of legal transactions, several types of contracts can be distinguished.[137]

1. Based on the number of parties entering into the agreement, a distinction can be made between *bilateral agreements* and *multilateral agreements*.
2. Considering the form in which a contract is concluded, a distinction is made between *formal contracts*, which require a specific form, and *informal contracts*. In the Czech Republic, the *principle of the formlessness of contracts* is common. An example of a formal contract is a contract for the sale of real estate, which according to the Czech legal system requires a written form.
3. Depending on the remuneration under the contract, a distinction can be made between *fee-based contracts, gratuitous contracts*, and *mixed contracts* (the remuneration is less than the usual value of the performance).
4. Considering the manner in which ownership over a thing is transferred, one can distinguish between *consensual contracts* and *real contracts* ('consensus' in Roman law means a consensual statement of the parties' will). In the case of consensual contracts, the legal relationship is already established when the contract itself is concluded (e.g., contract of mandate). In the case of real contracts, in addition to consensus, the actual performance of legal acts, the handing over of the object of the contract, or the delivery of the thing (e.g., loan agreement) is required for a legal relationship to be established.

137 The division of contracts and its discussion was developed by the author together with mec. Jana Samkova of the law firm Hajduk & Partneři. The study was prepared using such sources as the Czech Civil Code (*Občanský zákoník*), *Právní překlad v teorii a praxi. Nový občanský zákoník* (Chromá, 2014), and *Občanský zákoník V. Závazkové právo. Obecná část (§ 1721–2054)* (Hulmák a kol., 2014).

5. *Synallagmatic* and *asynallagmatic contracts* can be distinguished. Synallagmatic contracts are those in which the performance of both parties is mutually dependent on each other (the obligation to perform is conditional on the simultaneous performance of the other party to the contract). This is not only about the reciprocity of rights and obligations but also about mutual conditionality of performance (e.g., under a sales contract, the buyer is obliged to pay the price of the purchased goods, while the seller is obliged to hand over the object of the contract after the buyer has paid its price). Asynallagmatic contracts, on the other hand, can include, for example, a donation contract (with no performance obligation on the part of thc opposing party).
6. A distinction is made between *named* (specified) *contracts* and *unnamed* (unspecified) *contracts* – similar to the Polish legal system – see the description below.
7. Some contracts take into account *the obligatory legal relationship*: contracts that **secure** the obligatory legal relationship (*security transfer contracts*), contracts that have the effect of **changing** the obligatory legal relationship (e.g., assignment of an obligation), and contracts that have the effect of **cancelling** the obligatory legal relationship (*novation*).

Contracts can also be distinguished by considering their characteristic element:

1. *Consumer contracts* are generally not any special type of contract. A characteristic feature of this type of contract is that it is concluded between a trader and a consumer.
2. *Adhesion contracts* are contracts concluded in an adversarial manner. This is a type of contract, the basic terms of which have been defined (imposed) by one of the parties or drafted in accordance with its guidelines. The weaker party does not have the opportunity to influence the terms of the contract (often bank contracts, contracts containing general terms and conditions, or form contracts).
3. A *future contract* is a contract imposing on one of the parties, after having been called upon to do so by the first party, an obligation to conclude, within an accepted period of time, a contract the content of which has been, at least in general terms, agreed in advance.
4. A *contract for the benefit of a third party* is governed by § 1767 and § 1768 of the NOZ[138]. It is a contract between two parties whereby the

138 Nový občanský zakoník/Czech New Civil Code

debtor is obliged to perform for the benefit of a third party who is not a party to the contract. An example of a contract for the benefit of a third party could be, for example, an insurance contract.

The formal division of civil law contracts in the Czech legal system according to Act 89/2012, Civil Code (*Občanský zakoník*), §§ 2055–2893 is as follows:

- *Díl 1 – Převedení věci do vlastnictví jiného – darování, koupě, směna*[139];
- *Díl 2 – Přenechání věci k užití jinému – výprosa, výpůjčka, nájem, pacht, licence, zápůjčka, úvěr*[140];
- *Díl 3 – Pracovní poměr*[141];
- *Díl 4 – Závazky ze schovacích smluv – úschova, skladování*[142];
- *Díl 5 – Závazky ze smluv příkazního typu – příkaz, zprostředkování, komise, zasílatelství, obchodní zastoupení*[143];
- *Díl 6 – zájezd*[144];
- *Díl 7 – závazky ze smluv o přepravě – přeprava osob, přeprava věci, provoz dopravního prostředku*[145];
- *Díl 8 – dílo*[146];
- *Díl 9 – péče o zdraví*[147];
- *Díl 10 – Kontrolní činnost*[148];
- *Díl 11 – Závazky ze smlouvy o účtu, jednorázovém vkladu, akreditivu a inkasu – účet, jednorázový vklad, akreditivu, inkaso*[149];

---

139 Part 1 – Transfer of title to property to other persons – donation, purchase, exchange

140 Part 2 – Transfer of property for the use of others – precarium, loan, lease, pacht, licence, loan of property

141 Part 3 – Employment relationship

142 Part 4 – Deposit contract liabilities – deposit services, storage

143 Part 5 – Obligations under contracts of mandate – contract of mandate, agency, forwarding, commercial representation

144 Part 6 – Organised trips

145 Part 7 – Transport contract liabilities – transport of persons, transport of property, operation of means of transport

146 Part 8 – Work

147 Part 9 – Health care

148 Part 10 – Control activities

149 Part 11 – Accounts payable, single payment, letter of credit and collection agreements

- *Díl 12 – Závazky ze zaopatřovacích smluv – důchod, výměnek*[150];
- *Díl 13 – Společnost*[151];
- *Díl 14 – Tichá společnost*[152];
- *Díl 15 – Závazky z odvážných smluv – pojištění, sázka, hra a los.*[153]

3.1.2. Sources of Polish law: Typology of civil law contracts in the Polish legal system

Like the Czech legal system, the Polish legal system is based on the continental legal system, and the tradition of written, civil law. The most important law in Poland is the Constitution of the Republic of Poland (hereafter the Constitution),[154] which is the main source of law. This document regulates not only the rights and freedoms of the citizen, but also the entire Polish legal system, the organisation of institutions, the judicial system, and the organs of local self-government. Other legal instruments in Poland are laws, ratified international agreements, and regulations.[155]

A *statute* is an instrument which is the source of the law in Poland; it regulates the most important issues in the life of citizens, for example, the rules of the profession of a sworn translator, the budget, and the legal status of citizens. Resolutions of an internal nature are issued by the Council of Ministers.

Ratified international agreements are also legal instruments in Poland. Some international agreements require parliamentary and presidential approval in order to be ratified. These include such important issues as international alliances, political and military treaties, the rights and duties of citizens, and Poland's membership of international organisations.

---

150 Part 12 – Liabilities under benefit agreements – pension benefit

151 Part 13 – Company

152 Part 14 – Silent Company

153 Part 15 – Liabilities under contracts of chance/aleatory – insurance, betting, gaming, and lottery

154 The text of the Polish Constitution has been published on the website of the Sejm (www.sejm.gov.pl). The Constitution has been published in Polish as well as in English, German, French, and Russian translations.

155 'Źródłami powszechnie obowiązującego prawa Rzeczypospolitej Polskiej są: Konstytucja, ustawy, ratyfikowane umowy międzynarodowe oraz rozporządzenia, a także akty prawa miejscowego – na obszarze działania kompetentnych organów (art. 87 Konstytucji RP)' (compare with Radwański, Olejniczak, 2016: 3).

Regulations are legal instruments that are issued by government bodies. These bodies are indicated in the Constitution.

For smaller administrative units (in accordance with the administrative division applicable in Poland), the binding legal instruments are the *acts of local law*.

Tab. 29: Hierarchy of sources of law in Poland

The Constitution
Ratified international agreements
Regulations
EU directives and decisions
Laws
Government regulations
Local legislation

Source: Own elaboration based on information at www.e-justice.europa.eu

a In preparing information on the sources of law in the Czech Republic and Poland, the author of this work relied on written sources, information obtained during her studies for legal translators at the Faculty of Law of Charles University in Prague, as well as consultations with Polish and Czech lawyers. During the preparation of the tabular statement on the hierarchy of sources of law in Poland, there was some inaccuracy in the interpretation of the primacy of EU law. While in the Czech Republic this fact is strongly emphasised, in Poland the issue seems to be contentious, more precisely there is disagreement concerning the conflict between EU law and the Polish Constitution. While the data presented in the table is as true as possible, the author asked a Polish lawyer, mec. Tomasz Szaflarski, for a comment on the divergence of Czech and Polish interpretations, more specifically on the situation in Poland. Counsel pointed out the source of the discrepancy and how the question of recognition of the primacy of EU law was interpreted: 'I. One school invokes the Constitution and from its literal wording draws the conclusion that the Constitution has absolute precedence, as it follows from Article 8(1) of the Constitution: "The Constitution is the supreme law of the Republic of Poland" and with Article 87(1) of the Constitution: "The sources of universally binding law of the Republic of Poland are: Constitution, laws, ratified international agreements and regulations". In addition, there is also the provision of Article 91 [Primacy of ratified agreement over laws]: "1. A ratified international agreement, once it has been promulgated in the Journal of Laws of the Republic of Poland, is part of the national legal order and is directly applicable, unless its application depends on the enactment of a law. 2. An international agreement ratified with the prior consent of a law takes precedence over a law if that law cannot be reconciled with the agreement. 3. If it results from an agreement ratified by the Republic of Poland constituting an international organisation, the law enacted by it shall be applied directly, taking precedence in the event of a conflict with laws." From this article, supporters of the school of superiority of the Polish Constitution over EU law conclude that Article 91(3) allows secondary law to take precedence over Polish law, but only over the law and not over the Constitution. A possible conflict cannot be removed by acknowledging

the primacy of a derived law norm over a constitutional norm. The Constitution therefore remains – by virtue of its special force – the supreme law of the Republic of Poland in relation to all international agreements binding the Republic of Poland. And by virtue of the supremacy of legal force resulting from Article 8(1) of the Constitution, it enjoys primacy of validity and application within the territory of the Republic of Poland. II. However, there are representatives of the doctrine who put forward the thesis of the supremacy of EU law even over the Polish Constitution. One of the fundamental principles of EU law is the primacy of EU law over the national law of the Member States. Poland, by joining the EU, accepted these principles. This principle does not limit state sovereignty. It was introduced to guarantee uniform legal protection for citizens throughout the European Union. The priority rule states that:
– Member State must ensure the effectiveness of Union law;
– a state may not introduce provisions in its legislation that are contrary to the EU legal order;

Księga trzecia of the Polish Civil Code (hereafter the Civil Code) contains regulations on obligations. This act defines the issue of liabilities as follows: 'Art. 353. *§ 1. Zobowiązanie polega na tym, że wierzyciel może żądać od dłużnika świadczenia, a dłużnik powinien świadczenie spełnić. § 2. Świadczenie może polegać na działaniu albo na zaniechaniu*'.

There is no normative definition of a contract in the Polish legal system; it has been assumed that a contract is 'a declaration of will made by the parties to a specific legal relationship, directed towards producing specific legal effects. A declaration of intent should be made by any means as long as the will of the person concerned is sufficiently disclosed'.[156]

There are many possibilities to classify and divide contracts in the Polish legal system – the following are some of the most important from a practical point of view:

1. Considering the effects of contracts, a distinction can be made between *binding* (obligatory) *contracts* and *dispositive contracts*. Obligatory contracts are contracts whose essence is an obligation on the part of the debtor to provide a performance consisting of the disposition of his right in favour of the creditor. Obligatory contracts entail the creation of an obligation, i.e., an increase in liabilities, such as a contract of sale.

156 Based on an answer to a question on the existence of a definition of contract in the Polish Civil Code given on 30.09.2011 by a lawyer at www.e-prawnik.pl: accessed from https://e-prawnik.pl/porady-prawne/kodeks-cywilny-a-pojecie-umowy.html [1.06.2021].

Dispositive contracts are contracts that do not oblige anyone to provide performance but directly produce legal effects in the form of a transfer, transformation, encumbrance, or abolition, e.g., a release from debt.

2. Regarding the number of parties on whom the obligation to provide performance rests, a distinction can be made between *unilaterally binding contracts* and *bilaterally (multilaterally) binding contracts*. In the case of unilaterally binding contracts, the obligation to provide is on one party, so that one party is the debtor and the other is the creditor, e.g., in a donation contract. On the other hand, in the case of bilaterally binding contracts, the obligation to perform is borne by two parties. This means that each party is both debtor and creditor, e.g., a contract of work or a contract of mandate. A *reciprocal contract* is a special type of bilateral contract, in which one party provides benefits that are equivalent to those of the other party.
3. Considering the necessity of transferring actual power over a thing, *consensual contracts* and *real contracts* are distinguished. Consensual contracts come into effect when consensual declarations of intent are made without the need for the object to be delivered, e.g., contract of sale, contract of work, or contract of mandate. Real contracts require the delivery of an object in order to be valid, in addition to the submission of declarations of intent. The transfer of de facto authority is key here, the thing may be handed over with the declaration of intent or later but in connection with it, e.g., a custody agreement.
4. Based on the existence of a so-called causa (cause), *abstract* and *causal contracts* can be distinguished. Causal contracts are contracts whose validity depends on the existence and validity of a causa. The doctrine lists, among others: a causa where the purpose is to release oneself from an obligation incumbent on the adopter *(causa solvendi)*, a causa where the purpose is to acquire a right or other pecuniary benefit by the adopter *(causa obligandi vel acquirendi)*, a causa where an act is performed with the intention of adopting without obtaining an equivalent *(causa donandi)*, and a causa where a party has obtained a benefit without legal basis and is obliged to return it *(causa ob rem)*. Abstract (detached) contracts are contracts in which the existence of a causa is not necessary for the effectiveness of the legal act. In Polish law, abstract legal acts are an exception; the issuance of a bill of exchange is an example of such an act.

5. Contracts of *chance* are a special type of contract – a necessary element of such a contract is uncertainty. Contracts of chance include, for example, insurance contracts and life annuity contracts.
6. Considering the basis of contract regulation, *named*, *unnamed*, and *mixed contracts* are distinguished. Named contracts are those which are covered by the law and have a specific statutory regulation defining the mutual rights and obligations of the parties, e.g., a contract for work (Article 627 of the Civil Code et seq.) or a contract of mandate (Article 734 of the Civil Code et seq.). Unnamed contracts, on the other hand, are contracts concluded within the limits of the principle of freedom of contract. Their content is not governed by the applicable rules, which is linked to the fact that they allow for the satisfaction of individual needs of the contracting parties, e.g., a factoring agreement. Mixed contracts are characterised by a combination of elements of the two types of contracts indicated above, most often consisting of the conclusion of a named contract with the simultaneous introduction of peculiar differences resulting from arrangements made by the parties.
7. In Poland, the principle of freedom of contract applies. When considering the scope of freedom of contract, a distinction is made between *freely negotiated contracts* and *adhesion contracts*. Freely negotiated contracts are concluded as a result of independent bargaining. In contrast, the content of adhesion contracts is unilaterally shaped by one of the counterparties, usually the economically stronger one. The other party is left free only to enter into or opt out of the contract. A characteristic feature of adhesion contracts is their indiscriminate nature; examples of such contracts include those concluded by consumers with a trader who uses general terms and conditions, e.g., bank contracts.
8. Considering the existence of a *pecuniary* benefit equivalent to the benefit made, a distinction is made between *paid* and *unpaid* contracts. Contracts for pecuniary consideration are those in which each party obtains a specific pecuniary benefit, not necessarily monetary, e.g., a contract of sale, or a contract for work. Contracts without consideration, on the other hand, are those in which there is no element of pecuniary gain on the part of one of the parties – they serve to make a free gift, such as a donation contract.

3.1.3. Analysis of the lease agreement

Characteristics of a lease agreement in the Polish and Czech Civil Codes.

Tab. 30: Lease agreement – basic characteristics

Lease agreement	
Definition from Czech Civil Code	**Definition from Polish Civil Code**
§ 2201 Nájemní smlouvou se pronajímatel zavazuje přenechat nájemci věc k dočasnému užívání a nájemce se zavazuje platit za to pronajímateli nájemné. § 2202 Předmět nájmu (1) Pronajmout lze věc nemovitou i nezuživatelnou věc movitou. Pronajmout lze i část nemovité věci; co se dále stanoví o věci, použije se i pro nájem její části. (2) Pronajmout lze i věc, která v budoucnu teprve vznikne, je-li ji možné dostatečně přesně určit při uzavření nájemní smlouvy.	Art. 659 § 1. Przez umowę najmu wynajmujący zobowiązuje się oddać najemcy rzecz do używania przez czas oznaczony lub nieoznaczony, a najemca zobowiązuje się płacić wynajmującemu umówiony czynsz.. § 2. Czynsz może być oznaczony w pieniądzach lub w świadczeniach innego rodzaju.
Basic terminology as defined in the polish and czech civil codes	
nájem	najem
nájemce	najemca
pronajímatel	wynajmujący
nájemní smlouva	umowa najmu
věc	przedmiot najmu
nájemné	czynsz najmu
Features of a lease agreement	
Named contract, consensual, pecuniary, obligation, mutual. The subject matter of a lease agreement can be either movable or immovable property. The object of the lease cannot be rights.	
Essence of a lease agreement	
The essence of a lease is an obligation on the part of the lessor to give the lessee a thing to use, either for a definite or indefinite period. The lessor is obliged to pay the agreed rent to the lessee.	
Provisions governing a lease agreement	
§§ 2201–2331 NOZ	Articles 659-692 of the Civil Code

Source: 1. Act No. 89/2012 Coll.; 2. *Občanský zákoník*; Polish Civil Code, Act of 23 April 1964; 3. Dabrowski, 2019: 156.

Example No. 1	Context / text excerpt in Czech
Context: Title page of the lease agreement Smlouva o nájmu ***bytu***	
Proposals for translation:	**Translation universals**
T1: Umowa najmu *lokalu mieszkaniowego*	DT
T2: Umowa najmu *mieszkania*	S
T3: Umowa najmu *lokalu mieszkalnego*	N
Comment: The T1 translation uses the expression *lokal mieszkaniowy*. There is only one attestation for this expression in the NKJP, coming from the classified ads section of the *Dziennik Polski*. One may suspect that the translator's behaviour is the result of linguistic interference, for in Czech we are dealing with the expression *bytová jednotka*. This indicates a transfer of discourse. A better solution, which can be seen in the T3 translation, is to use the equivalent *lokal mieszkalny* for which there are numerous attestations in the NKJP; this expression is also used in the Polish Civil Code. For T3, normalisation has been applied, while for T2, simplification has been applied – the expression *lokal mieszkalny* has been simplified to *mieszkanie*.	
Example No. 2	**Context / text excerpt in Czech**
Context: Article title in the contract čl. I. ***Úvodní** ustanovení*	
Proposals for translation:	**Translation universals**
T1: Postanowienia *wstępne*	N
T2: Postanowienia *początkowe*	DT
T3: Postanowienia *wstępne*	N
Comment: Normalisation has been applied to the T1 and T3 translations. Although the expression *postanowienia wstępne* is not attested in the NKJP, when analysing parallel texts, one comes across such an expression in the texts of authentic Polish civil law contracts. *Postanowienia początkowe* is a form of literal translation from Czech. It is used very rarely in authentic texts, and there is no attestation in the NKJP for this expression. In the Czech InterCorp corpus, we find attestation (×1) for the expression *postanowienia początkowe* and attestation (×2) for the expression *postanowienia wstępne*.	

Example No. 3	Context / text excerpt in Czech
Pronajímatel prohlašuje, že je ***k okamžiku uzavření této smlouvy*** vlastníkem bytové jednotky č. 1, nacházející se v budově čp. 1 v ulici K. H. Máchy, Hradec Králové. Jedná se o ***byt o velikosti 1+kk ve 3. nadzemním podlaží o podlahové ploše 36,3 m2***	
Proposals for translation:	**Translation universals**
T1: Wynajmujący oświadcza, że *w chwili zawarcia niniejszej umowy* jest […]. Jest to mieszkanie *o wymiarach 1+aneks kuchenny na 3 piętrze o powierzchni 36,3 m2.*	N, S, N, DT, DT, S
T2: Wynajmujący oświadcza, że *w momencie zawarcia niniejszej umowy* jest […]. Chodzi o mieszkanie *o wymiarach pokój+aneks kuchenny [1+kk] na 3 kondygnacji naziemnej o powierzchni podłogi 36,3 m2.*	N, DT, DT, DT
T3: Wynajmujący oświadcza, że *na moment zawarcia niniejszej umowy* pozostaje […]. Mowa *o mieszkaniu jednopokojowym z kuchnią oraz łazienką, na trzecim piętrze, o powierzchni użytkowej 36,3 m2.*	N, S, N, N
Comment: The translators used the expressions *na moment / w momencie / w chwili* as the equivalent of the expression *k okamžiku.* For all these possibilities, there are numerous attestations in the NKJP. The translations have been adapted to the standards of the target language. The translators undertook the translation of the last part of the sentence, using both simplification and normalisation (example T3) and discourse transfer (T1, T2). In the T1 and T2 samples, a strong influence of the source language is evident at the syntactic level, resulting in an unfortunate expression of *o wymiarach pokój+aneks/1+aneks*; the T3 translator has avoided this calque by using a simplification and the descriptive equivalent of a *mieszkanie jednopokojowe z kuchnią oraz łazienką*, resulting in a better and clearer reception of the translation. Also, the seemingly simple expression *podlahová plocha* does not have an obvious translation. Translator T1 simplified the expression by using the equivalent *powierzchnia* area (simplification), translator T2 used a faithful translation (discourse transfer), and translator T3 attempted to normalise it by using the equivalent *powierzchnia użytkowa*, but this is clearly not the correct translation due to the different semantic fields of the expressions of *powierzchnia mieszkania* and *powierzchnia użytkowa mieszkania* (for the calculation of usable surface area, the parts of the dwelling with haunches are usually subtracted).	

Example No. 4	Context / text excerpt in Czech
čl. II. Předmět nájmu Předmětem nájmu je nadepsaná bytová jednotka sestávající se z obývacího pokoje, kuchyňského koutu, předsíně, koupelny a WC. Byt je standardně vybaven, ***má podlahovou krytinu*** ve všech místnostech. Tento byt pronajímatel přenechává nájemci ***do užívání výlučně za účelem bydlení***.	
Proposals for translation:	**Translation universals**
T1: […] we wszystkich pokojach znajdują się *wykładziny*. Wynajmujący przekazuje wskazane mieszkanie najemcy wyłącznie *do użytku mieszkaniowego*.	DT, DT
T2: […] posiada *wykładzinę* we wszystkich pomieszczeniach. Wynajmujący pozostawia niniejsze mieszkanie najemcy *do wykorzystywania na cele mieszkaniowe*.	DT, DT
T3: […] *panele* we wszystkich pomieszczeniach. Przedmiotowe mieszkanie wynajmujący oddaje w najem najemcy wyłącznie *w celach mieszkalnych*.	S, N
Comment: The challenge for the translator, in this case, is the translation of the expression *podlahová krytina*. Today's homes are very rarely fitted with floor coverings; it is more common to find tiles or panels. In order to match the text to the recipient (so as not to mislead them as to what is actually on the floor in the flat – panel, carpet, or tile, for example), the safest solution would be to use the neutral equivalent *pokrycie podłogowe*. We do not find attestations for such an expression in the NKJP, but it is used frequently in texts found in the EUR-Lex database. In the T3 sample, the translator applied a simplification, using the equivalent of *panele*. In the case of T1, the translation of the last sentence shows a strong interference at the syntactic level. Also the equivalent for *do użytku mieszkaniowego* was used, which is not found in Polish – rather the expressions *w celach mieszkalnych* / *na cele mieszkaniowe* are used. For these equivalents one can also find numerous attestations in the NKJP. The expression *pronajímatel přenechává nájemci* was translated using discourse transfer: *przekazuje, pozostawia* or using the target language norm: *oddaje w najem*.	

Example No. 5	**Context / text excerpt in Czech**
čl. III Doba nájmu 1/ ***Pronajímatel pronajímá*** touto smlouvou nájemci k účelům bydlení byt ***specifikovaný*** v čl. I. odst. 1/ této smlouvy. Nájem se sjednává na dobu určitou, v délce trvání od xxxxx do xxxxx.	
Proposals for translation:	**Translation universals**
T1: Wynajmujący *wynajmuje* Najemcy mieszkanie *określone* w […].	DT, DT
T2: Wynajmujący na mocy niniejszej umowy *wynajmuje* najemcy na cele mieszkaniowe mieszkanie *wyszczególnione* w […].	DT, DT
T3: Wynajmujący *oddaje w najem* na podstawie niniejszej umowy najemcy w celach mieszkalnych mieszkanie *opisane* […].	N, N
Comment: The expression *pronajímatel pronajímá* was translated faithfully by translators T1 and T2 (discourse transfer), while translator T3 used an equivalent in the form of the verbo-nominal expression *oddaje w najem*, which is more commonly found in authentic texts of Polish rental agreements (normalisation). The expression *byt specifikovaný* was translated as *mieszkanie określone* (T1 – discourse transfer), *mieszkanie wyszczególnione* (T2 – discourse transfer), and *mieszkanie opisane* (T3 – normalisation).	
Example No. 6	**Context / text excerpt in Czech**
Na žádost nájemce může být dohodou smluvních stran nájemní vztah dále prodloužen a to novou nájemní smlouvou nebo dodatkem ke smlouvě podepsanou všemi účastníky smlouvy. ***Nájemce požádá o*** prodloužení smlouvy nejméně 2 měsíce před jejím ukončením.	
Proposals for translation:	**Translation universals**
T1: *Na wniosek* najemcy […]. *Najemca wnosi* o […].	DT, DT
T2: *Na wniosek* najemcy […]. *Najemca złoży wniosek* o […].	DT, DT
T3: *Na życzenie* najemcy […]. *Najemca obowiązany jest zgłosić zainteresowanie* przedłużeniem umowy […].	N, E

Comment: The phrase *na žádost nájemce* was translated faithfully by the T1 and T2 translators as *na wniosek*, indicating a transfer of discourse. The T3 translator applied normalisation and used the expression *na życzenie*. The expression *nájemce požádá* has been translated by the T3 translator, expressing explicitly the message contained in the source text – *najemca obowiązany jest zgłosić zainteresowanie*. This treatment has resulted in a neater sentence construction, which also sounds closer to the Polish norm. The T1 and T2 translators translated closer to the source text, so a linguistic calque was created at the syntactic level (discourse transfer).	
Example No. 7	**Context / text excerpt in Czech**
Pronajímatel i nájemce je oprávněn ukončit nájemní vztah písemnou výpovědí s tříměsíční lhůtou počínající běžet od prvního dne následujícího měsíce po doručení výpovědi, pronajímatel z důvodu specifikovaných § 2288 NOZ.	
Proposals for translation:	**Translation universals**
T1: *Wynajmujący i najemca są uprawnieni* do wypowiedzenia najmu [...].	DT
T2: *Wynajmujący i najemca uprawnieni są* do zakończenia stosunku najmu [...].	DT
Wynajmującemu oraz najemcy przysługuje prawo rozwiązania umowy [...].	N
Comment: In the example above, interference in the T1 and T2 translations is evident. The expression *Pronajímatel i nájemce je oprávněn* was translated with Czech sentence formation (discourse transfer), using the equivalent expression *wynajmujący i najemca uprawnieni są*. In contrast, the T3 translation used syntax characteristic of Polish legal and juridical texts. The equivalent expression w*ynajmującemu oraz najemcy przysługuje prawo* testifies to normalisation.	

Example No. 8	Context / text excerpt in Czech
čl. IV Povinnosti smluvních stran 1/ Pronajímatel se zavazuje zejména: a) zajistit nájemci ***plný a nerušený*** výkon práv spojených s ***užíváním bytu***, právo užívat společné prostory, zařízení domu a požívat plnění, jejichž poskytování je s nájmem bytu spojeno.	
Proposals for translation:	**Translation universals**
T1: Wynajmujący zobowiązuje się […] zapewnić najemcy *pełne i niezakłócone* wykonywanie praw związanych z *użytkowaniem mieszkania*, prawa do korzystania z części wspólnych, wyposażenia domu oraz […].	DT, N, N
T2: Wynajmujący zobowiązuje się […] zapewnić dla najemcy *pełne i niezakłócone* wykonywanie praw związanych z *korzystaniem z mieszkania*, prawo do korzystania z pomieszczeń wspólnych, wyposażenia domu i […].	DT, N, N
T3: Wynajmujący zobowiązuje się […] do zapewnienia najemcy *kompleksowego i niezakłóconego* korzystania z praw przysługujących mu z tytułu *użytkowania lokalu*, prawa do korzystania z pomieszczeń wspólnych, wyposażenia budynku oraz […].	E, N
Comment: For the expression *plný a nerušený výkon práv*, the T1 and T2 translators used a literal translation, but one that was also in line with the standard of the target language – *pełne i niezakłócone wykonywanie praw*. The T3 translator made use of explicitation, using the equivalent *kompleksowy* for the lexeme *plný*. This treatment is not ideal for this example, but it does not prevent the content from being properly understood. The expression *užívání bytu* has been translated with the following equivalents: *użytkowanie mieszkania* (T1), *korzystanie z mieszkania* (T2), and *użytkowanie lokalu* (T3). The T1 and T2 translations are the closest to the norm of the target language, and we find numerous attestations for each of these possibilities in the NKJP. For the equivalent used in the T3 translation, we find two attestations in the NKJP, and it is a less common expression for leases.	

Example No. 9	Context / text excerpt in Czech
Nájemce se zavazuje zejména: a) ***užívat byt dohodnutým způsobem*** a odstranit závady a poškození, které způsobil v domě sám nebo osoby, které s ním žijí ve společné domácnosti,	
Proposals for translation:	**Translation universals**
T1: Najemca zobowiązuje się [...] *użytkować mieszkanie w uzgodniony sposób* [...].	DT
T2: Najemca zobowiązuje się [...] *korzystać z mieszania w uzgodniony sposób* [...]	DT
T3: Najemca zobowiązuje się [...] do *użytkowania lokalu zgodnie z przeznaczeniem* oraz [...].	N
Comment: The expression *užívat byt dohodnutým způsobem* was translated by the T1 translator in a literal way, preserving the Czech sentence formation (discourse transfer). The T2 translator took a similar approach (discourse transfer) in his translation, using the equivalent *korzystać z mieszkania w uzgodniony sposób*. The closest to the target language standard is the T3 translator – he has used the expression *zgodnie z przeznaczeniem*, for which there are numerous attestations available in the NKJP corpus.	
Example No. 10	Context / text excerpt in Czech
Nájemné a úhrady za plnění poskytovaná s užíváním bytu 1/ Nájemné bez služeb spojených s užíváním bytu za předmět nájmu se stanoví dohodou obou stran ve výši xxxxx Kč. K nájemnému bude nájemce hradit zálohu na služby s nájmem spojené, konkrétně částku xxxx Kč jako zálohu na úhradu elektrické energie a vodného, stočného.	
Proposals for translation:	**Translation universals**
T1: *Czynsz i opłaty za usługi związane z użytkowaniem lokalu mieszkaniowego.*	N, E
T2: *Czynsz i zapłata za usługi świadczone wraz z korzystaniem z mieszkania.*	DT

T3: *Czynsz oraz płatności za świadczenia z tytułu korzystania z lokalu mieszkalnego.*	E, N
Comment: The title of the article *Nájemné a úhrady za plnění poskytovaná s užíváním bytu* has been translated by the T3 translator as *Czynsz oraz płatności za świadczenia z tytułu korzystania z lokalu mieszkalnego*. The explicitation present in the translation is confirmed by the use of the expression *z tytułu*, which is common in legal language. The T2 translation uses the equivalent of the above expression phrased as *Czynsz i zapłata za usługi świadczone wraz z korzystaniem z mieszkania*. This sentence shows a strong influence of the original language at the syntactic level. The translation is faithful to the original content (discourse transfer). Translator T1 used both normalisation (translation closest to the norm of the target language) and explicitation: *Czynsz i opłaty za usługi związane z użytkowaniem lokalu mieszkaniowego* (adding the expression *związane*, as well as the expression *lokal mieszkalny* instead of *mieszkanie*).	
Example No. 11	**Context / text excerpt in Czech**
Nájemné, poplatky za služby v bytě jsou splatné vždy ***nejpozději k*** 10. dni stávajícího měsíce.	
Proposals for translation:	**Translation universals**
T1: Czynsz, opłaty za usługi w mieszkaniu płatne są zawsze *najpóźniej do* 10 dnia bieżącego miesiąca.	DT
T2: Czynsz, opłaty za usługi w mieszkaniu są płatne zawsze *najpóźniej do* 10. dnia bieżącego miesiąca.	DT
T3: Czynsz najmu, opłaty z tytułu usług dodatkowych związanych z najmem, płatne są zawsze *do* 10-go dnia danego miesiąca.	S, N
Comment: In the T1 and T2 translations, a linguistic calque is evident: the expression *nejpozději k* has been translated by both translators as *najpóźniej do* (discourse transfer). The T3 sample used simplification (omitting *najpóźniej*), bringing the translation into line with the standard of the target language (normalisation).	
Example No. 12	**Context / text excerpt in Czech**
čl. VI. Práva a povinnosti spojené s nájmem bytu 1/ ***Nájemce přebírá*** předmět nájmu v takovém stavu, jaký je uveden v předávacím protokolu, který je jako příloha číslo 1 nedílnou součástí této nájemní smlouvy.	

Proposals for translation:	**Translation universals**
T1: *Najemca przejmuje* przedmiot najmu […].	DT
T2: *Najemca przejmuje* przedmiot najmu […].	DT
T3: *Najemca odbiera* przedmiot najmu […].	E
Comment: The expression *nájemce přebírá* was translated in samples T1 and T2 literally (discourse transfer). The translator in sample T3 used explicitation ('taking possession of the flat' understood in this context as its reception at the time of handover), translating the above expression as the *najemca odbiera* possession. A good solution could also be the use of an equivalent *obejmuje*, according to the provisions of the Civil Code (cf. Art. 692 CC: 'The provisions on termination of the lease by the purchaser of the leased property shall not apply to the lease of residential premises, unless the tenant *nie objął jeszcze* of the premises').	
Example No. 13	**Context / text excerpt in Czech**
Nájemce je povinen ***užívat byt***, společné prostory a ostatní zařízení v domě specifikovaném v čl. I. odst. 1/ této smlouvy ***řádně*** a řádně požívat plnění, jejichž poskytování je spojeno ***s užíváním bytu a společnými prostory***.	
Proposals for translation:	**Translation universals**
T1: Najemca jest zobowiązany do *należytego korzystania* z mieszkania, części wspólnych i innych udogodnień w domu określonych w art. I. ust. 1/ niniejszej umowy i właściwego korzystania ze świadczenia, którego realizowanie jest związane *z użytkowaniem mieszkania i części wspólnych*.	N, N
T2: Najemca zobowiązany jest *do korzystania* z mieszkania, przestrzeni wspólnych i pozostałego wyposażenia w domu wyszczególnionego w art. I. ust. 1/ niniejszej umowy *należycie* oraz należycie korzystać z usług, świadczenie których związane jest z korzystaniem *z mieszkania i przestrzeni wspólnych*.	N, DT
T3: Najemca obowiązany jest użytkować lokal mieszkalny, części wspólne oraz pozostałe wyposażenie lokalu opisane w Art. I. ust. 1/ niniejszej umowy *właściwym sposobem*, jak również odpowiednio korzystać ze świadczeń, które związane są *z użytkowaniem lokalu oraz pomieszczeń wspólnych*.	N, DT

Comment: The expression *užívat byt řádně* has been translated as *należyte korzystanie* (T1), *korzystanie należycie* (T2), and *właściwym sposobem* (T3). In the parallel texts, we encounter the equivalents used by each translator (normalisation). The fragment of the sentence *s užíváním bytu a společnými prostory* was best rendered by the T1 translator, using the expression *z użytkowaniem mieszkania i części wspólnych*, which is closest to the texts of Polish rental agreements (normalisation); in the case of T2 and T3, a stronger influence of the source text on the translation (discourse transfer) is evident.	
Example No. 14	**Context / text excerpt in Czech**
Nájemce je povinen při výkonu svých práv dbát, aby ***v domě*** specifikovaném v čl. I. odst. 1/ této smlouvy bylo vytvořeno prostředí zajišťující ostatním nájemcům výkon jejich práv. Nájemce je povinen odstranit závady a poškození, které způsobil sám, nebo těmi, kdo s ním bydlí. Nestane-li se tak ani po předchozím upozornění pronajímatele, budou závady a poškození odstraněny na náklady nájemce.	
Proposals for translation:	**Translation universals**
T1: Realizując swoje prawa najemca zobowiązany jest do zapewnienia, aby *w domu* […].	DT
T2: Najemca zobowiązany jest przy wykonywaniu swoich praw dbać, aby *w domu* […].	N
T3: Najemca korzystając ze swoich praw obowiązany jest zadbać o to, by *w budynku* […].	N
Comment: Example T1 indicates linguistic calque. Examples T2 and T3 testify to normalisation and confirm the translators' correct understanding of the source text's message.	
Example No. 15	**Context / text excerpt in Czech**
čl. VII. Odpovědnost nájemce Nájemce je povinen pronajímateli bez zbytečného odkladu oznámit všechny závady v bytě, jejichž odstranění je povinností pronajímatele. V případě opomenutí této povinnosti ***odpovídá nájemce pronajímateli*** za veškeré škody tímto opomenutím způsobené.	

Proposals for translation:	**Translation universals**
T1: […] W przypadku zaniechania tego obowiązku *najemca odpowiada wobec wynajmującego* za wszelkie szkody spowodowane tym zaniechaniem.	N
T2: […] W przypadku pominięcia niniejszego obowiązku *najemca odpowiada wynajmującemu* za wszelkie szkody związane z niniejszym pominięciem.	DT
T3: […] W przypadku zaniechania obowiązku informacyjnego *najemca ponosi odpowiedzialność przed wynajmującym* za wszelkie szkody wynikłe z tytułu tegoż zaniechania.	E
Comment: The expression *odpovídá nájemce pronajímateli* was translated by the T3 translator using explicitation (clarification of the statement *najemca ponosi odpowiedzialność przed wynajmującym)*. In the case of the T2 translation, a linguistic calque has been created by interference, which changes the meaning of the sentence, while the expression itself is incorrect: *najemca odpowiada wynajmującemu*. The T1 translator has normalised the translation, using the equivalent *najemca odpowiada wobec wynajmującego*. (cf. art. 668 c.c. § 1. „Najemca może rzecz najętą oddać w całości lub części osobie trzeciej do bezpłatnego używania albo w podnajem, jeżeli umowa mu tego nie zabrania. W razie oddania rzeczy osobie trzeciej zarówno najemca, jak i osoba trzecia *są odpowiedzialni względem wynajmującego za to*, że rzecz najęta będzie używana zgodnie z obowiązkami wynikającymi z umowy najmu“).	
Example No. 16	**Context / text excerpt in Czech**
Nájemce ***odpovídá pronajímateli*** za škody způsobené jím, spolubydlícími osobami a dalšími osobami, jimž umožnil do bytu a domu přístup. Stejná odpovědnost se vztahuje na škody způsobené domácími zvířaty nájemce či zvířaty, jimž nájemce umožnil přístup do domu nebo bytu. Nájemce je povinen tyto škody vlastním nákladem odstranit, a to nejpozději do 15 dnů ode dne jejich vzniku. V případě porušení této povinnosti ***je nájemce povinen uhradit pronajímateli*** vzniklou škodu.	

Proposals for translation:	Translation universals
T1: Najemca *odpowiada wobec wynajmującego* za szkody wyrządzone […] W przypadku naruszenia tego obowiązku *najemca jest zobowiązany do pokrycia wynajmującemu* poniesionej szkody.	DT, DT
T2: Najemca *odpowiada wynajmującemu* za szkody spowodowane […] W przypadku naruszenia niniejszego obowiązku najemca *zobowiązany jest zapłacić wynajmującemu powstałą szkodę*.	N
T3: Najemca *ponosi odpowiedzialność przed wynajmującym* za szkody […] W przypadku naruszenia powyższego obowiązku *najemca obowiązany jest naprawić szkodę*.	N
Comment: In the case of the translation of the expression *nájemce odpovídá pronajímateli*, the situation is like that discussed in example 15. The expression *je nájemce povinen uhradit pronajímateli* was translated in sample T1 as *najemca jest zobowiązany do pokrycia wynajmującemu*; a linguistic calque is evident here at the level of the sentence formation, while the translation itself is characterised by literalism (discourse transfer). Translators T2 and T3 have simplified and normalised their translations, using the following translations, respectively: *zobowiązany jest zapłacić wynajmującemu powstałą szkodę* and *najemca obowiązany jest naprawić szkodę*.	
Example No. 17	**Context / text excerpt in Czech**
Skončení najmu Nájem zanikne uplynutím doby uvedené v čl. III/. odst. 1/ této smlouvy, písemnou dohodou mezi pronajímatelem a nájemcem, nebo písemnou výpovědí uvedenou shora. Ke dni skončení nájmu je nájemce povinen předmět nájmu ***vyklidit a odevzdat nájemci***. Po skončení nájmu není nárok na náhradní bydlení či podnájem.	
Proposals for translation:	**Translation universals**
T1: *Wypowiedzenie najmu* […]. Na dzień zakończenia najmu najemca zobowiązany jest opróżnić przedmiot najmu i *przekazać go najemcy*. […]	DT

T2: *Skończenie najmu* […] Do dnia skończenia najmu najemca zobowiązany jest posprzątać przedmiot najmu i zwrócić najemcy *[tłum.: powinno być wynajmującemu]*. […]	DT
T3: *Zakończenie najmu* […] Na dzień zakończenia umowy najmu najemca obowiązany jest opróżnić oraz zwrócić *najemcy [błąd w źródle, wynajmującemu]*. […]	N
Comment: The title of the article *Skončení najmu* was mistranslated by the T1 translator (the expression *skończenie najmu* is not the norm for the target language; a literal translation was used, resulting in a linguistic calque) and the T2 translator (the equivalent termination of *wypowiedzenie najmu* has a different meaning). The correct equivalent is the translation used in the T3 translation. There was an error in the source text in the quoted passage. None of the translators sanitised the translation – two of them (T2 and T3) opted for bracketed commentary, while translator T1 used a faithful translation, complete with error (discourse transfer).	
Example No. 18	**Context / text excerpt in Czech**
čl. IX. ***Závěrečná ustanovení*** ***1/ Ve věcech touto smlouvou neupravených se vztahy mezi smluvními stranami řídí příslušnými ustanoveními občanského zákoníku a ostatními obecně právními předpisy.***	
Proposals for translation:	**Translation universals**
T1: *Postanowienia końcowe. W sprawach nieuregulowanych niniejszą umową stosunki pomiędzy stronami regulują odpowiednie przepisy Kodeksu Cywilnego oraz inne ogólne przepisy prawa.*	N
T2: *Postanowienia końcowe. W sprawach nieuregulowanych w niniejszej umowie stosunki pomiędzy stronami umowy kierują się właściwymi postanowieniami Kodeksu cywilnego oraz pozostałymi przepisami prawa.*	DT
T3: *Postanowienia końcowe. W sprawach nieuregulowanych niniejszą umową zastosowanie mają właściwe zapisy kodeksu cywilnego oraz pozostałe powszechnie obowiązujące przepisy.*	N

Comment: In the T3 translation, the pronominal array and sentence structure indicate a strong normalisation and adaptation of the text to a Polish audience. In the T2 translation, a linguistic calque (*stosunki kierują się*) has emerged, which unfortunately negatively affects the quality of the translation (discourse transfer). The T1 translator used a translation close to the norm of the target language.	
Example No. 19	**Context / text excerpt in Czech**
Tato smlouva se vyhotovuje ve dvou stejnopisech, z nichž každá ze smluvních stran obdrží po jednom vyhotovení.	
Proposals for translation:	**Translation universals**
T1: *Niniejsza umowa jest sporządzona w dwóch egzemplarzach*, z których każda ze stron umowy otrzyma po jednym egzemplarzu.	DT
T2: *Niniejsza umowa została zawarta w dwóch jednobrzmiących egzemplarzach*, z których każda ze stron umowy otrzyma po jednym egzemplarzu.	N, E
T3: *Niniejsza umowa została sporządzona w dwóch jednobrzmiących egzemplarzach*, po jednym dla każdej ze stron.	N
Comment: In the T1 translation, the strong influence of the source text is evident – the translator has retained the present tense, and such sentence wording is not in line with the Polish norm for texts of this nature (discourse transfer). The wording of the sentence in translations T2 and T3 is closer to the Polish reader, although in the T2 translation the translator used an additional explicitation (the original does not mention the *zawarciu umowy*, but *sporządzeniu*; the translator implicitly considered the drafting of a contract to be synonymous with its conclusion, which is not so obvious).	
Example No. 20	**Context / text excerpt in Czech**
Tato smlouva může být doplněna nebo měněna jen písemnými a řádně číslovanými dodatky, které budou podepsány oběma stranami této smlouvy.	
Proposals for translation:	**Translation universals**
T1: *Niniejsza Umowa może być zmieniana lub modyfikowana tylko poprzez pisemne i należycie ponumerowane dodatki (aneksy), które zostaną podpisane przez obie strony niniejszej umowy.*	DT

T2: *Niniejsza umowa może zostać uzupełniona lub zmieniona wyłącznie w formie pisemnych i należycie ponumerowanych aneksów, które zostaną podpisane przez obie strony niniejszej umowy.*	DT
T3: *Zmiany lub uzupełnienia umowy wymagają wyłącznie pisemnych, numerowanych aneksów, podpisanych przez obydwie strony.*	N
Comment: At the level of the punctuated sentence formation used by the T3 translator, a strong normalisation is evident – this way of sentence construction is characteristic of Polish civil law contracts. The T1 and T2 translations have a copied Czech sentence formation (discourse transfer) and a translation close to the source text.	
Example No. 21	**Context / text excerpt in Czech**
Účastníci smlouvy prohlašují, že si smlouvu přečetli, s jejím obsahem souhlasí a rozumí mu, že je výrazem jejich pravé a svobodné vůle, smlouva nebyla uzavřena v tísni či za nápadně nevýhodných podmínek, na důkaz čehož připojují své podpisy.	
Proposals for translation:	**Translation universals**
T1: *Strony umowy oświadczają, że zapoznały się z umową, zgadzają się z jej treścią i rozumieją ją, że jest to wyraz ich prawdziwej i dobrowolnej woli, że umowa nie została zawarta pod naciskiem lub na wyraźnie niekorzystnych warunkach, o czym świadczą ich podpisy.*	DT
T2: *Strony umowy oświadczają, że przeczytały umowę, zgadzają się z jej treścią i rozumieją ją, że jest wyrażeniem ich rzeczywistej i wolnej woli, umowa nie została zawarta pod presją lub na rażąco niedogodnych warunkach, w dowód czego dołączają swoje podpisy.*	DT
T3: *Strony umowy oświadczają, że umowę przeczytały, zgadzają się co do jej treści, rozumieją ją oraz, że umowa jest wyrazem ich prawdziwej i wolnej woli, że umowa nie została zawarta pod naciskiem lub przy niekorzystnych warunkach, na dowód czego składają swoje podpisy.*	DT

Comment: The quoted passage of text is characteristic of virtually all Czech civil law contracts. The closing statement of intent in Czech has a very elaborate and detailed wording, a provision of this nature in Polish civil law contracts is much poorer. Each of the translators had to make a faithful translation close to the original text, this is seen above all at the level of syntax and sentence formation (discourse transfer).	
Example No. 22	**Context / text excerpt in Czech**
*V **Hradci Králové*** dne xxxxx	
Proposals for translation:	**Translation universals**
T1: *W Hradec Králové*, dnia xxxxx	DT
T2: *Hradec Králové*, dnia xxxxx	N
T3: *Hradec Kralove*, dn. Xxxxx	N
Comment: A seemingly simple and obvious expression specifying the place and date of signing a contract also poses a challenge for the translator, as can be seen in the example above. In Polish, the name of the locality in the nominative is normally used, followed by the date of signing of the deed after a comma. In Czech it is customary to use the *V+miejscownik nazwy miejscowości* construction. The T1 translator did not use the locative of the place name, hence the expression *W Hradec Králové* should be considered incorrect. The T2 and T3 translations have the correct forms for Polish.	

3.1.3.1. *Summary*

1. What universals have been identified in the lease translations?

Example number	E (explicitation)	S (simplification)	N (normalisation)	R (reduction)	DT (discourse transfer)
1		•	•		•
2			•		•
3		•	•		•
4		•	•		•
5			•		•
6	•		•		•
7			•		•
8	•		•		•
9			•		•
10	•		•		•
11		•	•		•
12	•				•
13	•		•		•
14			•		•
15			•		•
16			•		•
17			•		•
18			•		•
19	•		•		•
20			•		•
21					•
22			•		•

2. Frequency of universals of a given type in translations of the lease agreement

Example number	E (explicitation)	S (simplification)	N (normalisation)	R (reduction)	DT (discourse transfer)
1		•	•		•
2			••		•
3		•••	••••••		•••••
4		•	••		••••
5			••		••••
6	•		•		••••
7			•		••
8	•		•••••		••
9			•		••
10	••		••		•
11		•	•		••
12	•				••
13	•		•		•
14			••		•
15			••••		••
16			••		••
17			•		••
18			••		•
19	•		••		•
20			•		••
21					•••
22			••		•
Total:	7	6	42	0	46

3. Graph of the frequency of translation universals in translations of the lease agreement

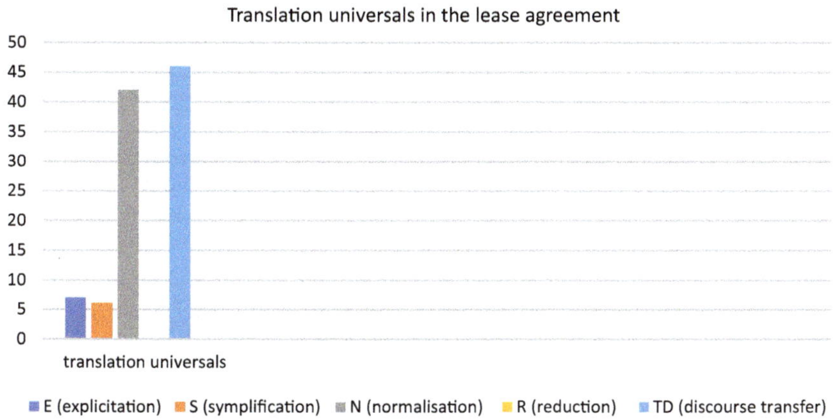

Source: Author's own elaboration.

3.1.4. Analysis of the donation agreement

Characteristics of a donation contract in the Polish and Czech Civil Codes.

Tab. 31: Donation agreement – basic characteristics

<table>
<tr><th colspan="2">Donation agreement</th></tr>
<tr><th>Definition from Czech Civil Code</th><th>Definition from Polish Civil Code</th></tr>
<tr><td>§ 2055
(1) Darovací smlouvou dárce bezplatně převádí vlastnické právo k věci nebo se zavazuje obdarovanému věc bezplatně převést do vlastnictví a obdarovaný dar nebo nabídku přijímá.</td><td>Article 888
§ 1. Przez umowę darowizny darczyńca zobowiązuje się do bezpłatnego świadczenia na rzecz obdarowanego kosztem swego majątku.</td></tr>
<tr><td colspan="2">Basic terminology as defined in the Polish and Czech Civil Codes</td></tr>
<tr><td>dárce
obdarovaný
darovací smlouva
věc/dar</td><td>darczyńca
obdarowany
umowa darowizny
darowizna / przedmiot umowy darowizny</td></tr>
<tr><td colspan="2">Features of a donation agreement</td></tr>
<tr><td colspan="2">Unilaterally binding, consensual, named contract, enabling the transfer of property without consideration, free of charge contract</td></tr>
<tr><td colspan="2">Essence of a donation agreement</td></tr>
<tr><td colspan="2">The essence of a donation contract is a commitment by the donor to provide a gratuitous benefit to the recipient at the expense of his or her estate.</td></tr>
<tr><td colspan="2">Provisions governing a donation agreement</td></tr>
<tr><td>§§ 2055–2078 NOZ</td><td>Articles 888-902 of the Civil Code</td></tr>
</table>

Source: 1. Act No. 89/2012 Coll.; 2. *Občanský zákoník*; Polish Civil Code, Act of 23 April 1964; 3. Dąbrowski, 2019: 204.

Example No. 1	**Context / text excerpt in Czech**
.... Zapsán v obchodním rejstříku Městského soudu v Praze, ***oddíl* x, *vložka*** x	
Proposals for translation:	**Translation universals**
T1: *sygnatura akt* xxx	N
T2: *section… entry.*	DT
T3: *sekcja… pozycja*	DT
Comment: In sample T1, the translator normalised the translation by using the equivalent present in the Polish extract from the Companies Register (parallel text). In the T2 and T3 samples, the translators adopted the strategy of using a translation that was as close as possible to the culture of the source language (which may be an example of exoticisation).	
Example No. 2	**Context / text excerpt in Czech**
Context: Preambuła umowy ***IČO [identifikační číslo]***: xxx DIČ: CZxxxxxx bankovní spojeni: xxxx číslo účtu: xxxxx/xxx	
Proposals for translation:	**Translation universals**
T1: *numer identyfikacyjny*	DT
T2: *KRS*	
T3: *REGON*	N
Comment: The Czech IČO is recognised in the business community as the equivalent of the Polish REGON number. The T1 sample is an example of discourse transfer, as the utterance is constructed directly under the influence of the Czech text. The T3 sample is an example of typical normalisation. The T2 sample is a mistranslation and is not considered in the study.	

Example No. 3	Context / text excerpt in Czech
Context: Preambuła umowy IČO [identifikační číslo]: xxx DIČ: CZxxxxxx ***bankovní spojení*:** **xxxx** číslo účtu: xxxxx/xxx	
Proposals for translation:	**Translation universals**
T1: *instytucja finansowa*	N
T2: *bank*	N, S
T3: *nazwa banku*	N
Comment: Each translator aimed in the translation to use an equivalent that is an adaptation to the norms of the target language. The translators' behaviour is indicative of normalisation. The use of simplification is evident in the T2 translation.	
Example No. 4	**Context / text excerpt in Czech**
[…] uzavírají podle S 2055 zákona č. 89/2012 Sb., občanského zákoníku, ve znění pozdějších předpisů, a v souladu s usnesením vlády České republiky č. 334/1999, ve znění usnesení vlády České republiky č. 534/2000, č. 1187/2001, č. 903/2003 a č. 174/2009, k ***poskytování sponzorských darů*** státními podniky a podniky s většinovou majetkovou účastí státu tuto darovací smlouvu (dále také označovanou jako „smlouva“)	
Proposals for translation:	**Translation universals**
T1: *udzielanie darowizn*	N
T2: *przekazywanie darowizn sponsorskich*	DT
T3: *przekazywanie darowizn sponsorskich*	DT
Comment: Discourse transfer was used in the T2 and T3 samples. A literal translation was adopted for the expression *sponzorský dar*. In the NKJP reference corpus we do not find attestations for such an expression, while attestations for the expression *przekazywanie darowizn* are seen. On the other hand, the expression *udzielanie darowizn* used in the T1 sample occurs only in texts originating from the internet; no attestations for such an expression appear in the NKJP corpus.	

Example No. 5	Context / text excerpt in Czech
[…] uzavírají podle S 2055 zákona č. 89/2012 Sb., občanského zákoníku, ve znění pozdějších předpisů, a v souladu s usnesením vlády České republiky č. 334/1999, ve znění usnesení vlády České republiky č. 534/2000, č. 1187/2001, č. 903/2003 a č. 174/2009, k poskytování sponzorských darů státními podniky a podniky s většinovou majetkovou účasti státu ***tuto darovací smlouvu (dále také označovanou jako „smlouva“)***	
Proposals for translation:	**Translation universals**
T1: […] *niniejszą umowę darowizny (dalej jako „umowa“)*	N
T2: […] *niniejszej umowy darowizny (zwane dalej również „umową“)*	DT
T3: […] *niniejszą umowę darowizny (zwaną dalej również „umową“)*	DT
Comment: The T1 sample is a typical normalisation. Expressions specific to parallel texts – Polish contents of donation agreements or civil law contracts in general – have been used, as can be seen in the author's corpus. The other two attempts are discourse transfer, evident at the level of preserving sentence structure and formation (the impact of the source text on the translation).	
Example No. 6	**Context / text excerpt in Czech**
Předmětem této smlouvy je ***poskytnuti finančního daru*** (dále jen „dar“) obdarovanému za účelem podpory projektu.	
Proposals for translation:	**Translation universals**
T1: […] *udzielenie darowizny pieniężnej*	N
T2: […] *przekazanie darowizny pieniężnej*	N
T3: […] przekazanie darowizny finansowej	DT
Comment: The NKJP reference corpus contains attestations for the expression *darowizna pieniężna*, but none for the expression *darowizna finansowa*. Each translator tried to convey the message in the translation that it was about the transfer of money. The first two attempts are examples of normalisation, while the third attempt is an example of discourse transfer.	

Example No. 7	Context / text excerpt in Czech
Context: Tytuł artykułu umowy 1. ***Předmět smlouvy a jeho účel***	
Proposals for translation:	**Translation universals**
T1: *przedmiot umowy oraz cel umowy*	E
T2: *przedmiot umowy oraz jego cel*	DT
T3: *przedmiot umowy i jego cel*	DT
Comment: In sample T1, the translator used explicitation, adding that the *cel umowy* is in question. In samples T2 and T3, the strong influence of the source text on the translation is apparent, resulting in an unfortunate linguistic calque, misleading the recipient of the translation, as it is not the purpose of the object of the contract, but the purpose of the contract (this can be inferred by also supporting the analysis of parallel texts in the work).	

Example No. 8	Context / text excerpt in Czech
Dar je určen obdarovanému k pokrytí části nákladů vyvolaných realizací projektu.	
Proposals for translation:	**Translation universals**
T1: *Darowizna jest przeznaczona dla obdarowanego w celu pokrycia części kosztów związanych z realizacją projektu.*	DT
T2: *Darowizna jest przeznaczona dla obdarowanego na pokrycie części kosztów spowodowanych realizacją projektu.*	DT
T3: *Darowizna przeznaczona jest dla obdarowanego na pokrycie części kosztów związanych z realizacją projektu.*	DT
Comment: In each of the samples, the strong influence of the Czech sentence formation on the Polish translation can be observed. Such behaviour qualifies as discourse transfer.	

Example No. 9	**Context / text excerpt in Czech**
Context: Tytuł punktu umowy II. ***Závazky smluvních stran***	
Proposals for translation:	**Translation universals**
T1: *zobowiązania stron*	S
T2: *zobowiązania kontrahentów*	E
T3: *zobowiązania stron umowy*	DT
Comment: In sample T1, a simplification procedure is evident. In sample T2, the translator adopted the functional equivalent *kontrahent* for the expression *smluvní strana*, which can be considered an example of explicitation. The T3 translator used the translation that is closest to the original.	

Example No. 10	**Context / text excerpt in Czech**
Dárce se zavazuje jednorázově poukázat na účet obdarovaného uvedený v záhlaví této smlouvy dar ve výši xxxx,- Kč (slovy: xxxxx korun českých), ***a to do 30 dnů*** ode dne, v němž bude dárci prokazatelné doručen originál této smlouvy podepsaný oběma smluvními stranami.	
Proposals for translation:	**Translation universals**
T1: [...] *w terminie 30 dni*	E
T2: [...] *w ciągu 30 dni*	N
T3: [...] *w ciągu 30 dni*	N
Comment: Translations T2 and T3 show translator behaviour indicative of normalisation. The author of the T1 translation applied an explicitation, adding that the *termin* is meant. This manner of expression is evident in untranslated texts, in authentic texts of civil law contracts.	

Example No. 11	Context / text excerpt in Czech
Za prokazatelné doručení podle tohoto ustanovení se považuje doručení do sídla dárce (popř. jinou adresu, kterou dárce příjemci předem písemné oznámí) ve formě doporučeného dopisu, kurýrem nebo osobně.	
Proposals for translation:	**Translation universals**
T1: *za rzeczywiste doręczenie* zgodnie z niniejszym paragrafem uznaje się	E
T2: *dowodem doręczenia* według tego przepisu jest	DT
T3: *dowodem doręczenia* według tego przepisu jest doręczenie	DT
Comment: The above example deals with the interesting issue of delivery service (in the case of this text, the delivery of the printed contract on the other party). None of the translators are likely to have been tempted to look into the corpus of the Polish language. This is because it contains the expression *doręczenie uważa się za dokonane* (the certification comes, for example, from Article 44 of the Code of Civil Procedure), which would be very helpful in this translation. The T1 translation, which is an explicative expression of the content contained in the source text, could be the closest to the expectations of the audience. Samples T2 and T3 are examples of strong interference; discourse transfer can also be considered to occur here.	
Example No. 12	**Context / text excerpt in Czech**
Toto ustanoveni o doručování je speciální k ustanoveni článku IV. Odst. 5. Této smlouvy;	
Proposals for translation:	**Translation universals**
T1: *Powyższy zapis dotyczący doręczeń jest szczególnym zapisem* w odniesieniu do postanowień art.	DT
T2: *To postanowienie o doręczeniu jest wyjątkowe* w stosunku do postanowień art. ...	DT
T3: *Niniejsze postanowienie o doręczeniu jest szczególne* w stosunku do postanowień artykułu	DT
Comment: The example above shows the strong influence of the source text on the syntax of the content in Polish. A discourse transfer was applied here, which can be seen in each of the three samples.	

Example No. 13	**Context / text excerpt in Czech**
Dárce určuje jako ***kontaktní osobu*** při dalších jednáních: jméno a příjmení: xxxxxx xxxxxx adresa: xxxxxxxxx 140 53 Praha 4 tel.: +420 xxx xxx xxx e–mail: xxx.xxxxxxx@xxxxxx	
Proposals for translation:	**Translation universals**
T1: *osoba do kontaktów*	E
T2: *osoba kontaktowa*	DT
T3: *osoba kontaktowa*	DT
Comment: Several attestations are available in the NKJP for both the expressions *osoba do kontaktów* and *osoba kontaktowa*, so in each situation the translation should be understandable to the recipient both in terms of terminology and context. Unlike the T2 and T3 translations, where a literal translation faithful to the Czech version was used, the T1 translation used an expletive expression.	
Example No. 14	**Context / text excerpt in Czech**
Dárce určuje jako kontaktní osobu ***při dalších jednáních***: jméno a příjmení: xxxxxx xxxxxx adresa: xxxxxxxxx 140 53 Praha 4 tel.: +420 xxx xxx xxx e–mail: xxx.xxxxxxx@xxxxxx	
Proposals for translation:	**Translation universals**
T1: …osobą do kontaktów wyznaczoną *do prowadzenia dalszych rozmów* jest…	N
T2: … wyznacza jako osobę kontaktową do dalszych negocjacji…	DT
T3: …wyznacza jako osobę kontaktową *do dalszych negocjacji…*	DT
Comment: The translator in sample T1 used a syntax characteristic of Polish texts, with the use of the passive voice. He therefore adapted the translation to the norms of the target language. In samples T2 and T3, the strong influence of Czech syntax on the Polish translation is again evident.	

Example No. 15	Context / text excerpt in Czech
Obdarovaný dar přijímá ***a zavazuje se použit jej výhradně v souladu s účelem*** *uvedeným v článku I. této smlouvy.*	
Proposals for translation:	**Translation universals**
T1: […] *oraz zobowiązuje się do wykorzystania darowizny wyłącznie w celu* określonym w artykule I. niniejszej umowy.	E
T2: […] *i zobowiązuje się do korzystania z niej wyłącznie zgodnie z celem* określonym w artykule I. niniejszej umowy	DT
T3: […] *i zobowiązuje się do wykorzystania jej wyłącznie do celów* określonych w artykule I. niniejszej umowy.	N
Comment: The translators used the expressions *w celu*, *zgodnie z celem*, and *do celów* which have numerous attestations in the NKJP. In sample T2, interference at the syntactic level is evident. In sample T1, an explicitation is discernible; the translator emphasises that *obdarowany zobowiązuje się do wykorzystania darowizny*, whereas in the Czech text we see the pronoun *jej* when referring to the donation. In sample T3, the translator used the plural for the lexeme *cel*, while the Czech text uses the singular; this may indicate a sanitisation of the translation, an adaptation to the norms of the target language, as the Polish text of civil law contracts very often uses the plural in such constructions.	
Example No. 16	Context / text excerpt in Czech
Obdarovaný je povinen předložit dárci do 60 dnů po vyčerpání daru, nejpozději však do 31.1.2020, závěrečnou zprávu o použití daru.	
Proposals for translation:	**Translation universals**
T1: Obdarowany obowiązany jest przedstawić darczyńcy w terminie do 60 dni od daty wykorzystania środków pochodzących z darowizny, najdalej w terminie do 31.1.2020, raport końcowy dotyczący wykorzystania darowizny.	E
T2: Obdarowany jest zobowiązany do przedłożenia darczyńcy w terminie 60 dni po wyczerpaniu darowizny, nie później jednak niż do dnia 31 stycznia 2020 r., sprawozdanie końcowe z wykorzystania darowizny.	DT

T3: Obdarowany zobowiązany jest do przedstawienia darczyńcy końcowego sprawozdania o wykorzystaniu darowizny w ciągu 60 dni po wykorzystaniu darowizny, nie później jednak niż do 31 stycznia 2020 r.	N
Comment: In the T1 sample, the translator used explicitation three times. Explicative additions are evident in the expressions: *w terminie*, *środków pochodzących z [darowizny]*, and once again *w terminie*. In the T2 sample, interference is evident, which has led to a linguistic calque occurring in the expression *po wyczerpaniu darowizny*. In the T3 sample, normalisation is most evident in using the equivalent *sprawozdanie* for the Czech lexeme *závěrečná zpráva*.	
Example No. 17	**Context / text excerpt in Czech**
Obdarovany je povinen předložit dárci do 60 dnů po vyčerpání daru, nejpozději však do 31. 1. 2020, závěrečnou zprávu o použití daru. Závěrečná zpráva o použití daru musí obsahovat minimálně následující náležitosti: (i) ***základní popis projektu včetně popisu skutečností prokazujících účely daru vymezené v S 20 odst. 8 zákona č. 586/1992 Sb., o daních z příjmů, ve znění pozdějších předpisů***;	
Proposals for translation:	**Translation universals**
T1: podstawowy opis projektu wraz z opisem okoliczności potwierdzających cele darowizny określone w par. 20 ust. 8 ustawy nr 586/1992 Dz. U., o podatkach dochodowych, z późniejszymi zmianami	N
T2: podstawowy opis projektu, w tym opis faktów wskazujących na cele darowizny określone w § 20 ust. 8 ustawy nr 586/1992 Dz. U., o podatku dochodowym, z późniejszymi zmianami	N, DT
T3: podstawowy opis projektu, w tym opis faktów potwierdzających cele darowizny, o których mowa w § 20 ust. 8 ustawy nr 586/1992 Dz. U. Republiki Czeskiej, w sprawie podatków dochodowych, z późniejszymi zmianami	E, N
Comment: The expression *z późniejszymi zmianami* used by each translator is confirmation of the standardisation and adaptation of the translation to the norms of the Polish language (the target language). In the T2 translation, an interference can also be observed: the sentence formation is preserved, and the translation is very close to the source text at the level of the sentence, with *prokazujících úcely daru vymezené v* translated as *wskazujących na cele darowizny określone w*. In addition, the T3 translator used the explicative expression *Republiki Czeskiej* in relation to the Journal of Laws.	

Example No 18.	Context / text excerpt in Czech
Odstoupení od této smlouvy dle předchozího odstavce se tato smlouva od počátku ruší.	
Proposals for translation:	**Translation universals**
T1: Odstąpienie od niniejszej umowy, o którym mowa w poprzedzający punkcie, skutkuje jej rozwiązaniem w całości.	N
T2: Przez odstąpienie od niniejszej umowy zgodnie z poprzednim ustępem, niniejsza umowa zostaje anulowana od początku.	DT
T3: Po odstąpieniu od niniejszej umowy zgodnie z uprzednim ustępem niniejsza umowa zostaje rozwiązana od początku.	N
Comment: In the T1 translation, the normalisation of the translation is evident. The T1 translator aims to bring the translation into line with the norms of the Polish language, as does T3 translator. In both the T1 translation and the T3 translation, the translators used the expression *rozwiązanie umowy*, in contrast to the T2 translator, who used the expression *anulowanie umowy*. In the corpus of the Polish language, we find numerous attestations for the first expression, while for the second we find only one – indicating use in email correspondence. Interference and discourse transfer can be observed in T2 translation.	
Example No. 19	**Context / text excerpt in Czech**
Oznámení o odstoupení musí mít písemnou formu a pro jeho doručení druhé smluvní stran platí podmínky uvedené v čl. V. odst. 5 této smlouvy.	
Proposals for translation:	**Translation universals**
T1: Informacja o odstąpieniu od umowy wymaga formy pisemnej. Doręczenie informacji o odstąpieniu od umowy objęte jest zapisami podanymi w art. V ust. 5 niniejszej umowy.	N
T2: Zawiadomienie o odstąpieniu musi mieć formę pisemną, a warunki określone w artykule V ustęp 5 niniejszej Umowy mają zastosowanie do dostarczenia drugiej stronie.	DT
T3: Zawiadomienie o odstąpieniu musi mieć formę pisemną, a dla jego doręczenia drugiej stronie umowy obowiązują warunki wskazane w art. V. ust. 5 niniejszej umowy.	DT
Comment: The use of the passive voice in the T1 translation indicates the normalization of content. In contrast, the T2 and T3 translations show strong interference at the syntactic level.	

Example No. 20	Context / text excerpt in Czech
Smluvní strany nesou samy veškeré naklady a závazky vzniké jim v souvislosti s uzavřením této smlouvy, a to i v případě výše upraveného odstoupení.	
Proposals for translation:	**Translation universals**
T1: Każda ze stron sama ponosi wszelkie koszty i zobowiązania powstałe w związku z zawarciem niniejszej umowy, również w sytuacji potencjalnego odstąpienia, o którym mowa powyżej.	S, N
T2: Strony umowy ponoszą wszelkie koszty i zobowiązania poniesione przez nie w związku z zawarciem niniejszej umowy, nawet w przypadku odstąpienia, o którym mowa powyżej.	DT
T3: Strony umowy ponoszą wszelkie koszty i zobowiązania powstałe w związku z zawarciem niniejszej umowy, nawet w przypadku powyższego odstąpienia.	DT
Comment: T1 translator aims to normalise and simplify the wording of the content in Polish. The T2 and T3 translations show a strong imitation of Czech sentence formation, indicating discourse transfer.	
Example No. 21	Context / text excerpt in Czech
Obdarovaný není oprávněn uveřejňovat žádné informace týkající se obsahu této smlouvy, kromě osoby dárce, předmětu smlouvy a výše daru.	
Proposals for translation:	**Translation universals**
T1: Obdarowanemu nie przysługuje prawo upubliczniania jakichkolwiek informacji dotyczących treści niniejszej umowy, za wyjątkiem osoby darczyńcy, przedmiotu umowy oraz wysokości darowizny.	N
T2: Obdarowany nie jest uprawniony do publikowania jakichkolwiek informacji dotyczących treści niniejszej umowy, za wyjątkiem osoby darczyńcy, przedmiotu umowy oraz kwoty darowizny.	DT
T3: Obdarowany nie jest uprawniony do publikowania jakichkolwiek informacji dotyczących treści niniejszej umowy, za wyjątkiem osoby darczyńcy, przedmiotu umowy oraz kwoty darowizny.	DT

Comment: In the T1 translation, standardisation at the level of syntax and terminology can be observed, while in the T2 and T3 translations a strong interference is apparent – an expression that is a literal translation is used: *publikowanie informacji*. In this context in the Polish corpus, we find attestations for the expression *upublicznianie informacji* rather than *publikowanie informacji*.	
Example No. 22	Context / text excerpt in Czech
Smluvní strany jsou si vědomy toho, že v rámci plnění této smlouvy mezi nimi může dojít k předávání osobných údajů ve smyslu nařízení 2016/679 ze dne 27. Dubna 2016, obecne nařízení o ochráně osobnych údajů, a k vzájemnému poskytnutí informacji, které budou považovány za důvěrné.	
Proposals for translation:	Translation universals
T1: Strony umowy są świadome, że w ramach realizacji niniejszej umowy może dochodzić między nimi do przekazywania danych osobowych w rozumieniu rozporządzenia 2016/679 z dnia 27 kwietnia 2016 roku, powszechne rozporządzenie o ochronie danych osobowych, oraz do wzajemnego udzielania informacji, które uznawane są za poufne.	N, DT
T2: Kontrahenci są świadomi tego, że w ramach realizacji niniejszej umowy mogą być przekazywane między nimi dane osobowe w rozumieniu Rozporządzenia 2016/679 z dnia 27 kwietnia 2016 r. rozporządzenie o ochronie danych osobowych oraz o wzajemnym przekazywaniu informacji, które będą traktowane jako poufne.	DT
T3: Strony umowy są świadome, że w ramach realizacji niniejszej umowy mogą być przekazywane między nimi dane osobowe w rozumieniu rozporządzenia 2016/679 z dnia 27 kwietnia 2016 r., ogólnego rozporządzenia o ochronie danych osobowych oraz wzajemnego przekazywania informacji, które będą uważane za poufne.	DT
Comment: At the level of syntax, each translator aimed to render the content as faithfully as possible in Czech, which may indicate the strong influence of the source text on the translation (discourse transfer). In addition, standardisation is evident in the translations, with each translator referring to the accepted nomenclature in terms of EU regulations. Translated texts T2 and T3 contain the passive voice in the phrase *które będą uważane za poufne*, while in translation T1 the translator used the passive voice *które uznawane są za poufne*, an example of adapting the translation to the standards of the target language.	

Example No. 23	Context / text excerpt in Czech
Za důvěrné informace jsou považovány zejména informace výslovně označené za důvěrné a další informace mající důvěrnou povahu s ohledem na jejich obsah.	
Proposals for translation:	**Translation universals**
T1: Pod pojęciem informacji poufnych rozumiane są przede wszystkim informacje wyłącznie określone jako poufne oraz pozostałe informacje o charakterze poufnym z uwagi na ich treść.	S, N, DT
T2: Za poufne uważa się w szczególności informacje wyraźnie oznaczone jako poufne oraz inne informacje o charakterze poufnym w zakresie ich treści	DT
T3: Za poufne uważa się w szczególności informacje wyraźnie oznaczone jako poufne oraz inne informacje o charakterze poufnym w odniesieniu do ich treści.	DT
Comment: In the first part of the T1 translation, normalisation and explicitation are evident – the translator adapts the lexical and grammatical forms to the norms of the target language, using the passive voice and the usual form of expressing information of this nature *(pod pojęciem informacji poufnych)*. In the second part, as in the T2 and T3 translations, the transfer of discourse at the syntactic level is evident, with the aim to render the content as faithfully as possible in the target language.	
Example No. 24	**Context / text excerpt in Czech**
Obdarovaný se zavazuje poskytnout veškerou součinnost nezbytnou pro zajištění ochrany důvěrných informaci v souladu s dotčenými právními předpisy a ujednáními smluvních stran.	
Proposals for translation:	**Translation universals**
T1: Obdarowany zobowiązuje się udzielić wszelkiego zaangażowania w celu zapewnienia ochrony informacji poufnych zgodnie z właściwymi przepisami prawa oraz postanowieniami stron	N, DT, S
T2: Obdarowany zobowiązuje się do zapewnienia wszelkiej współpracy niezbędnej do zapewnienia ochrony informacji poufnych zgodnie z właściwymi przepisami prawa i uzgodnieniami stron umowy.	DT

T3: Obdarowany zobowiązuje się do zapewnienia wszelkiej współpracy niezbędnej do zapewnienia ochrony informacji poufnych zgodnie z właściwymi przepisami prawa i uzgodnieniami kontrahentów.	S, DT
Comment: The expressions *udzielić wszelkiego zaangażowania* and *zapewnienia wszelkiej współpracy* confirm the use of discourse transfer. In addition, the T1 translation uses a simplification at the end of the sentence, as does the T2 translation.	
Example No. 25	**Context / text excerpt in Czech**
Obdarovaný se zavazuje zajistit bezokladně souhlas dotčených subjektů osobnych údajů dárci.	
Proposals for translation:	**Translation universals**
T1: Obdarowany zobowiązuje się zapewnić niezwłocznie zgodę właściwych podmiotów przetwarzania danych osobowych.	E, S
T2: Obdarowany zobowiązuje się do niezwłocznego zapewnienia zgody osoby, której dane dotyczą na przetwarzanie i publikację danych osobowych przez darczyńcę.	S, DT
T3: Obdarowany zobowiązuje się do niezwłocznego uzyskania zgody osób, których dane dotyczą, na przetwarzanie i publikację danych osobowych przez darczyńcę.	E, S
Comment: In the T1 translation, an addendum in the form of a *przetwarzania* expression is visible, which qualifies as an explicitation in translation. In addition, the translator has simplified the syntax of the sentence. In the T2 translation, the translator applied the singular form to the noun *subjektů* and used the expression *zapewnienia*, indicating interference at the syntactic level. The T3 translator used an addendum at the level of expression for *na przetwarzanie i publikację danych osobowych*.	
Example No. 26	**Context / text excerpt in Czech**
Obdarovaný je povinen zaplatit smluvní pokutu dárci do 30 dní ode dne doručení písemné výzvy dárce.	
Proposals for translation:	**Translation universals**
T1: Obdarowany zobowiązany jest do zapłaty kary umownej na rzecz darczyńcy w terminie do 30 dni od daty doręczenia pisemnego wezwania darczyńcy.	E, S, N
T2: Obdarowany ma obowiązek zapłacić karę umowną darczyńcy w terminie 30 dni od dnia doręczenia pisemnego wezwania darczyńcy.	DT

T3: Obdarowany zobowiązany jest do zapłaty na rzecz darczyńcy kary umownej w terminie 30 dni od dnia doręczenia pisemnego wezwania darczyńcy.	E, S
Comment: The T1 translator used the complement in the expression *w terminie do*, and flattened the syntax by using the passive voice in the first part of the translation, which is often used in Polish civil law contract texts. The T3 translator did the same, and he too used an addendum, using the expression *w terminie*. At the level of syntax and sentence formation, the T2 translator applied discourse transfer.	
Example No. 27	**Context / text excerpt in Czech**
Zaplacení smluvní pokuty nemá vlív na povinnost obdarovaného zaplatit dárci úroky z prodlení a způsobenou škodu, a to vedle smluvní pokuty.	
Proposals for translation:	**Translation universals**
T1: Zapłata kary umownej pozostaje bez wpływu na obowiązek obdarowanego do zapłaty odsetek na rzecz darczyńcy i naprawy wyrządzonej szkody, prócz kary umownej.	E, S, N
T2: Zapłata kary umownej nie wpływa na zobowiązanie obdarowanego do zapłaty na rzecz darczyńcy odsetek za zwłokę i wyrządzoną szkodę, oprócz kary umownej.	DT
T3: Zapłata kary umownej nie wpływa na zobowiązanie obdarowanego do zapłaty na rzecz darczyńcy odsetek za zwłokę i wyrządzoną szkodę, oprócz kary umownej.	E, DT
Comment: The T1 translator used explicative expressions *pozostaje bez wpływu na* and *naprawy wyrządzonej szkody* and simplified the syntax to bring the text in line with the norms of the language of translation. In the T2 translation, the transfer of discourse at the syntactic level is evident. The T3 translation includes both explicative expressions and discourse transfer.	
Example No. 28	**Context / text excerpt in Czech**
Obdarovaný prokázal dárci před podpisem této smlouvy oprávnění osoby, která za obdarovaného tuto smlouvu podepsala.	
Proposals for translation:	**Translation universals**
T1: Obdarowany okazał darczyńcy przed podpisaniem niniejszej umowy upoważnienie osoby, która podpisała niniejszą umowę w imieniu obdarowanego.	DT
T2: Przed podpisaniem tej umowy obdarowany udowodnił darczyńcy uprawnienia osoby, która podpisała tę umowę w imieniu obdarowanego.	DT

T3: Przed podpisaniem niniejszej umowy obdarowany przedstawi darczyńcy upoważnienie osoby, która w imieniu obdarowanego podpisała niniejszą umowę.	DT
Comment: The interference occurring in the T2 translation led to the calque evident in the expression *obdarowany udowodnił darczyńcy* (a literal translation was used). The T3 translator used the future tense rather than the past perfect tense, as is evident in the T1 and T2 samples. At the level of syntax, each translator used a faithful translation close to the source text.	
Example No. 29	**Context / text excerpt in Czech**
Tato smlouva nabývá platnosti a účinnosti dnem jejího podpisu oběma smluvními stranami.	
Proposals for translation:	**Translation universals**
T1: Niniejsza umowa wchodzi w życie i staje się skuteczna z dniem podpisania jej przez obydwie strony umowy.	DT
T2: Niniejsza umowa wchodzi w życie z dniem jej podpisania przez obie strony.	S
T3: Niniejsza umowa wchodzi w życie i obowiązuje w dniu jej podpisania przez strony umowy.	S
Comment: Translator T1, using the expression *staje się skuteczna*, applied discourse transfer, while translators T1 and T2 simplified the translation.	
Example No. 30	**Context / text excerpt in Czech**
Tato smlouva se vyhotovuje ve dvou (2) stejnopisech, z nichž každá ze smluvních stran obdrží jedno (1) vyhotovení.	
Proposals for translation:	**Translation universals**
T1: Niniejsza umowa została sporządzona w dwóch (2) egzemplarzach, po jednym (1) dla każdej ze stron.	S, N
T2: Niniejsza umowa została sporządzona w dwu (2) egzemplarzach, przy czym każda strona otrzyma po jednej (1) kopii.	DT
T3: Niniejsza umowa zostaje sporządzona w dwóch (2) egzemplarzach, po jednym (1) egzemplarzu dla każdej ze stron.	E, S, N
Comment: In the T2 translation, a strong discourse transfer is evident. In the T1 and T3 translations, syntactic simplification has been applied and the translation has been normalised, although in the T3 translation, explicitation can still be seen at the level of expression *dla każdej ze stron*.	

3.1.4.1. Summary

1. What universals have been identified in translations of the donation agreement?

Example number	E (explicitation)	S (simplification)	N (normalisation)	R (reduction)	DT (discourse transfer)
1			•		•
2			•		•
3		•	•		
4			•		•
5			•		•
6			•		•
7	•				•
8					•
9	•	•			•
10	•		•		
11	•				•
12					•
13	•		•		•
14			•		•
15	•		•		•
16	•		•		•
17	•		•		•
18			•		•
19			•		•
20		•	•		•
21			•		•
22			•		•
23		•	•		•
24		•	•		•
25	•	•			•
26	•	•	•		•
27	•	•	•		•
28					•
29		•			•
30		•	•		•

2. Frequency of universals of a given type in translations of the donation agreement

Example number	E (explicitation)	S (simplification)	N (normalisation)	R (reduction)	DT (discourse transfer)
1			•		••
2			•		•
3		•	•••		
4			•		••
5			•		••
6			••		•
7	•				••
8					•••
9	•	•			•
10	•		••		
11	•				••
12					•••
13	•		•		••
14			•		••
15	•		•		•
16	•		•		•
17	•		•••		•
18			••		•
19			•		••
20		•	•		••
21			•		••
22			•		•••
23		•	•		•••
24		••	•		•••
25	••	•••			•
26	••	••	•		•
27	••	•	•		••
28					•••
29		••			•
30		••	••		•
Total:	14	16	29		51

3. Graph of the frequency of translation universals in translations of the donation agreement

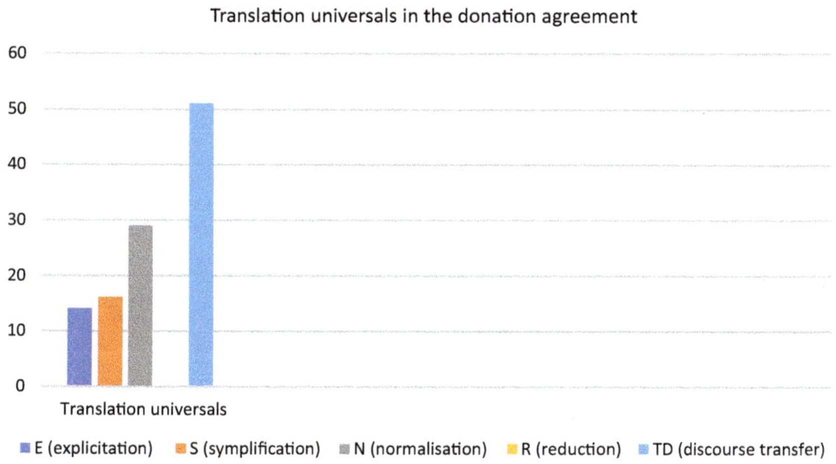

Source: Author's own elaboration.

3.1.5. Analysis of contract for a work of art

Characteristics of a contract for a work of art in the Polish and Czech Civil Codes.

Tab. 32: Contract for a work of art – basic characteristics

<table>
<tr><th colspan="2">Work contract</th></tr>
<tr><th>Definition from Czech Civil Code</th><th>Definition from Polish Civil Code</th></tr>
<tr><td>§ 2586
(1) Smlouvou o dílo se zhotovitel zavazuje provést na svůj náklad a nebezpečí pro objednatele dílo a objednatel se zavazuje dílo převzít a zaplatit cenu.
(2) Cena díla je ujedná dostatečně určitě, je-li dohodnut alespoň způsob jejího určení, anebo je-li určena alespoň odhadem. Mají-li strany vůli uzavřít smlouvu bez určení ceny díla, platí za ujednanou cena placená za totéž nebo srovnatelné dílo v době uzavření smlouvy a za obdobných smluvních podmínek.
§ 2587
Dílem se rozumí zhotovení určité věci, nespadá-li pod kupní smlouvu, a dále údržba, oprava nebo úprava věci, nebo činnost s jiným výsledkem. Dílem se rozumí vždy zhotovení, údržba, oprava nebo úprava stavby nebo její části.</td><td>Art. 627
Przez umowę o dzieło przyjmujący zamówienie zobowiązuje się do wykonania oznaczonego dzieła, a zamawiający do zapłaty wynagrodzenia.</td></tr>
<tr><th colspan="2">Basic terminology as defined in the Polish and Czech Civil Codes</th></tr>
<tr><td>dílo
smlouva o dílo
cena
zhotovitel
objednatel</td><td>dzieło
umowa o dzieło
cena
przyjmujący zamówienie
zamawiający</td></tr>
<tr><th colspan="2">Features of a work contract</th></tr>
<tr><td colspan="2">Contract of obligation, mutual, consensual, pecuniary. A contract for a work of art results in a specific outcome.</td></tr>
<tr><th colspan="2">Essence of a work contract</th></tr>
<tr><td colspan="2">The essence of a contract for a work of art is the obligation of the ordering party to complete a specific work, as well as the obligation of the ordering party to pay the price (remuneration).</td></tr>
<tr><th colspan="2">Provisions governing a work contract</th></tr>
<tr><td>§§ 2586–2635 NOZ</td><td>Articles 627-646 of the Civil Code</td></tr>
</table>

Source: 1. Act No. 89/2012 Coll.; 2. *Občanský zákoník*; Polish Civil Code, Act of 23 April 1964; 3. Dąbrowski, 2019: 145.

Example No. 1	**Context / text excerpt in Czech**
Předmětem této smlouvy je závazek zhotovitele provést pro objednatele za podmínek stanovených touto smlouvou dílo – „Terénní úpravy včetně osazení zábradlí a zámkové dlažby“, a to ***řádně, včas a v dohodnutém rozsahu a kvalitě.***	
Proposals for translation:	**Translation universals**
T1: [...] *prawidłowo, terminowo oraz w uzgodnionym zakresie i jakości.*	DT
T2: [...] *należycie, terminowo oraz w uzgodnionym zakresie i jakości.*	N
T3: [...] *należycie, terminowo oraz we właściwym zakresie i jakości.*	N
Comment: The T1 translator translated the lexeme *řádně* using an equivalent close to the source expression *prawidłowo*. The other translators have adapted the text to the terminological usus of the Polish language. The lexeme *należycie* is used, among others, in the Commercial Code and the Code of Offences and is used in such word compounds as *należyte zabezpieczenie, należyte wykonanie usługi,* and *należyte prowadzenie pojazdu.*	
Example No. 2	**Context / text excerpt in Czech**
1.2. Objednatel ***se zavazuje řádně a včas provedené dílo od zhotovitele převzít*** a zaplatit za jeho provedení zhotoviteli cenu podle čl. III. této smlouvy.	
Proposals for translation:	**Translation universals**
T1: Zleceniodawca *zobowiązuje się przejąć należycie i terminowo wykonaną pracę od Wykonawcy* [...].	DT, DT
T2: Zamawiający *zobowiązuje się należycie i terminowo wykonane dzieło odebrać od wykonawcy* [...].	N, N
T3: Zamawiający *zobowiązuje się do odbioru dzieła zrealizowanego przez wykonawcę należycie i terminowo* oraz do zapłaty [...]	N, S, N

Comment: The main problem of the analysed sentence is its array, which determines the correct communication of the source text. In the case of translator T1, an array close to the original text was used, resulting in an unfortunate calque that creates an ambiguous message (it is unclear whether *zleceniodawca ma przejąć należycie i terminowo pracę* whether *zleceniodawca wykonał należycie i terminowo pracę*). Translator T2 avoided the calque by using the correct sentence formation, while translator T3 took advantage of simplifying and adapting the text to the audience by changing the sentence formation completely. Attention should also be paid to the translation of the lexeme *dílo* – in a work contract we are talking about the lexeme *dzieło*, not the *praca* as it appears in the T1 translation.	
Example No. 3	**Context / text excerpt in Czech**
Zhotovitel se zavazuje ***provést dílo*** v souladu s touto smlouvou a ***dle položkového rozpočtu***, jež tvoří přílohu č. 1 této smlouvy, a to v souladu s obecně závaznými předpisy České republiky a technickými normami závaznými v České republice.	
Proposals for translation:	**Translation universals**
T1: Wykonawca zobowiązuje się *wykonać prace* zgodnie z niniejszą umową i *zgodnie z pozycją kosztorysową*, która stanowi […].	DT, DT
T2: Wykonawca zobowiązuje się *wykonać dzieło* zgodnie z niniejszą umową i *zgodnie z kosztorysem jednostkowym*, tworzącym […].	N, DT
T3: Wykonawca zobowiązuje się *wykonać dzieło zgodnie z* niniejszą umową oraz *kosztorysem*, który […].	N, N, S
Comment: The Civil Code uses the expression *wykonać dzieło* in relation to the completion of the work. The NKJP, the EUR-Lex text database, and parallel texts contain just such an expression – in this situation, translations T2 and T3 are in line with the terminological usage of the Polish language, while translation T1 is a calque of Czech. In Polish civil law contracts, it is most common to see simply *kosztorysy*, a word that means a statement of costs related to the performance of something/work, for example, *kosztorys budowy/remontu/planowanych działań* (based on the NKJP and the author's corpus). Translator T3 used simplification and normalisation, while translators T1 and T2 used descriptive equivalents close to the source text.	

Example No. 4	Context / text excerpt in Czech
Cena za zhotovení díla dle této smlouvy byla dohodnuta mezi smluvními stranami jako nejvýše přípustná a nepřekročitelná na částku XXX Kč ***bez DPH*** (slovy: XXX).	
Proposals for translation:	**Translation universals**
T1: *Cena za wykonanie prac* w ramach niniejszej umowy została uzgodniona pomiędzy stronami umowy jako maksymalna dopuszczalna i nieprzekraczająca XXX CZK *bez VAT* […].	DT, DT
T2: *Cena za realizację dzieła* zgodnie z niniejszą umową została uzgodniona przez strony umowy jako maksymalna i nieprzekraczalna na kwotę XXX *CZK netto* […].	N, N
T3: *Wysokość wynagrodzenia za wykonanie dzieła* zgodnie z niniejszą umową jest maksymalna i nieprzekraczalna, wynosi XXX CZK *bez podatku VAT*.	N, E
Comment: In the T1 translation, the translator used the literal translation twice. The T2 translator sought to apply the norm of the target language, but the closest to the usus of the target language is the T3 translation, in which its author used the expression *wysokość wynagrodzenia za wykonanie dzieła*, which is a direct reference to the nomenclature used in the Civil Code. For the last part of the translation, an explicitation – the addendum *bez* ***podatku*** *VAT* – was used.	
Example No. 5	**Context / text excerpt in Czech**
Cena dle čl. 3.1. této smlouvy nezahrnuje ***daň z přidané hodnoty***, která bude zhotovitelem účtována ve výši dle platných právních předpisů a v souladu s platebními podmínkami uvedenými v čl. IV. této smlouvy.	
Proposals for translation:	**Translation universals**
T1: Cena zgodnie z art. 3.1. niniejszej umowy nie zawiera *podatku od towarów i usług*, który […].	DT
T2: Cena zgodnie z art. 3.1. niniejszej umowy nie obejmuje *podatku od towarów i usług*, który […].	DT

T3: Zgodnie z art. 3.1. niniejszej umowy cena nie obejmuje *podatku VAT*, który [...]	N
Comment: *Daň z přidané hodnoty*, Czech abbreviation *DPH*, is nothing more than *VAT*, i.e., *podatek od towarów i usług*. Each of the translations is correct, however, in Polish the abbreviation *VAT* is most commonly used for this tax, so translations T1 and T2 indicate discourse transfer, while translation T3 indicates normalisation.	
Example No. 6	**Context / text excerpt in Czech**
Cena za zhotovení díla dle čl. 3.1. této smlouvy zahrnuje ***veškeré náklady zhotovitele*** související s ***provedením díla*** a je cenou konečnou v rozsahu položkového rozpočtu, jež tvoří přílohu č. 1 této smlouvy.	
Proposals for translation:	**Translation universals**
T1: Cena za wykonanie prac zgodnie z art. 3.1. niniejszej umowy obejmuje *wszystkie koszty wykonawcy* związane z *wykonaniem robót* [...].	DT
T2: Cena za wykonanie dzieła zgodnie z art. 3.1. niniejszej umowy obejmuje *wszystkie koszty wykonawcy* związane z *wykonaniem dzieła* [...].	DT, DT, N
T3: Zgodnie z art. 3.1. niniejszej umowy cena zawiera *wszelkie koszty po stronie wykonawcy* związane z *wykonaniem dzieła* [...]	N, E, N
Comment: At the level of sentence formation, the T1 and T2 translations show a strong influence of the source language, while in the T3 translation the punctuated sentence formation is more in line with the norm of the target language. In addition, the T3 translation uses an explicitation in the expression concerning the costs incurred by the contractor: *wszelkie koszty* ***po stronie*** *wykonawcy*, while the T1 and T2 translators made a faithful translation. It should also be noted that in the T1 translation there is a third option for translating the expression *provedení díla*: *wykonanie robót*. While synonymic expressions and the avoidance of repetition are highly desirable, often in contracts the end audience expects the use of uniform terminology throughout the text.	

Example No. 7	Context / text excerpt in Czech
Platby budou provedeny výhradně v Kč. Objednatel neposkytne zálohu. Smluvní strany se dohodly, že provedené práce budou fakturovány vždy k poslednímu dni kalendářního měsíce, a to na základě vzájemně odsouhlaseného soupisu provedených prací a dále pak k termínu předání a převzetí dokončeného díla. Objednatel uplatní pozastávku ve výši XXX % z celkové ceny díla, která bude uvolněna po předání a převzetí hotového díla bez vad a nedodělků. Faktury budou mít splatnost 14 dnů od potvrzení objednatelem.	
Proposals for translation:	**Translation universals**
T1: Płatności *będą dokonywane* wyłącznie w CZK. Zleceniodawca *nie zapewni kaucji.*	DT
T2: Płatności *zostaną wykonane* wyłącznie w CZK. Zamawiający *nie udzieli zaliczki.*	DT
T3: Płatności *realizowane będą* wyłącznie w walucie CZK. *Kaucja nie jest wymagana.*	N
Comment: In Polish civil law contracts, in the wording of payment methods, the most common expression used is *płatności są/będą realizowane* (attestations in reference corpora), while the expressions *dokonywać płatności / wykonać płatność* are also used in Polish. However, special attention should be paid to the translation of the lexeme *záloha*. The translators used two equivalents: *kaucja* and *zaliczka*. They have different semantic fields (in civil law contracts, a deposit and advance payment are still applicable in addition to the deposit), which can consequently lead to a factual error. *Zaliczka* represents a portion of the amount due in advance, while *kaucja* represents a security (e.g., performance/retention of the contract). *Zaliczka* is usually non-refundable, although the tax regulations allow for this possibility; *kaucja* is usually returned to the depositor in full upon fulfilment of the obligation, although here too the regulations allow it to be set off against receivables/obligations (*zadatek*, unlike these two forms of payment, is non-refundable). It is important to use the correct translation to communicate the meaning of the message. In the author's opinion, both the equivalent *zaliczka* and the equivalent *kaucja* are acceptable in the translation of the contract in question, while the equivalent *kaucja* is the most appropriate (in the case of work contracts, it is usually the security of the obligation that is involved). The term *zaliczka* would be more appropriate if partial payments, so-called advance payments, were described.	

Example No. 8	Context / text excerpt in Czech
Objednatel je povinen všechny platby dle této smlouvy platit ***bezhotovostním převodem*** na bankovní účet zhotovitele, jež je uveden v záhlaví této smlouvy nebo na jiný bankovní účet, který zhotovitel objednateli pro tento účel písemně sdělí.	
Proposals for translation:	**Translation universals**
T1: Zleceniodawca jest zobowiązany do uiszczenia wszystkich płatności wynikających z niniejszej umowy *przelewem bezgotówkowym* na rachunek bankowy Wykonawcy, który jest wskazany w nagłówku niniejszej umowy lub na inny rachunek bankowy, o czym wykonawca powiadomi zleceniodawcę na piśmie.	DT, DT
T2: Zamawiający zobowiązany jest wszelkie płatności zgodnie z niniejszą umową dokonywać *przelewem bezgotówkowym* na rachunek bankowy wykonawcy, podanego w nagłówku niniejszej umowy lub na inny rachunek bankowy, podany pisemnie zamawiającemu przez wykonawcę w tym celu.	DT, DT
T3: Zamawiający obowiązany jest dokonać wszystkich płatności *przelewem* na rachunek bankowy wykonawcy podany w preambule niniejszej umowy lub na inny rachunek bankowy, który wykonawca przekaże w formie pisemnej zamawiającemu.	N, S, N
Comment: There is a calque in the T1 and T2 translations – the expression *bezhotovostní převod* has been translated literally as *przelew bezgotówkowy*. In Polish, the correct term is *przelew* (bank transfer – by definition it is a non-cash operation, there are no cash transfers) or *transakcja bezgotówkowa*. The T3 translator applied the terminological usus of the target language and simplification. Also, at the level of sentence syntax, the T3 translation is closer to the target audience, while the T1 and T2 translations bear the mark of source-like translation.	
Example No. 9	**Context / text excerpt in Czech**
Zhotovitel se zavazuje provést pro objednatele dílo v celém rozsahu dle klimatických podmínek do XXX. Zhotovením díla se rozumí jeho provedení řádně a včas v souladu s touto smlouvou, ***stavebně technickými požadavky na výstavbu*** a právními předpisy České republiky.	

Proposals for translation:	Translation universals
T1: Ukończenie robót oznacza ich prawidłowe i terminowe wykonanie zgodnie z niniejszą umową, *wymaganiami techniczno-budowlanymi dla budownictwa* oraz przepisami prawa Republiki Czeskiej.	DT
T2: Przez wykonanie dzieła rozumie się należyte i terminowe wykonanie zgodnie z niniejszą umową, *wymaganiami techniczno-budowlanymi dot. budowy* oraz przepisami prawa Republiki Czeskiej.	DT
T3: Wykonanie dzieła rozumiane jest jako terminowe i należyte jego wykonanie zgodnie z niniejszą umową, *warunkami techniczko-budowlanymi dla obiektów budowlanych* oraz przepisami prawa Republiki Czeskiej.	N
Comment: The expression *stavebně technické požadavky na výstavbu* is analysed in this example. Translators T1 and T2 used a faithful translation, while translator T3 translated according to the terminological usus of the Polish language, using the equivalent *warunki techniczno-budowlane dla obiektów budowlanych* (another equivalent for which attestations are available in the reference corpora is *wymogi techniczno-budowlane dla obiektów budowlanych*).	
Example No. 10	**Context / text excerpt in Czech**
Zhotovitel je povinen dílo v termínu uvedeném v čl. 5. 1. této smlouvy řádně dokončit a po provedení všech případně ***předepsaných zkoušek a revizí*** jej předat objednateli způsobem stanoveným v čl. VIII této smlouvy. Objednatel je povinen takto provedené dílo od zhotovitele převzít.	
Proposals for translation:	**Translation universals**
T1: Wykonawca jest zobowiązany do należytego zakończenia prac w terminie określonym w artykule 5.1 niniejszej umowy i przekazania ich zleceniodawcy w sposób określony w artykule VIII niniejszej umowy po wszystkich możliwych przewidzianych *testach i rewizjach*.	DT
T2: Wykonawca zobowiązany jest dokończyć dzieło w terminie podanym w art. 5.1. niniejszej umowy w należyty sposób, a po wykonaniu wszystkich ewentualnie wskazanych *prób i przeglądów* przekazać go zamawiającemu w sposób określony w art. VIII. niniejszej umowy.	DT

T3: Wykonawca obowiązany jest dokończyć dzieło w należyty sposób w terminie wskazanym w art. 5.1. niniejszej umowy, zaś po przeprowadzeniu wszystkich wymaganych *prób i rewizji* przekazać je zamawiającemu w sposób opisany w art. VIII niniejszej umowy.	N
Comment: For the expression *předepsané zkoušky a revize*, the translators used three different equivalents: *testy i rewizje, próby i przeglądy*, and *próby i rewizje*. According to the Polish terminological usus, the most adequate translation is T3. In the case of the acceptance of construction works, *rewizji* (internal, external) and *prób* (leakage, pressure) are most often required. The T1 and T2 translators used a source-like translation.	
Example No. 11	**Context / text excerpt in Czech**
Práva a povinnosti objednatele Objednatel je povinen předat ihned po podpisu smlouvy staveniště zhotoviteli, na kterém bude dílo zhotovitelem zhotovováno. Termín předání staveniště zhotoviteli je ***závislý na připravenosti objednatele a nabytí právní moci stavebního povolení***. Předání staveniště bude zaznamenáno ve stavebním deníku, který je povinen zhotovitel po celou dobu provádění díla vést a který bude vždy k dispozici na místě provádění díla.	
Proposals for translation:	**Translation universals**
T1: Termin przekazania placu budowy wykonawcy uzależniony jest *od gotowości zleceniodawcy i nabycia mocy prawnej zezwolenia na budowę.*	DT, N
T2: Termin przekazania terenu budowy wykonawcy zależny jest *od przygotowania zamawiającego oraz uprawomocnienia się zezwolenia na budowę.*	N, N
T3: Termin przekazania terenu budowy uzależniony jest *od gotowości zamawiającego, jak również terminu uprawomocnienia się pozwolenia na budowę.*	N, N
Comment: *Uprawomocnienie się* is understood as *nabycie mocy prawnej decyzji*, in Polish civil law contract texts one usually encounters the simplified form *uprawomocnienie*. Translators T2 and T3 used the target language standard, while translator T1 used a faithful translation. The expression *stavební povolení* can be translated as both *pozwolenie na budowę* and *zezwolenie na budowę* in Polish.	

Example No. 12	**Context / text excerpt in Czech**
Objednatel má právo kdykoliv provést kontrolu provádění díla, a to včetně kontroly dodržování předpisů bezpečnosti práce apod. O této kontrole může objednatel kdykoliv ***učinit zápis do stavebního deníku s návrhem příslušných opatření.***	
Proposals for translation:	**Translation universals**
T1: Zleceniodawca może w każdej chwili *dokonać wpisu w dzienniku budowy z propozycją wdrożenia odpowiednich środków.*	DT
T2: Z tej kontroli zamawiający może kiedykolwiek *sporządzić wpis do dziennika budowy z propozycją właściwych działań.*	DT
T3: *Raport pokontrolny wraz z propozycją zastosowania właściwych środków może zostać odnotowany w dzienniku budowy* w dowolnym momencie przez zamawiającego.	N, E
Comment: The T1 and T2 translators used a faithful translation – this is evident both at the level of syntax and terminology. The T3 translator made a free translation in an effort to adapt it to the recipient. One can also notice an explicitation in the translation of the lexeme *zápis*, which has been translated as *raport pokontrolny*.	
Example No. 13	**Context / text excerpt in Czech**
Objednatel či jím pověřený stavebně technický dozor má právo kdykoliv nahlédnout do stavebního deníku a učinit do něj záznam a zhotovitel je povinen toto objednateli či stavebně technickému dozoru kdykoliv umožnit.	
Proposals for translation:	**Translation universals**
T1: Zleceniodawca lub upoważniony przez niego nadzór techniczno-budowlany ma prawo w każdej chwili dokonać wglądu do dziennika budowy i dokonać w nim wpisu, a wykonawca ma obowiązek w każdym czasie umożliwić to zleceniodawcy lub nadzorowi techniczno-budowlanemu.	DT
T2: Zamawiający lub upoważniony przez niego nadzór techniczno-budowlany ma prawo do wglądu do dziennika budowy kiedykolwiek oraz do dokonywania w nim wpisów, a wykonawca zobowiązany jest kiedykolwiek umożliwić to zamawiającemu lub nadzorowi techniczno-budowlanemu.	DT

T3: Zamawiający bądź upoważniony przez niego nadzór techniczno-budowlany może dokonać w dowolnym momencie wglądu do dziennika budowy, jak również wprowadzić w nim adnotację. Wykonawca obowiązany jest umożliwić powyższe zarówno zamawiającemu jak i potencjalnemu nadzorowi techniczno-budowalnemu.	N, S
Comment: Translators T1 and T2 used a source-like translation, while translator T3 adapted the translation to the target audience. He simplified the sentence structure by dividing one longer statement into two shorter ones. Translators T1 and T2 matched the sentence formation of the translation to the original text.	
Example No. 14	**Context / text excerpt in Czech**
Práva a povinnosti zhotovitele Zhotovitel je povinen ***na své náklady a na své nebezpečí*** zhotovit dílo dle této smlouvy, a to v rozsahu, kvalitě a termínech podle této smlouvy.	
Proposals for translation:	**Translation universals**
T1: Wykonawca zobowiązany jest do wykonania prac w ramach niniejszej umowy *na własny koszt i ryzyko*, w zakresie, jakości i terminach wynikających z niniejszej umowy.	N
T2: Wykonawca zobowiązany jest *na swój koszt i na swoje ryzyko* wykonać dzieło zgodnie z niniejszą umową, w zakresie, jakości i terminach zgodnie z niniejszą umową.	DT
T3: Wykonawca obowiązany jest *na własny koszt i ryzyko* wykonać dzieło zgodnie z niniejszą umową, w zakresie i jakości oraz terminach wskazanych w niniejszej umowie.	N
Comment: Translators T1 and T3 used a translation preserving the usus of the target language (normalisation), while translator T2 used literal translation (discourse transfer). Analysing the available corpus of civil law contracts, the expression used by translators T1 and T3 is more common than the translation used by translator T2.	

Example No. 15	**Context / text excerpt in Czech**
Zhotovitel je povinen při realizaci díla dodržovat veškeré platné normy a bezpečnostní předpisy, ***veškeré zákony a jejich prováděcí vyhlášky***, které se týkají jeho činnosti.	
Proposals for translation:	**Translation universals**
T1: Wykonawca zobowiązany jest do przestrzegania wszystkich obowiązujących norm iI przepisów bezpieczeństwa, *wszelkich przepisów ustawowych i wykonawczych*, które dotyczą jego działalności.	E
T2: Wykonawca zobowiązany jest do przestrzegania wszelkich obowiązujących norm i przepisów bezpieczeństwa, *wszelkich ustaw oraz zarządzeń wykonawczych do nich*, które dotyczą jego czynności, przy realizacji dzieła.	N, E
T3: Wykonawca obowiązany jest do przestrzegania podczas wykonywania dzieła wszelkich obowiązujących norm oraz przepisów bezpieczeństwa, *ustaw oraz przepisów wykonawczych*, które dotyczą jego działań.	R, N, S
Comment: Each translator aimed to faithfully convey the message of the source text; however, different terminology was used. The translation closest to the norm of the target language is T3 (a reduction was used, removing the lexeme *wszelkich*). The T2 translator was also guided by the norms of the target language when choosing equivalents. The T1 translator used explicitation – in the case of the lexeme *zákony* he used the equivalent *przepisy ustawowe*. In the T2 translation, the explicitation is evident in the addition of *zarządzeń wykonawczych* ***do nich***.	

3.1.5.1. *Summary*

1. What universals have been identified in translations of the work contract?

Example number	E (explicitation)	S (simplification)	N (normalisation)	R (reduction)	DT (discourse transfer)
1			•		•
2		•	•		•
3		•	•		•
4	•		•		•
5			•		•
6	•		•		•
7			•		•
8		•	•		•
9			•		•
10			•		•
11			•		•
12	•		•		•
13		•	•		•
14			•		•
15	•	•	•	•	

2. Frequency of universals of a given type in translations of the work contract

Example number	E (explicitation)	S (simplification)	N (normalisation)	R (reduction)	DT (discourse transfer)
1			••		•
2		•	••••		••
3		•	•••		•••
4	•		•••		••
5			•		••
6	•		•••		•••
7			•		••
8		•	••		••••
9			•		••
10			•		••
11			•••••		•
12	•		•		••
13		•	•		••
14			••		•
15	••	•	••	•	

3. Graph of the frequency of translation universals in translations of the work contract

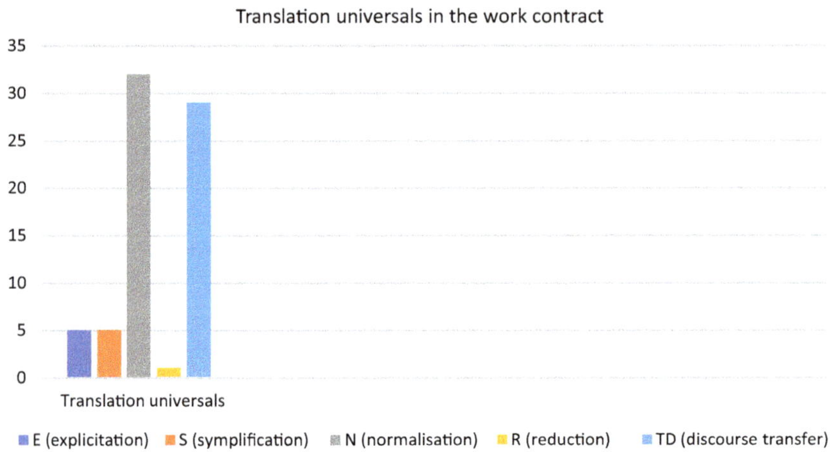

Source: Author's own elaboration.

3.1.6. Analysis of the sales contract

Characteristics of a sales contract in the Polish and Czech Civil Codes.

Tab. 33: Sales contract – basic characteristics

Sales contract	
Definition from Czech Civil Code	**Definition from Polish Civil Code**
§ 2079 (1) Kupní smlouvou se prodávající zavazuje, že kupujícímu odevzdá věc, která je předmětem koupě, a umožní mu nabýt vlastnické právo k ní, a kupující se zavazuje, že věc převezme a zaplatí prodávajícímu kupní cenu. (2) Neplyne-li ze smlouvy nebo zvyklostí něco jiného, jsou prodávající a kupující zavázáni splnit své povinnosti současně.	Article 535 § 1 Przez umowę sprzedaży sprzedawca zobowiązuje się przenieść na kupującego własność rzeczy i wydać mu rzecz, a kupujący zobowiązuje się rzecz odebrać i zapłacić sprzedawcy cenę. § 2 (repealed)
Basic terminology as defined in the Polish and Czech Civil Codes	
kupní smlouva kupní cena prodávající kupující předmětem koupě	umowa sprzedaży cena sprzedawca kupujący rzecz / przedmiot umowy
Features of a sales contract	
Consensual, pecuniary, reciprocal contract. As a result of a sales contract, a double effect (obligation and disposition) is created.	
Essence of a sales contract	
The essence of a sales contract is the seller's obligation to transfer ownership to the buyer and deliver the item, as well as the buyer's obligation to pay the price and take delivery of the item.	
Provisions governing a sales contract	
§§ 2079–2183 NOZ	Articles 535-602 of the Civil Code Formę oraz tryb zawarcia umowy sprzedaży regulują przepisy ogólne art. 73–81 oraz art. 66–72.

Source: 1. Act No. 89/2012 Coll.; 2. *Občanský zákoník*; Polish Civil Code, Act of 23 April 1964; 3. Dąbrowski, 2019: 115.

Example No. 1	**Context / text excerpt in Czech**
čl. II. Prohlášení ***prodávajícího*** Prodávající tímto prohlašuje, že je ***výhradním vlastníkem*** prodávaného motorového vozidla uvedeného v čl. Ill této smlouvy, a že mu nejsou známy žádné okolnosti, které by ***bránily převodu*** tohoto vozidla.	
Proposals for translation:	**Translation universals**
T1: Oświadczenie *sprzedającego* […] *jedynym właścicielem* […], które uniemożliwiłyby *przekazanie* tego pojazdu.	DT, N
T2: Oświadczenie *sprzedawcy* […] *wyłącznym właścicielem* […], które *stanowiłyby przeszkodę w zbyciu* niniejszego pojazdu.	DT, DT
T3: Oświadczenie *sprzedającego* […] *jedynym właścicielem* […] okoliczności *uniemożliwiające mu jego sprzedaż*.	N
Comment: Na samym początku umowy występuje problem znalezienia właściwego ekwiwalentu leksemu *prodávající*. Przez tłumaczy T1 oraz T2 został on przetłumaczony jako *sprzedający*, czyli osoba, która dokonuje zbycia posiadanej rzeczy. Tłumacz T2 dokonał przekładu, stosując odpowiednik *sprzedawca*, bardziej kojarzący się z osobą, która obsługuje w sklepie klientów, dokonując czynności mających na celu sprzedaż danej rzeczy. W uzusie języka polskiego w sytuacjach podobnych do występującej w analizowanej umowie sprzedaży częściej stosuje się wyrażenie *sprzedający*, choć w polskim k.c. dla określenia zbywcy stosowany jest leksem *sprzedawca*, a nie *sprzedający*, zatem obydwie formy są poprawne. Wyrażenie *výhradní vlastník* zostało przetłumaczone przez tłumacza T1 oraz T3 z użyciem normalizacji, w umowach cywilnoprawnych najczęściej wykorzystywane jest wyrażenie *jedyny właściciel*. Tłumacz T2 zastosował przekład wierny *wyłączny właściciel* – jest to tłumaczenie właściwe, a wyrażenie to również często spotykane jest w umowach w języku polskim. Czeski rzeczownik *převod* w umowie sprzedaży ma na celu wyrażenie czynności oznaczającej przekazanie bądź wydanie przedmiotu sprzedaży, w rozumieniu przeniesienia praw do rzeczy. Każdy z tłumaczy starał się dostosować przekład do norm języka docelowego, choć przekład T1 nie podkreśla jednoznacznie faktu zbycia, lecz samo fizyczne przekazanie przedmiotu, co z kolei wskazuje na użycie kalki językowej.	

Example No. 2	**Context / text excerpt in Czech**
čl. Ill. Předmět smlouvy/Předmětem této smlouvy je prodej a koupě níže uvedeného motorového vozidla./Tovární značka: Iveco/ Typ model: Eurocargo/Barva vozidla: bílá/Rok výroby: XXX/Identifikační číslo vozidla (VIN): XXX/Zdvihový objem motoru XXX cm3/Registrační značka vozidla (SPZ): XXX/***Číslo velkého technického průkazu***: XXX/***Číslo ověření o registraci vozidla*** XXX ***(malý technický průkaz)/STK platná do*** XXX/***Počet ujetých kilometrů*** XXX/Počet klíčů: XXX	
Proposals for translation:	**Translation universals**
T1: *Numer karty technicznej: XXX/Numer weryfikacyjny rejestracji pojazdu XXX (dowód rejestracyjny)/Przegląd techniczny ważny do XXX/Przebieg w km XXX*	DT, S
T2: *Numer karty pojazdu: XXX/Numer certyfikatu rejestracji pojazdu: XXX (dowód rejestracyjny)/Przegląd ważny do: XXX/Liczba przejechanych kilometrów: XXX/*	N, DT
T3: *Numer karty pojazdu: XXX/Number of vehicle registration confirmation: XXX (dowód rejestracyjny)/Badanie techniczne ważne do XXX/Przebieg: XXX*	N, S
Comment: In translating texts such as the above excerpt, translators need to demonstrate their knowledge of documents operating in the culture of the target language. The use of parallel texts and corpora is of great importance here. Each translator applied standardisation, matching the nomenclature of the vehicle's formal documents as they appear in the Polish administrative circuit. Only in the T1 translation, in the expression *numer weryfikacyjny rejestracji pojazdu*, is interference evident, as the translation is strongly influenced by the source language. In the T2 translation there is also an example of discourse transfer in the expression *liczba przejechanych kilometrów.* In Polish, the simplification *przebieg (pojazdu)* should be used instead.	

Example No. 3	Context / text excerpt in Czech
čl. IV. ***Kupní cena*** Dohodnutá cena ***prodávaného motorového vozidla včetně příslušenství*** činí XXX Kč bez DPH (slovy: XXX). Kupní cenu kupující zaplatí: převodem na bankovní účet prodávajícího* č: XXX v den podpisu smlouvy.	
T1: *Cena zakupu* […] *sprzedawanego pojazdu mechanicznego wraz z wyposażeniem* […].	DT, DT
T2: *Cena sprzedaży* […] *sprzedawanego pojazdu mechanicznego wraz z akcesoriami* […]	N, DT
T3: *Cena sprzedaży* […] *sprzedawanego pojazdu wraz z wyposażeniem* […]	N, S
Comment: The naming of the civil law contract in question requires knowledge of the Polish and Czech Civil Codes, or at least parallel texts, from the very beginning of the search for equivalence. In the T1 translation, the translator has made a faithful translation, whereas the accepted standard of the target language is *cena/umowa sprzedaży* rather than *cena/umowa zakupu*. Translators T2 and T3 applied a normalisation procedure, matching the equivalent to the standards of the target language. There is also a strong interference in the translation of the expression *prodávaného motorového vozidla včetně příslušenství* in the T2 and T3 translations. The T3 translator has simplified the sentence structure, correctly reading the intentions of the author of the contract, who sells the vehicle together with accesories called *wyposażenie* (*akcesoria* is a less frequently used expression in this context, rather, car equipment is referred to as *wyposażenie*; *motorové vozidlo* is also used, although in a literal translation it means *pojazd mechaniczny*, in the corpus of civil law contracts in most cases it appears as an equivalent of *pojazd/samochód*).	

Example No. 4	Context / text excerpt in Czech
čl. V. Prohlášení kupujícího Kupující je srozuměn se skutečností, ***že kupuje věc již užívanou*** a prohlašuje, že se ***podrobně a pečlivě*** seznámil s technickým stavem vozidla, ***jeho obsluhou*** a že s ním byla provedena zkušební jízda.	
Proposals for translation:	**Translation universals**
T1: […], *že kupuje przedmiot będący już w użyciu* i oświadcza, że *dokładnie* zapoznał się ze stanem technicznym pojazdu i *jego eksploatacją*. Dodatkowo potwierdza, że przeprowadzono jazdę próbną.	DT, R, DT
T2: […], *że kupuje rzecz używaną* i oświadcza, iż szczegółowo i *dokładnie* zapoznał się ze stanem technicznym pojazdu, *jego obsługą* i że dokonał w nim jazdy próbnej.	S, N, R, DT
T3: […], *iż kupuje używany pojazd*, że zapoznał się *dokładnie* z jego stanem technicznym, *instrukcją obsługi* oraz, że przeprowadzono jazdę próbną.	S, R, N, E
Comment: The T1 translator, acting under the influence of the source text, used a linguistic calque, using for the expression *kupuje věc již užívanou* the equivalent *kupuje przedmiot będący już w użyciu*. Other translators have simplified the translation, bringing it into line with the standards of the target language. In relation to the expression *podrobně a pečlivě*, each translator used a reduction and used the equivalent *dokładnie*. The lexeme *obsluha*, meaning in the case of the contract in question the instructions for operating the vehicle, was translated differently by each translator. Translator T3 used standardisation (*instrukcja obsługi*), translator T2 used faithful translation (*obsługa*), while translator T1 translated closer to machine and equipment operation (*eksploatacja*). In the case of the T1 translator, his or her behaviour can also be classified as explicitation.	

Example No. 5	**Context / text excerpt in Czech**
čl. VI. Povinnosti kupujícího Nahlášení změn v ***evidenci držitelů motorových vozidel*** zajistí kupující a to na svůj náklad, k čemuž mu tímto prodávající uděluje plnou moc.	
Proposals for translation:	**Translation universals**
T1: Kupujący zapewni zgłoszenie zmian *w ewidencji właścicieli pojazdów mechanicznych* na swój koszt, do czego mu niniejszym sprzedający udzieli pełnomocnictwa.	DT
T2: Zgłoszenie zmian *w ewidencji posiadaczy pojazdów mechanicznych* zapewni kupujący na swój koszt, do czego sprzedawca udziela mu niniejszym pełnomocnictwa.	DT
T3: Zgłoszenie zmian *w wydziale komunikacji* leży w gestii kupującego. Wszelkie koszty z tym związane ponosi kupujący, zaś sprzedający udziela w tym celu kupującemu pełnomocnictwa.	E, E, R
Comment: The analysis of the above example should be done in terms of the overall, whole sentence. Translators T1 and T2 have retained the Czech sentence structure and formation in the Polish translation, indicating strong interference. Each of these translators points to the *ewidencję posiadaczy* (or *właścicieli*, as in the T1 translation) *pojazdów mechanicznych*. The T3 translator adopted a different translation strategy, namely, to use simplification, dividing the whole sentence into three shorter ones, and explicitation. He took the Polish institution of the *wydział komunikacji*, where the activities in question are carried out, as an *ewidencja*, and also explicated by introducing the lexemes *sprzedający* and *kupujący* in the second part of the utterance instead of personal pronouns (an explicative expression of content that implicitly follows from the content).	

Example No. 6	**Context / text excerpt in Czech**
Kupující bere na vědomí, že prodávající bezprostředně po podpisu smlouvy ***zruší pojištění odpovědnosti za škodu způsobenou provozem motorového vozidla*** a kupující je tedy povinen bezodkladně vozidlo pojistit.	
Proposals for translation:	**Translation universals**
T1: […] *anuluje ubezpieczenie odpowiedzialności cywilnej za szkody spowodowane eksploatacją pojazdu mechanicznego* […]	DT
T2: […] *rozwiąże ubezpieczenie odpowiedzialności cywilnej z tytułu użytkowania pojazdów* […]	N
T3: […] *wypowie polisę ubezpieczenia* OC […]	S, R
Comment: The T1 translator has made a faithful translation and retained the sentence structure of the source text, indicating discourse transfer. The T2 translator made use of standardisation, bringing the translation into line with the norms of the Polish language. The T3 translator has made a significant simplification in expressing the intention of the author of the contract (a 'third-party liability insurance policy for damage caused by the use of a vehicle' is simply 'a third-party liability policy'). The above example demonstrates not only the translators' competence, but also their familiarity with texts in current circulation in Polish, as well as their ability to understand the meaning of the transmitted content.	

3.1.6.1. Summary

1. What universals have been identified in translations of the sales contract?

Example number	E (explicitation)	S (simplification)	N (normalisation)	R (reduction)	DT (discourse transfer)
1			•		•
2		•	•		•
3		•	•		•
4	•	•	•	•	•
5	•			•	•
6		•	•	•	•

2. Frequency of universals of a given type in translations of the sales contract

Example number	E (explicitation)	S (simplification)	N (normalisation)	R (reduction)	DT (discourse transfer)
1			••		•••
2		••	••		••
3		•	••		•••
4	•	••	••	•••	•••
5	••			•	••
6		••	•	•	•
Total:	3	7	9	5	14

3. Graph of the frequency of translation universals in translations of the sales contract

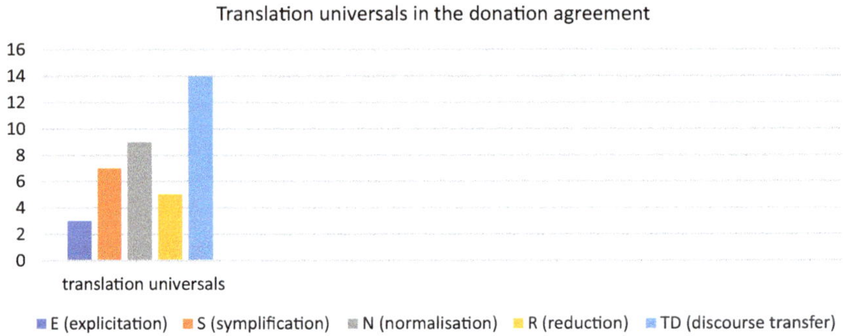

Source: Author's own elaboration.

3.1.7. Analysis of the contract of mandate

Characteristics of a contract of mandate in the Polish and Czech Civil Codes.

Tab. 34: Contract of mandate – basic characteristics

Contract of mandate	
Definition from Czech Civil Code	**Definition from Polish Civil Code**
§ 2430 Příkazní smlouvou se příkazník zavazuje obstarat záležitost příkazce.	Article 750 Do umów o świadczenie usług, które nie są uregulowane innymi przepisami, stosuje się odpowiednio przepisy o zleceniu.
Basic terminology as defined in the Polish and Czech Civil Codes	
příkazní smlouva příkazník příkazce záležitost	umowa zlecenia zleceniobiorca zleceniodawca zlecenie / przedmiot umowy
Features of a contract of mandate	
A named contract, whether paid or unpaid, a contract of endeavour, consensual and reciprocal in nature	
Nature of a contract of mandate	
The purpose of a contract of mandate is to regulate the provision of services in the form of the performance of a legal act for another person. Through such a contract, the contractor undertakes to perform a specific legal act for the benefit of the principal.	
Provisions governing a contract of mandate	
§§ 2430–2444 NOZ	Art. 750 c.c.

Source: 1. Act No. 89/2012 Coll.; 2. *Občanský zákoník*; Polish Civil Code, Act of 23 April 1964; 3. Dąbrowski, 2019: 179.

Example No. 1	**Context / text excerpt in Czech**
Advokátní kancelář se touto Smlouvou zavazuje poskytnout Klientovi právní služby spočívající ***v právním zastoupení*** statutárního mesta Brna v soudním rízení vedeném Krajským soudem v Brně jako soudem odvolacím ve věci pod SP. zn. XXX, žalobce statutární město Brno, žalovaný XXX s.r.o., IČ: XXX, o odvolání žalovaného proti rozsudku Městského soudu v Brně ze dne XXX, č. j. XXX, ***o zaplacení XXX Kč s přísl.***, smlouva o dílo (XXX).	
Proposals for translation:	**Translation universals**
T1: Na mocy niniejszej Umowy kancelaria adwokacka zobowiązuje się świadczyć na rzecz Klienta usługi prawne polegające *na reprezentacji prawnej* miasta statutowego Brno […] *o zapłatę XXX CZK z należnościami ubocznymi*, umowa o dzieło (XXX).	DT, N, E
T2: Kancelaria Adwokacka na postawie niniejszej Umowy zobowiązuje się świadczyć usługi prawne dla Klienta, polegające *na reprezentowaniu prawnym* miasta statutowego Brno […] *o zapłatę XXX – CZK wraz z należnościami ubocznymi*, umowa o dzieło.	DT, N, E
T3: Na mocy niniejszej umowy Kancelaria adwokacja zobowiązuje się świadczyć na rzecz Klienta usługi polegające *na reprezentacji* miasta statutowego Brno […] *w sprawie zapłaty XXX – CZK wraz z należnościami ubocznymi*, umowa o dzieło.	R, E
Comment: The expression *v právním zastoupení* has been translated as *reprezentacja prawna* (T1 and T3) and as *reprezentowanie prawne* (T2). In the case of T1 and T3, the norm of the target language was preserved, while in the case of T2, a rather unfortunate linguistic calque was created. Numerous attestations for the expression *reprezentowanie prawne* can be found in the EUR-Lex database. The expression *o zaplacení XXX Kč s přísl.* has been translated with fidelity to the source text by translators T1 and T2. Each of the translators applied the terminological usus of the Polish language, using the equivalent *należności uboczne* – there are numerous attestations in the NKJP for such an expression with usage in the Civil Code and the Journal of Laws. Explicitation is also evident in this case, as the content expressed by the abbreviation *s přísl.* is rendered in its full meaning in Polish – this is in accordance with the art of translation, as also indicated by the Polish Code of the Sworn Translator. The expression *o zaplacení* was translated with fidelity to the source text by translators T1 and T2, while translator T3 applied a closer translation strategy, using the equivalent *w sprawie*.	
Example No. 2	**Context / text excerpt in Czech**
Předmětem plnění jsou rovněž všechna potřebná související jednání ***včetně písemných vyjádření.***	

Proposals for translation:	**Translation universals**
T1: Przedmiotem świadczenia są również wszelkie niezbędne negocjacje z tym związane, *w tym oświadczenia pisemne.*	N
T2: Przedmiotem świadczenia są także wszelkie konieczne rozmowy z tym związane *łącznie z pisemnymi opiniami.*	E
T3: Przedmiotem świadczenia są również wszelkie niezbędne czynności *z uwzględnieniem sporządzania właściwych pism.*	E
Comment: The subject of the analysis is the translation of the expression *včetně písemných vyjádření. Písemná vyjádření* in the context of legal proceedings are all written submissions by the parties to the proceedings (EUR-Lex), written comments (EUR-Lex, Gazette, NKJP), or letters / written statements made by attorneys (in this case a law firm) on behalf of their principals. It can be considered that each translator tried to faithfully convey the meaning of the content of the source text. The equivalent *oświadczenia pisemne* used by translator T1 is closest to the terminological usus of the target language, while the translation proposals of translators T2 and T3 – *pisemne opinie, właściwe pisma* – exemplify the explicative expression of the content contained in the original language.	
Example No. 3	**Context / text excerpt in Czech**
Klient se touto Smlouvou ***zavazuje zaplatit*** za poskytnuté právní služby odměnu dle podmínek stanovených touto Smlouvou.	
Proposals for translation:	**Translation universals**
T1: Na mocy niniejszej Umowy *klient zobowiązuje się do uiszczenia wynagrodzenia* za świadczone usługi prawne zgodnie z warunkami określonymi w niniejszej Umowie.	N
T2: *Klient* na postawie niniejszej Umowy *zobowiązuje się do zapłaty wynagrodzenia* za świadczone usługi prawne zgodnie z warunkami określonymi w niniejszej Umowie.	N
T3: *Klient* na podstawie niniejszej umowy *zobowiązuje się pokryć koszty* świadczonych usług prawnych zgodnie z warunkami w niej zawartymi.	E

Comment: In translations T1 and T2, the expression *wynagrodzenie* appears as the basis for payment. The expression *wynagrodzenie za usługi s* appears in both the Civil Code and the Journal of Laws, and numerous attestations of it can also be found in the NKJP. In the situation referred to in the agreement under review, such a translation proposal is the closest to the standard of the target language. In the T3 translation there is a strong explicitation, the translator used the equivalent *pokryć koszty*, adapting the translation to the perspective of the recipient of the law firm's services (for the client, the lawyers' fees are a cost); numerous attestations can be found for such an expression in the NKJP, but in a slightly different context: *pokryć koszty sądowe/pogrzebu/wywozu ścieków/odśnieżania/opinii rzeczoznawców/postępowania sądowego.* Regarding services, attestations are available for expressions such as *koszty usług medycznych/akwizycyjnych/**prawników/ prawniczych**/bankowych*. The attestation for the expression *koszty usług prawników* services comes from the *Gazeta Ubezpieczeniowa* newspaper, while the attestation for the expression *koszty usług prawniczych* comes from the transcripts of the proceedings of the Polish Parliament. It should be recognised that the most reliable source of knowledge for the translator in this case is the attestations from legal and juridical texts.	
Example No. 4	**Context / text excerpt in Czech**
Klient současně s podpisem této Smlouvy ***výslovně uděluje*** Advokátní ***kanceláři plnou moc k jednání jeho jménem*** v mezích této Smlouvy.	
Proposals for translation:	**Translation universals**
T1: Z chwilą podpisania niniejszej Umowy *klient wyraźnie udziela* Kancelarii Adwokackiej *pełnomocnictwa do działania w jego imieniu* w granicach niniejszej Umowy.	N, DT
T2: *Klient* równocześnie z podpisaniem niniejszej Umowy *wyraźnie udziela* Kancelarii Adwokackiej pełnomocnictwa *do reprezentowania w jego imieniu* w zakresie niniejszej Umowy.	N, DT
T3: Z chwilą podpisania niniejszej Umowy *Klient udziela pełnomocnictwa* Kancelarii prawnej *do występowania w jego imieniu* w zakresie określonym w niniejszej Umowie.	R, N

<table>
<tr><td colspan="2">Comment:
There is an expression in Polish legal nomenclature udzielić pełnomocnictwa and this is what was used by each of the translators, which demonstrates the use of the standard of the target language. Regarding powers of attorney granted to law firms, verbo-nominal phrases such as: udzielać pełnomocnictwa do występowania/zastępowania/reprezentowania/działania w imieniu (based on authentic texts – powers of attorney). Each translator adapted his or her translation to the standard of the target language. Translator T3 used a reduction, omitting the equivalent lexeme výslovně (translators T1 and T2 made the translation preserving the usus of the source language). Polish powers of attorney do not – as is the Czech custom – use message reinforcement in the form of emphasising that the client gives the power of attorney voluntarily, unambiguously, unquestionably, and explicitly.</td></tr>
<tr><td>Example No. 5</td><td>Context / text excerpt in Czech</td></tr>
<tr><td colspan="2">Advokátní kancelář a Advokáti jsou povinni chránit a prosazovat práva a oprávněné zájmy Klienta a řídit se jeho pokyny. Pokyny Klienta však nejsou vázáni, jsou-li v rozporu s právním nebo stavovským předpisem.</td></tr>
<tr><td>Proposals for translation:</td><td>Translation universals</td></tr>
<tr><td>T1: […] zobowiązani są do ochrony i egzekwowania praw i uzasadnionych interesów […] są sprzeczne z przepisami prawa lub statutu.</td><td>N, N, DT</td></tr>
<tr><td>T2: […] chronić i egzekwować prawa i uprawnione interesy […] sprzeczne z przepisami prawa lub przepisami zawodowymi.</td><td>N, N, N</td></tr>
<tr><td>T3: […] chronić i egzekwować prawa oraz uzasadnione interesy […] niezgodne z przepisami prawa lub zasadami wykonywania zawodu</td><td>N, N, N</td></tr>
</table>

Comment: Two expressions are analysed in this example: *oprávněné zájmy* and *v rozporu s právním nebo stavovským předpisem*. In the Polish nomenclature, the expressions *prawnie uzasadniony interes* (legal and juridical texts) and *uzasadniony interes* (attestations in the NKJP in journalistic texts, the Journal of Laws, the Civil Code, and the Offences Code) are used. The equivalent used by the T2 translator is an unfortunate linguistic calque, the result of adapting the translation to the source text. The terminological usus of the Polish language allows the use of the equivalent *sprzeczny z przepisami / niezgodny z przepisami* for the expression *v rozporu s předpisem* (note that while in Czech the lexeme *předpis* occurs in the singular, the Polish parallel texts use the plural; the adaptation to the norm of the target language is evident in this case in every translation attempt). The translators adopted different translation techniques for the lexeme *stavovský předpis*. In the EUR-Lex text database, the most common equivalent is *zasady wykonywania zawodu / regulamin etyki zawodowej*. In the case of the T2 and T3 translations, the translations are closest to the Polish language norm, the T2 translation proposal is probably a translator's mistake (the translator may have meant *stanovy*, hence the mistranslation of the *statut*).	
Example No. 6	**Context / text excerpt in Czech**
Advokátní kancelář a Advokáti ***jsou povinni zachovávat mlčenlivost*** o všech skutečnostech, o nichž se dozvěděli v souvislosti s poskytováním právních služeb. ***Povinnosti může Advokátní kancelář nebo Advokáta zprostit pouze Klient.***	
Proposals for translation:	**Translation universals**
T1: Kancelaria i Adwokaci *zobowiązani są do zachowania w tajemnicy* wszystkich faktów, z którymi zapoznali się w związku ze świadczeniem usług prawnych. Jedynie Klient może *zwolnić* Kancelarię lub Adwokata *z ciążących na nich zobowiązań*.	N, E
T2: Kancelaria Adwokacka i Adwokaci *są zobowiązani do zachowania poufności* o wszystkich faktach, o których dowiedzieli się w związku ze świadczeniem usług prawnych. Z obowiązku może Kancelarię Adwokacką lub Adwokata *zwolnić* wyłącznie Klient.	N, N
T3: Kancelaria adwokacja oraz jej pracownicy *zobowiązani są do zachowania poufności* w zakresie wszelkich informacji, o których dowiedzieli się w związku z świadczeniem usług na rzecz Klienta. Powyższy obowiązek *może zostać zniesiony* wyłącznie przez Klienta.	N, N

Comment: The expression *povinni zachovávat mlčenlivost* is used very frequently in civil law contracts, mainly about protecting business secrets of companies and know-how. The following equivalents of the above expression can be found in comparative corpora: *zobowiązani do nieujawniania informacji* (translation by modulation technique), *zobowiązani do zachowania poufności*, *zobowiązani do zachowania tajemnicy służbowej*, *zobowiązani do zachowania tajemnicy zawodowej*, *zobowiązani do poufnego traktowania informacji*, and *zobowiązani do zachowania poufności*. Given the cited attestations, each translator can be considered to have adapted the translation to the standard of the target language. The expression *zprostit povinnosti* has been translated as *zwolnić z obowiązku*, *zwolnić z ciążących zobowiązań*, and *obowiązek może zostać zniesiony*. As for the sense of the message, it was best preserved in the T1 translation, while in the T2 and T3 translations the translators tried to match the equivalents to the norm of the target language, using elaborate sentence structure and punctuation.	
Example No. 7	**Context / text excerpt in Czech**
Klient souhlasí s tím, aby Advokátní kancelář zakázku či poradenství realizované na základě této Smlouvy ***uváděla jako svou referenci***, a to v rozsahu názvu Klienta, kontaktní osoby, obecného popisu poskytovaných právních služeb a doby poskytování.	
Proposals for translation:	**Translation universals**
T1: Klient wyraża zgodę na to, aby Kancelaria Adwokacka *wskazywała* zlecenie czy doradztwo realizowane na podstawie niniejszej Umowy jako swoją referencję, w zakresie nazwy Klienta, osoby kontaktowej, ogólnego opisu świadczonych usług prawnych oraz okresu świadczenia.	DT
T2: Klient wyraża zgodę, żeby Kancelaria Adwokacka *prezentowała* zlecenie lub doradztwo wykonywane na podstawie niniejszej Umowy jako swoją referencję, w zakresie nazwy Klienta, konkretnej osoby, ogólnego opisu świadczonych usług prawnych oraz czasu świadczenia.	DT
T3: Klient akceptuje *powoływanie się* przez Kancelarię Adwokacką na świadczone na jego rzecz usługi i zlecenia realizowane w ramach niniejszej umowy w swoich listach referencyjnych, w zakresie nazwy Klienta, osoby do kontaktów, ogólnego opisu usług oraz okresu świadczenia.	N

Comment: It can be concluded that the translation of the analysed sentence from the source text was quite a challenge for the translators. The sentence is elaborate and syntactically very strongly embedded in the grammatical and stylistic structures of Czech. When translating such sentences, there is a risk of numerous linguistic calques or copying the sentence formation from the source text. The message from the source text is that the client does not mind if the law firm mentions its name and information about the services it has provided for them in its reference letters. Translation is a challenge for the translator primarily because of the structure of the sentence and the amount of information it contains. Translators T1 and T2 used a translation strategy close to the source text (exoticisation), while translator T3 tried to construct the Polish sentence in such a way that it was as close as possible to the target audience (domestication).	
Example No. 8	**Context / text excerpt in Czech**
Advokátní kancelář se zavazuje informovat včas Klienta o důležitých skutečnostech souvisejících s poskytováním právních služeb a ***poučit jej o jeho oprávněných nárocích*** a lhůtách, v nichž je třeba je uplatňovat, jakož i o jeho povinnostech vyplývajících z právních a jiných předpisů.	
Proposals for translation:	**Translation universals**
T1: *Kancelaria* zobowiązuje się do informowania Klienta w odpowiednim czasie o istotnych faktach związanych ze świadczeniem usług prawnych oraz *do informowania go o jego uzasadnionych roszczeniach* i terminach, w jakich należy je zrealizować, a także o jego obowiązkach wynikających z przepisów prawa i innych.	R
T2: *Kancelaria Adwokacka* zobowiązuje się do terminowego informowania Klienta o ważnych faktach związanych ze świadczeniem usług prawnych oraz *do pouczenia go o jego uprawnionych roszczeniach* i terminach, w których należy je zastosować, a także o jego obowiązkach wynikających z przepisów prawa i innych.	DT
T3: *Kancelaria* zobowiązuje się do terminowego informowania Klienta w sprawie wszelkich istotnych kwestii związanych ze świadczonymi usługami, *informowania go w zakresie przysługujących mu praw* i właściwych terminów, w których należy powyższych praw dochodzić, jak również o obowiązkach wynikających przepisów prawa oraz pozostałych przepisów.	R, R, S, N

Comment: An extended sentence with the transmission of a lot of information caused considerable difficulty for the translators. Translators T1 and T3 made a reduction, translating the expression *advokátní kancelář* as *kancelaria*, rather than *kancelaria adwokacka*, as translator T2 did. Translators T1 and T2 applied a translation strategy close to the source text, translating the passage *poučit jej o jeho oprávněných nárocích* practically literally: *do informowania go o jego uzasadnionych roszczeniach / do pouczenia go o jego uprawnionych roszczeniach.* While the lexeme *nárok* itself does indeed mean a claim, in the context of the entire sentence, however, it refers to the client's rights, which the client can claim and which the law firm should inform the client about. The actual meaning of the sentence is therefore best conveyed by the T3 translation. The translator simplified the translation, made the necessary reduction, and adapted the message to the standards of the target language.	
Example No. 9	**Context / text excerpt in Czech**
Advokátní kancelář sdělí na požádání Klientovi odhadovaný rozsah ***právních služeb*** a výši odměny. Pokud Klient s tímto rozsahem a odměnou nesouhlasí, je povinen tuto skutečnost Advokátní kanceláři bez zbytečného odkladu sdělit, ***jinak se má zato, že je schválil.***	
Proposals for translation:	**Translation universals**
T1: Na żądanie *Kancelaria* przedstawi Klientowi szacunkowy zakres *usług prawnych* oraz wysokość wynagrodzenia. Jeżeli Klient nie zgadza się z tym zakresem i wynagrodzeniem, zobowiązany jest bez zbędnej zwłoki poinformować Kancelarię, *w przeciwnym razie uważa się, że je zatwierdził.*	R, DT, DT
T2: *Kancelaria Adwokacka* na wniosek Klienta poinformuje go o szacunkowym zakresie *usług prawnych* oraz o wysokości wynagrodzenia. Jeżeli Klient nie wyraża zgodę na ten zakres i wynagrodzenie, zobowiązany jest bez zbędnej zwłoki przekazać niniejszy fakt Kancelarii Adwokackiej, *inaczej uważa się, że go zatwierdził.*	R, DT, DT, DT
T3: Na życzenie klienta *kancelaria* przedstawi klientowi szacunkowy zakres *usług* oraz wysokość wynagrodzenia. W przypadku braku akceptacji ze strony klienta zakresu usług oraz wysokości wynagrodzenia obowiązany jest on niezwłocznie poinformować o tym fakcie kancelarię, w przeciwnym razie *uznaje się, iż klient powyższe zaakceptował.*	R, R, S
Comment: The translators used reduction when translating expressions such as *advokátní kancelář* (*kancelaria*, not *kancelaria prawna*) and *právní služby* (*usługi*, not *usługi prawne*), aiming to simplify the message without unnecessary repetition. For fragment *jinak se má zato, že je schválil* the T1 and T2 translators translated using a source-like strategy, while the T3 translator made a simplification, making the translation seem clearer.	

Example No. 10	Context / text excerpt in Czech
Klient se zavazuje poskytovat Advokátní kanceláři včas úplné a pravdivé informace a předkládat jí veškeré ***listinné materiály*** potřebné k řádnému výkonu činnosti podle této Smlouvy, jakož i ***poskytnout jinou potřebnou součinnost.***	
Proposals for translation:	**Translation universals**
T1: Klient zobowiązuje się do terminowego przekazywania Kancelarii pełnych i zgodnych z prawdą informacji oraz do przekazywania jej wszelkich *materiałów dokumentacyjnych* niezbędnych do prawidłowego wykonywania czynności wynikających z niniejszej Umowy, a także do *zapewnienia innej niezbędnej współpracy.*	E, DT
T2: Klient zobowiązuje się udzielić Kancelarii Adwokackiej terminowo pełne i prawdziwe informacje oraz przedstawiać jej wszelkie ***materiały piśmienne*** konieczne do należytego wykonywania czynności zgodnie z niniejszą Umową, a także *udzielać innego koniecznego współdziałania.*	DT, N
T3: Klient zobowiązuje się przekazywać kancelarii terminowo pełne i prawdziwe informacje, jak również przedstawiać wszelkie *dokumenty w formie pisemnej* niezbędne do prawidłowego wykonywania czynności zgodnie z niniejszą umową, jak również *udzielać innego niezbędnego współdziałania.*	N, N
Comment: In the case of the expression *listinné materiály*, the T2 translator has used the unfortunate equivalent *materiały piśmienne*, so that the translation must be considered incorrect. The text of the agreement refers to *w formie pisemnej* (T3), and the T1 translator used an explicative expression, writing explicitly about documentary materials. For the expression *poskytnout jinou potřebnou součinnost* an adequate equivalent according to the NKJP attestations derived from the Civil Code should be the expression *udzielić innego niezbędnego współdziałania*, used by the T2 and T3 translators.	

Example No. 11	**Context / text excerpt in Czech**
Klient se zavazuje uvědomit stanoveným způsobem Advokátní kancelář ***s dostatečným předstihem*** o svých požadavcích na poskytování právních služeb podle této Smlouvy.	
Proposals for translation:	**Translation universals**
T1: Klient zobowiązuje się do poinformowania Kancelarii w określony sposób o wymogach świadczenia usług prawnych na podstawie niniejszej Umowy *z odpowiednim czasowym wyprzedzeniem.*	E
T2: Klient zobowiązuje się powiadomić w określony sposób Kancelarię Adwokacką *z odpowiednim wyprzedzeniem* o swoich wymaganiach dot. świadczenia usług prawnych zgodnie z niniejszą Umową.	N
T3: Klient zobowiązuje się informować kancelarię zgodnie z przyjętym sposobem, *z odpowiednim wyprzedzeniem*, w zakresie swoich oczekiwań dotyczących świadczenia usług na podstawie niniejszej umowy.	N
Comment: According to the Polish terminological usus, the correct equivalent of the term *s dostatečným předstihem* would be the expression *z odpowiednim wyprzedzeniem.* It was used by translators T2 and T3, and translator T1 additionally used explicitation, completing the translation with the adjective *czasowym.* There are only two attestations in the NKJP for the expression *z odpowiednim czasowym wyprzedzeniem*, the dominant majority being *z odpowiednim wyprzedzeniem.*	
Example No. 12	**Context / text excerpt in Czech**
Odměna za poskytované právní služby ***se stanovuje jako smluvní odměna***, a to jako maximální ve výši:	
Proposals for translation:	**Translation universals**
T1: Wynagrodzenie za świadczone usługi prawne *jest ustalane umownie*, maksymalnie w wysokości:	R, DT
T2: Wynagrodzenie za świadczone usługi prawne *określa się jako wynagrodzenie umowne* w maksymalnej wysokości:	N
T3: Wynagrodzenie z tytułu świadczonych usług prawnych *przyjmuje się jako wynagrodzenie umowne* w maksymalnej wysokości:	N

Comment: The T1 translator used a source-similar translation with a reduction – he omitted the lexeme *wynagrodzenie* in the translation of the expression *se stanovuje jako smluvní odměna*. The T2 and T3 translators applied standardisation at the level of sentence syntax – using expressions such as *określa się / przyjmuje się*, they adapted the translation to the usus of the language of civil law contracts. Numerous attestations for such constructions can be found in parallel texts.	
Example No. 13	**Context / text excerpt in Czech**
Advokátní kancelář Klientovi účtuje polovinu dohodnuté sazby ***za každou započatou půlhodinu právních služeb***.	
Proposals for translation:	**Translation universals**
T1: Kancelaria pobiera od Klienta połowę ustalonej stawki *za każde rozpoczęte pół godziny obsługi prawnej*.	DT
T2: Kancelaria Adwokacka nalicza Klientowi połowę uzgodnionej stawki *za każdą rozpoczętą półgodzinę usług prawnych*.	DT
T3: Przyjmuje się, że kancelaria *za każde rozpoczęte 30 minut obsługi prawnej* pobierze klientowi połowę ustalonej stawki.	N
Comment: In the T3 translation, a strong alignment of the translation with the standard of the target language is evident. The translator, wishing to avoid using the expression *pół godziny*, made use of the modulation technique, describing the exact amount of time. This translation also resonates well due to the use of the *obsługa prawna* equivalent for the Czech term *právní služby*. This is a typical expression when referring to legal services provided to an entity. The T1 and T2 translators used a faithful translation; in addition, a calque of the lexeme *półgodzina* appeared in the T2 translation.	
Example No. 14	**Context / text excerpt in Czech**
Nedosažení zamýšleného výsledku právních případů není důvodem k nezaplacení či jednostrannému snížení smluvní odměny dle tohoto odstavce; ***nárok na náhradu škody v případě vadného poskytnutí služeb tím není dotčen***.	
Proposals for translation:	**Translation universals**
T1: Nieosiągnięcie zamierzonego wyniku spraw prawnych nie jest powodem do braku zapłaty lub jednostronnego obniżenia wynagrodzenia umownego zgodnie z niniejszym ustępem; *prawo do odszkodowania w przypadku wadliwego wykonania usług pozostaje nienaruszone*.	DT

T2: Nieosiągnięcie zamierzonego wyniku spraw prawnych nie jest powodem do niezapłacenia lub jednostronnego obniżenia wynagrodzenia umownego zgodnie z niniejszym ustępem; *roszczenie do odszkodowania w przypadku wadliwego świadczenia usług nie jest przez to naruszone.*	DT
T3: Nieosiągnięcie założonego wyniku procesowanych spraw nie stanowi podstawy do braku płatności bądź jednostronnego obniżenia wynagrodzenia w myśl niniejszego ustępu; *powyższe pozostaje bez wpływu na prawo do dochodzenia roszczeń odszkodowawczych w przypadku wadliwej obsługi prawnej.*	N
Comment: *Nárok na náhradu škody* is one of the more frequent constructions appearing in civil law contracts and concerns the right to claim damages. The aim of achieving the greatest possible convergence with the target language norm can be seen in the T3 translation – the translator used sentence constructions characteristic of civil law contracts, as confirmed by the analysis of the parallel texts. The text reads very naturally, so the normalisation of the translation can be confirmed. The T2 translation, like the T3 translation, is close to the original text in terms of preserving sentence formation.	
Example No. 15	Context / text excerpt in Czech
Klient je oprávněn tuto Smlouvu vypovědět bez uvedení důvodu písemnou výpovědí. Výpověď je účinná doručením druhé straně. V takovém případě je povinen uhradit Advokátní kanceláři odměnu za poskytnuté, ale dosud neuhrazené služby; nárok na odměnu dle odst. 46 této Smlouvy zůstává rovněž nedotčen.	
Proposals for translation:	**Translation universals**
T1: *Klient ma prawo wypowiedzieć niniejszą Umowę bez podania przyczyny za pisemnym wypowiedzeniem.* Wypowiedzenie jest skuteczne […].	DT
T2: *Klient uprawniony jest do wypowiedzenia niniejszej Umowy bez podania powodu w formie pisemnego wypowiedzenia.* Wypowiedzenie jest skuteczne […].	DT
T3: *Klientowi przysługuje prawo pisemnego wypowiedzenia niniejszej umowy bez podania przyczyny.* Wypowiedzenie staje się skutecznym […]	N
Comment: At the level of sentence formation, translations T1 and T2 are closest to the source text, while translator T3, using the *klientowi przysługuje prawo* construction, has standardised the translation. It is also more common in civil law contracts to find the expression *bez podania przyczyny* than the T2 translator's proposed equivalent *bez powodu.*	

Example No. 16	Context / text excerpt in Czech
Tato Smlouva ***se řídí příslušnými ustanoveními*** občanského zákonilku a zákona o advokacii.	
Proposals for translation:	**Translation universals**
T1: Niniejsza Umowa *podlega odpowiednim przepisom* Kodeksu cywilnego oraz ustawie o adwokaturze.	N
T2: Niniejsza Umowa *kieruje się właściwymi postanowieniami* Kodeksu cywilnego oraz ustawy o adwokaturze.	DT
T3: Niniejsza umowa *podlega właściwym przepisom* kodeksu cywilnego oraz ustawie o adwokaturze.	N
Comment: In the T2 translation, a linguistic calque or literal translation was created – from the Czech *se řídí* the equivalent *kieruje się* was created. The standard for such provisions in Polish agreements is most often the construction used in the T1 and T3 translations – *podlega odpowiednim/właściwym przepisom.*	

Example No. 17	Context / text excerpt in Czech
Smluvní strany tímto vylučují pro použití 1740 odst. 3 občanského zákonicu, který stanoví, že smlouva je uzavřena i tehdy, kdy ***nedojde k úplné shodě projevů vůle smluvních stran.***	
Proposals for translation:	**Translation universals**
T1: Strony umowy niniejszym wyłączają zastosowanie § 1740 ust.3 Kodeksu cywilnego, który stanowi, że umowa zostaje zawarta nawet wtedy, *gdy wyrazy woli stron umowy nie są w pełni uzgodnione.*	DT
T2: Strony umowy niniejszym wykluczają zastosowanie § 1740 ust. 3 Kodeksu cywilnego, który określa, że umowa jest zawarta także wtedy, *kiedy nie dojdzie do pełnej zgody oświadczenia woli stron umowy.*	DT
T3: Strony niniejszym wykluczają zastosowanie par. 1740 ust. 3 kodeksu cywilnego, który stanowi, że umowa jest zawarta również *w przypadku braku pełnej zgodności woli stron.*	S, N
Comment: The simplification applied in the T3 translation has helped to bring the translation closer to the standard of the target language. An expression that is not easy in Czech has been simplified using modulation. Translators T1 and T2 followed a translation strategy of keeping the translation close to the original text.	

3.1.7.1. Summary

1. What universals have been identified in translations of the contract of mandate?

Example number	E (explicitation)	S (simplification)	N (normalisation)	R (reduction)	DT (discourse transfer)
1	•		•	•	•
2	•		•		
3	•		•		
4			•	•	•
5			•		•
6	•		•		
7			•		•
8		•	•	•	•
9		•		•	•
10	•		•		•
11	•		•		
12			•	•	•
13			•		•
14			•		•
15			•		•
16			•		•
17		•	•		•

2. Frequency of universals of a given type in translations of the contract of mandate

Example number	E (explicitation)	S (simplification)	N (normalisation)	R (reduction)	DT (discourse transfer)
1	•••		••	•	••
2	••		•		
3	•		••		
4			•••	•	••
5			•••••••••		•
6	•		•••••		
7			•		••
8		•	•	•••	•
9		•		••••	•••••
10	•		•••		••
11	•		••		
12			••	•	•
13			•		••
14			•		••
15			•		••
16			•		•
17		•	••		••

3. Graph of the frequency of translation universals in translations of the contract of mandate

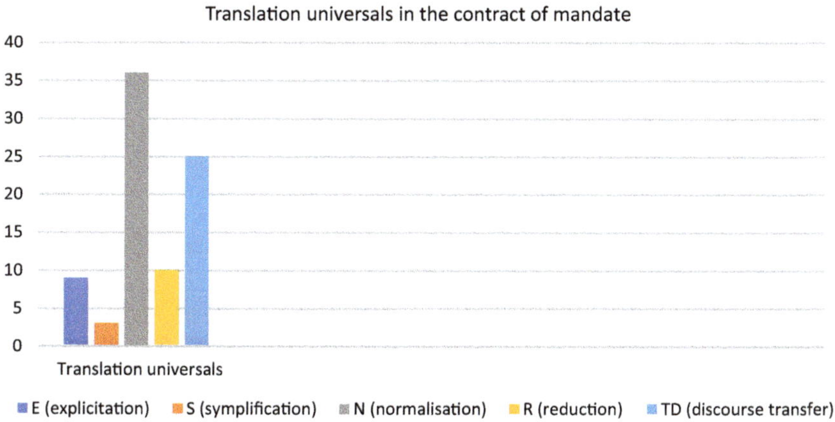

Source: Author's own elaboration.

3.1.8. Analysis of the cooperation agreement

Characteristics of a cooperation agreement in the Polish and Czech Civil Codes.

Tab. 35: Cooperation agreement – basic characteristics

Cooperation agreement A cooperation agreement as such is not defined in the Polish Civil Code, but its drafting and conclusion are possible on the basis of Article 353, which covers the principles of freedom of contract.[a] By modifying typical civil law contracts, it is possible to create a separate unnamed contract, such as a cooperation agreement. The situation is similar in the Czech legal system. For this type of contract, the regulations described in § 1746 NOZ apply. In the Czech Republic, the most common is the so-called *umowa ramowa (rámcová smlouva)* or *umowa o współpracy ramowej (smlouva o rámcové spolupráci)*.	
Definition from Czech Civil Code	**Definition from Polish Civil Code**
§ 1746 (1) Zákonná ustanovení upravující jednotlivé typy smluv se použijí na smlouvy, jejichž obsah zahrnuje podstatné náležitosti smlouvy stanovené v základním ustanovení pro každou z těchto smluv. (2) Strany mohou uzavřít i takovou smlouvu, která není zvláště jako typ smlouvy upravena.	Art. 353 [Zasada swobody umów] Strony zawierające umowę mogą ułożyć stosunek prawny według swego uznania, byleby jego treść lub cel nie sprzeciwiały się właściwości (naturze) stosunku, ustawie ani zasadom współżycia społecznego.
Basic terminology as defined in the Polish and Czech Civil Codes	
smlouva o spolupráci předmět smlouvy/služba/zakázka zadavatel poskytovatel	umowa współpracy zlecenie zleceniodawca zleceniobiorca
FEATURES OF A COOPERATION AGREEMENT	
A non-negotiable, pecuniary or gratuitous, bilateral or multilateral contract	
Essence of a cooperation agreement	
The essence of a cooperation agreement lies in the parties to the agreement achieving a jointly set objective through their interaction. The interaction of the parties – and therefore the rights and obligations of each of them – is defined in the provisions of the contract.	
Provisions governing a cooperation agreement	
§ 1746 NOZ	Article 353 of the Civil Code.

Source: 1. Act No. 89/2012 Coll.; 2. *Občanský zákoník*; Polish Civil Code, Act of 23 April 1964; 3. Radwański, Olejniczak, 2016: 129.

a The principle of freedom of contract is 'a legal norm granting civil law subjects the general competence to freely shape contractual relations through contracts and, moreover, to interpret and apply specific legal norms in favour of this competence' (Radwański, Olejniczak, 2016: 129).

Example No. 1	**Context / text excerpt in Czech**
Zadavatel je vlastníkem technologie XXX. Vzhledem k tomu, že zadavatel má v úmyslu získat marketingovou podporu a zajistit doplňkové služby XXX, ***vyhlásil zadavatel*** dne XXX ***výběrové řízení na uzavření smlouvy o spolupráci***, jejímž předmětem bude zajištění požadovaných služeb v souladu s ust. § 178 zákona č. 134/2016 Sb., v platném znění. Jedná se tedy o tzv. koncesi malého rozsahu, přičemž nejde o zadávací řízení v režimu zákona č. 134/2016 Sb. Ve výběrovém řízení zvítězila nabídka předložená poskytovatelem. Poskytovatel je připraven zajistit veškeré požadované služby jako nedělitelný celek.	
Proposals for translation:	**Translation universals**
T1: […] zamawiający *ogłosił* w dniu XXX *przetarg na zawarcie umowy o współpracy*, której przedmiotem będzie […]	N, DT
T2: […] zamawiający w dniu XXX *ogłosił przetarg na zawarcie umowy o współpracy*, przedmiotem której będzie […].	N, DT
T3: […] zamawiający *ogłosił* w dniu XXX *przetarg nieograniczony na zawarcie umowy współpracy*, przedmiotem której będzie […]	E, N
Comment: The T3 translator used an explicitive expression, translating *výběrové řízení* as the Polish expression *przetarg nieograniczony*. It should be noted that it must be clear from the contract that this is a restricted/unrestricted tender (which is not yet apparent in the quoted passage), otherwise there may be a miscommunication. In addition, translator T3 used the expression *umowa współpracy*, while the other translators used the equivalent *umowa o współpracy*. Each of the above possibilities is in line with the norm of the target language, although it can be argued that the second is a faithful translation.	
Example No. 2	**Context / text excerpt in Czech**
Předmětem této smlouvy je vzájemná spolupráce ***při zajištění marketingové podpory a doplňkových služeb*** XXX.	
Proposals for translation:	**Translation universals**
T1: Przedmiotem niniejszej umowy jest wzajemna współpraca *w zakresie wsparcia marketingowego i usług dodatkowych* XXX.	S
T2: Przedmiotem niniejszej umowy jest wzajemna współpraca *przy zapewnieniu wsparcia marketingowego oraz usług uzupełniających* XXX.	DT
T3: Przedmiot niniejszej umowy stanowi wzajemna współpraca podczas *zabezpieczenia wsparcia marketingowego oraz usług uzupełniających* XXX.	N

Comment: The expression *při zajištění marketingové podpory a doplňkových služeb* was translated faithfully by translators T2 and T3, while translator T1 applied simplification by eliminating the lexeme *zajištění*. Each of the translations can be considered to meet the standard of the target language.	
Example No. 3	**Context / text excerpt in Czech**
Obchodní a cenová politika související s realizací požadovaných služeb je plně v kompetenci poskytovatele, který je však povinen respektovat omezení uvedená v článku 5. této smlouvy a zadávací dokumentaci. Rovněž ***veškerý výnos plynoucí z realizace požadovaných služeb náleží poskytovateli*.**	
Proposals for translation:	**Translation universals**
T1: Również *wszystkie przychody wynikające z realizacji żądanych usług przysługują wykonawcy*.	DT, N
T2: Także *wszelki przychód wynikający z realizacji wymaganych usług przynależy usługodawcy*.	DT
T3: Wszystkie *przychody uzyskane w drodze realizacji zamawianych usług przysługują usługodawcy*.	N, S
Comment: The T1 translation, in terms of sentence structure and terminology used, is a faithful translation, although it should be noted that the T1 translator, like the T3 translator, used the plural in translating the lexeme *výnos*, which is in line with the terminological usus of the Polish language. Admittedly, the reference corpora also include attestations for the expression *uzyskany przychód*, however, the predominant form is *uzyskane przychody* (in contrast, earned income is often referred to as *dochód za rok / uzyskany dochód*). The T3 translator adapted the translation to the standard of the target language by simplifying the sentence structure. The T2 translator also kept the sentence formation close to the original text, e.g., through the expression *przynależy usługodawcy*.	

Example No. 4	**Context / text excerpt in Czech**
Poskytovatel zajistí realizaci požadovaných služeb jako jeden nedělitelný celek, k čemuž mu zadavatel tímto výslovně uděluje oprávnění. Rizika spojená s realizací uvedených služeb nese poskytovatel. Pro vyloučení pochybností se uvádí, že poskytovatel bude plnit své závazky podle této smlouvy ***na vlastní riziko a bez jakéhokoli dalšího nároku na zdroje městské části Brno-střed*** (s výjimkou nároku popsaného touto smlouvou).	
Proposals for translation:	**Translation universals**
T1: W celu uniknięcia wątpliwości stwierdza się, że wykonawca wypełni swoje zobowiązania wynikające z niniejszej umowy *na własne ryzyko i bez dalszych roszczeń do źródeł dzielnicy Brno-střed* (z wyjątkiem roszczenia opisanego w niniejszej umowie).	DT, DT
T2: W celu wykluczenia wątpliwości podaje się, iż usługodawca będzie wykonywał swoje zobowiązania zgodnie z niniejszą umową *na własne ryzyko i bez jakiegokolwiek innego roszczenia do zasobów dzielnicy Brno-śródmieście* (za wyjątkiem roszczenia opisanego w niniejszej umowie).	N, DT
T3: Celem wykluczenia wszelkich wątpliwości strony zgodnie przyjmują, iż usługodawca zobowiązuje się realizować swoje zobowiązania w myśl niniejszej umowy *na własne ryzyko bez dochodzenia roszczeń względem zasobów dzielnicy Brno-Śródmieście* (z wyłączeniem roszczeń uwzględnionych w niniejszej umowie).	N, S
Comment: The first element that proved to be a challenge in translation was the correct understanding of the meaning of the lexeme *zdroje*. It has been translated as *źródła* (literal translation) by the T1 translator and as *zasoby* by the T2 and T3 translators. In this contract, the idea is that the contractor should not pursue its financial claims against municipal funds, so the option proposed by the T2 and T3 translators seems to be the most understandable for the recipient. The expression *bez jakéhokoli dalšího nároku*, on the other hand, was translated using a source-like strategy by the T1 and T2 translators – *bez dalszych roszczeń / bez jakiegokolwiek innego roszczenia*. The T3 translator simplified the message by omitting the translation of the words *jakéhokoli dalšího*.	

Example No. 5	**Context / text excerpt in Czech**
Fakturace: Faktura bude ***předložena*** v každé sezóně vždy nejpozději do 5. Iedna za aktuálně probíhající sezónu provozu XXX, ve dvojím vyhotovení ***a je splatná do 15 kalendářních dní*** ode dne doručení faktury poskytovateli. Faktura musí obsahovat všechny údaje uvedené v 29 zákona č. 235/2004 Sb., o dani z přidané hodnoty, v platném znění.	
Proposals for translation:	**Translation universals**
T1: Fakturowanie: Faktura *będzie wystawiana* w każdym sezonie nie później niż do 5 stycznia za bieżący sezon funkcjonowania XXX, w dwóch egzemplarzach *z terminem płatności 15 dni* kalendarzowych od daty doręczenia faktury do wykonawcy.	E, N
T2: Fakturowanie: Faktura *zostanie przedstawiona* w każdym sezonie zawsze najpóźniej do 5 stycznia za aktualnie przebiegający sezon funkcjonowania XXX, w dwóch egzemplarzach *i jest płatna do 15 dni* kalendarzowych od dnia doręczenia faktury usługodawcy.	DT, DT
T3: Fakturowanie: Faktura *zostanie przekazana* w każdym sezonie zawsze najdalej do dnia 5-go stycznia za bieżący sezon działalności XXX, w dwóch egzemplarzach. *Termin płatności faktury wynosić będzie 15 dni* kalendarzowych licząc od daty doręczenia faktury usługodawcy.	E, N, S
Comment: Translator T1 translated the lexeme *předložena* using free translation, adapting it to the recipient. He did not translate the lexeme in question literally, as translator T2 did, using a faithful translation with the equivalent *zostanie przedstawiona*. Translator T1 used explicitation, expressing literally what was meant by presenting an invoice, or rather, issuing an invoice. Translator T3, on the other hand, broke out of this situation in yet another way, also by means of an explicitation, pointing to the fact not only that the invoice was issued, but also that it was handed over. With regard to the translation of the sentence fragment *a je splatná do 15 kalendářních dní*, translator T1 used normalisation through the use of the eqivalent *termin płatności*, while translator T2 used a faithful translation in an identical situation (albeit one that deviates slightly from the norm of the target language – the parallel texts usually contain the expression *termin płatności*). In addition to normalisation, translator T3 also used simplification by splitting one long sentence into two shorter ones.	

Example No. 6	Context / text excerpt in Czech
Chybná fakturace: Poskytovatel je oprávněn ***do data splatnosti*** vrátit fakturu, která neobsahuje požadované náležitosti, nebo která obsahuje jiné cenové údaje, než bylo sjednáno v této smlouvě. Doba splatnosti opravné faktury začíná znovu běžet ode dne doručení bezvadné faktury poskytovateli.	
Proposals for translation:	**Translation universals**
T1: *Błędnie wystawiona faktura*: Wykonawca jest uprawniony do zwrotu w terminie płatności faktury, która nie zawiera wymaganych danych lub zawiera inne dane cenowe niż uzgodnione w niniejszej umowie.	E, DT
T2: *Błędne fakturowanie*: Usługodawca uprawniony jest do dnia płatności zwrócić fakturę, która nie zawiera wymaganych wymogów lub która zawiera inne dane cenowe, aniżeli uzgodnione w niniejszej umowie.	DT, DT
T3: *Błędne fakturowanie*: usługodawcy przysługuje prawo zwrotu nieprawidłowo wystawionej faktury do dnia upłynięcia terminu płatności. Błędnie wystawiona faktura nie zawiera obowiązkowych danych lub zawiera inną cenę, niż przyjęta w niniejszej umowie.	DT, S, N
Comment: In the case of the expression *chybná fakturace*, translators T2 and T3 used a faithful translation, while translator T1 used an explicitation. Regarding the syntax of the sentence and its construction (punctuation, passive voice, division of one sentence into two shorter ones), translator T3 has simplified and normalised, while translators T1 and T2 have followed a faithful translation strategy.	
Example No. 7	Context / text excerpt in Czech
Smlouva nabývá platnosti a účinnosti dnem podpisu smlouvy oběma smluvními stranami, nejdříve však dnem jejího uveřejnění v registru smluv.	
Proposals for translation:	**Translation universals**
T1: *Umowa wchodzi w życie i jest skuteczna* z dniem podpisania umowy przez obie strony, nie wcześniej jednak niż z dniem jej opublikowania w rejestrze umów.	DT
T2: *Umowa wchodzi w życie* z dniem jej podpisania przez obie strony umowy, najwcześniej jednak z dniem jej opublikowania w rejestrze umów.	R

T3: *Umowa wchodzi w życie i staje się skuteczną* z dniem jej podpisania przez obydwie strony, najwcześniej jednakże w dniu jej publikacji w rejestrze umów.	DT
Comment: Translators T1 and T2 have kept the translation faithful to the expression *smlouva nabývá platnosti a účinnosti.* Translator T2 made a reduction by excluding the equivalent lexeme *účinnost* from the translation. However, for the proper communication of the content of the source text, the equivalent of this lexeme should be left in place. Indeed, the effectiveness of a contract implies the ability of the contract to produce the intended legal effects, while its mere entry into force does not guarantee this. In this case, a faithful translation is desirable.	
Example No. 8	**Context / text excerpt in Czech**
Smlouva se sjednává na dobu určitou do 15. 3. 2025, přičemž platnost a účinnost této smlouvy nastane nejpozději k datu zveřejnění této smlouvy v registru smluv.	
Proposals for translation:	**Translation universals**
T1: *Umowa zostaje zawarta* na czas określony do dnia 15 marca 2025 r., a ważność i skuteczność tej umowy nastąpi nie później niż w dniu jej opublikowania w rejestrze umów.	N, N
T2: *Umowa uzgodniona zostaje* na czas określony do 15.03.2025, przy czym umowa wejdzie w życie i będzie obowiązywać najpóźniej w dniu jej opublikowania w rejestrze umów.	DT, DT
T3: *Umowa zostaje zawarta* na czas określony, do dnia 15 marca 2025 roku. Umowa wejdzie w życie i stanie się skuteczną najdalej w dniu jej publikacji w rejestrze umów.	N, S
Comment: Translators T1 and T3 applied the usus of the target language, using the equivalent *umowa zostaje zawarta* for the expression *smlouva se sjednává.* Translator T2 used an inadequate expression. In addition, in terms of sentence structure, translator T3 used a simplification, splitting one longer utterance into two shorter ones, translator T2 used a sentence structure faithfully reflecting the Czech sentence formation, while translator T1 translated according to the standard of the target language.	

Example No. 9	Context / text excerpt in Czech
Poskytovatel se zavazuje, že veškerá reklama jím sjednaných reklamních partnerů bude v souladu s platnými právními předpisy, zejména pak ***se zákonem č. 40/1995 Sb., o regulaci reklamy a o změně a doplnění zákona č. 468/1991 Sb., o provozování rozhlasového a televizního vysílání, ve znění pozdejších předpisů.*** Poskytovatel se především výslovně zavazuje, že nedojde ke zveřejnění zakázané reklamy.	
Proposals for translation:	**Translation universals**
T1: Wykonawca zobowiązuje się, że wszelka reklama partnerów reklamowych przez niego zapewnionych będzie zgodna z obowiązującymi przepisami prawa, w szczególności *z ustawą nr 40/1995 Dz.U., o regulacji reklamy i o zmianie ustawy nr 468/1991 Dz.U., w sprawie funkcjonowania radiofonii i telewizji, z późniejszymi zmianami.*	DT, N
T2: Usługodawca zobowiązuje się, że wszelkie reklamy uzgodnionych przez niego partnerów reklamowych będą zgodne z obowiązującymi przepisami prawa, w szczególności zaś *z ustawą nr 40/1995 Sb., o regulacji reklamy i zmianach oraz uzupełnieniu ustawy nr 468/1991 Sb., o prowadzeniu transmisji radiowych i telewizyjnych, z późniejszymi zmianami.*	DT, N
T3: Usługodawca zobowiązuje się, że wszystkie ogłoszenia potencjalnych reklamodawców spełniać będą wymogi obowiązujących przepisów prawa, w szczególności zaś *ustawy nr 40/1995 Dz. U., w sprawie regulacji reklamy oraz uzupełnienia ustawy nr 468/1991 Dz. U., w sprawie transmisji radiowych i telewizyjnych, z późniejszymi zmianami.*	S, N

Komentarz:
A first glance at the beginning of the sentence gives the impression that translators T1 and T2 used a faithful, source-like translation, while translator T3 used a free translation, more adapted to the audience (we are referring in particular to the sentence formation, and the simplifications used when creating the equivalent expression *sjednaných reklamních partnerů*). An analysis of the second part of the sentence shows that creating equivalents for the names of laws or regulations is always problematic for translators. While it is possible to consult EUR-Lex and check the accepted standard for the naming of legal acts, the hitherto untranslated names of laws always pose a challenge for the translator. In this case, all the translators adopted practically identical equivalents in the form of *o / w sprawie regulacji reklamy i o zmianie ustawy* for the Czech name of the Act *o regulaci reklamy a o změně a doplnění zákona,* while in the case of the subsequent name of the Act *o provozování rozhlasového a televizního vysílání, ve znění pozdejších předpisů*, different equivalents were used. Translator T1 used the equivalent *w sprawie funkcjonowania radiofonii i telewizji*, which can be assessed as an effort to preserve the Polish terminological usus (there is a Broadcasting Act in Poland), for such an equivalent there are also numerous attestations in the EUR-Lex database. Translators T2 and T3 used an equivalent, using terminology close to the terminological usus of the target language – *w sprawie transmisji radiowych i telewizyjnych*. It may be considered that none of the above equivalents restricts the correct understanding of the meaning of the source text's message, however, translator T1 has adopted the applicable standard for the naming of the law in question.

Example No. 10	Context / text excerpt in Czech
Účetní vypořádání této smluvní pokuty bude realizováno ***v souladu s platnými účetními a daňovými právními předpisy***.	
Proposals for translation:	**Translation universals**
T1: Rozliczenie księgowe tej kary umownej zostanie przeprowadzone *zgodnie z obowiązującymi przepisami rachunkowymi i podatkowymi.*	R, N
T2: Księgowe rozliczenie niniejszej kary umownej zostanie zrealizowane *zgodnie z obowiązującymi przepisami księgowymi i podatkowymi.*	R, N
T3: Rozliczenie powyższej kary umownej będzie *zgodne z obowiązującymi przepisami prawa w zakresie podatków i księgowości.*	S, E

Comment: In the case under review, we can reflect on the adequate translation of terms such as *účetní předpisy / daňové předpisy / právní předpisy*. In general, *účetní předpisy* means accounting regulations (i.e., regulations on bookkeeping), *daňové předpisy* means tax regulations (i.e., regulations that regulate tax settlements), and *právní předpisy* means legal regulations. Typically, contracts will either include accounting provisions alone, tax provisions alone, or legal provisions alone. The sentence under consideration should include such a formulation which, as in the source text, covers all three types of provisions. The T1 and T2 translators left out the translation of the phrase *právní předpisy* in their translations, focusing on equivalents relating to translations of tax and accounting regulations, aiming to achieve an expression in line with the norm of the target language. Only the T3 translator kept the translation faithful, changing the structure of the statement while retaining the complete content of the message (he used simplification and explicitation to do so).	
Example No. 11	**Context / text excerpt in Czech**
V případě prodlení poskytovatele se zaplacením ***bezchybné faktury***, vystavené zadavatelem v souladu s čl. 3 této smlouvy, má zadavatel právo na smluvní pokutu ve výši 0,5 % z dlužné částky a to za každý den prodlení, až do úplného zaplacení. Smluvní pokuta se stává splatnou dnem následujícím po dni, ve kterém na ni vznikl nárok.	
Proposals for translation:	**Translation universals**
T1: W przypadku zwłoki wykonawcy w zapłacie *skorygowanej faktury* wystawionej przez zamawiającego zgodnie z art. 3 niniejszej umowy, zamawiającemu przysługuje kara umowna w wysokości 0,5 % od należnej kwoty za każdy dzień zwłoki do momentu jej pełnego zapłacenia.	E
T2: W przypadku zwłoki usługodawcy z zapłatą *prawidłowej faktury*, wystawionej przez zamawiającego zgodnie z art. 3 niniejszej umowy, zamawiający ma prawo do kary umownej w wysokości 0,5 % z zaległej kwoty za każdy dzień zwłoki aż do całkowitej zapłaty.	N
T3: W przypadku zwłoki w zapłacie *faktury niezawierającej błędów*, wystawionej przez zamawiającego zgodnie z art. 3 niniejszej umowy, zamawiającemu przysługuje prawo do naliczenia kary umownej w wysokości 0,5 % od kwoty zadłużenia, za każdy dzień zwłoki, aż do momentu otrzymania zapłaty w pełnej wysokości.	N

Comment: In the example in question, the expression *bezchybná faktura* is analysed. The literal equivalent *bezbłędna faktura* would unfortunately not convey the sense of the statement implied by the original text. With reference to the earlier paragraph of the agreement, it is clear from the wording that what is meant is an invoice that does not have deficiencies due to the statutory requirements for a fiscal document, as well as ordinary errors – for example, calculation errors or errors concerning a predetermined price. The T1 translator used the translation *skorygowanej faktury*, using explicitation (because he assumed that the content referred to an earlier paragraph of the contract, so that it was now referring to an invoice that had already been stripped of its earlier errors, so corrected). Unfortunately, this translation may turn out to be wrong if the recipient does not know the context of the entire contract. The T2 translator adopted the functional equivalent *prawidłowa faktura*, which fits as closely as possible to the message in the original text and is in line with the norm of the target language. The T3 translator aimed to include the error message in the translation, and so used the descriptive equivalent *faktura niezawierająca błędów*, which also captures the sense of the source language message.	
Example No. 12	**Context / text excerpt in Czech**
V případě vypovězení této smlouvy v souladu s čl. 5.2. a 7.1. této smlouvy a v případě porušení povinností poskytovatele uvedených v čl. 7.1. této smlouvy má zadavatel právo na jednorázovou smluvní pokutu ve výši XXX Kč. ***Smluvní pokuta se stává splatnou*** dnem následujícím po dni, ve kterém na ni vznikl nárok. Smluvní pokutou dle tohoto odstavce není dotčeno právo zadavatele na náhradu škody.	
Proposals for translation:	**Translation universals**
T1: Kara umowna *staje się płatna* następnego dnia po dniu powstania prawa do niej.	DT
T2: Kara umowna *jest płatna* z dniem następującym po dniu, w którym powstało do niej roszczenie.	DT
T3: *Wymagalność kary* umownej nastaje z dniem następującym po dniu, w którym powstało roszczenie do niej.	S, N
Komentarz: The T1 and T2 translators used a source-like translation strategy – a translation faithful to the source text. The T3 translator simplified the construction of the sentence by using the equivalent *wymagalność*, thus bringing the translation into line with the standard of the target language. In the NKJP for the lexeme *maturity* there are numerous attestations referring to the required date of payment of a claim, for example: *wymagalność świadczenia/składki/roszczenia/długu wierzytelności.*	

Example No. 13	Context / text excerpt in Czech
Uchazeč podpisem této smlouvy prohlašuje, ***že má vyrovnané závazky*** vůči statutárnímu městu Brnu, městským částem statutárního města Brna, právnickým osobám zřízeným nebo založeným statutárním městem Brnem, nebo některou z jeho městských částí včetně těch právnických osob, ve kterých má statutární město Brno nebo některá z jeho městských částí podíl, a zavazuje se, že tento stav udrží po celou dobu trvání smluvního vztahu.	
Proposals for translation:	**Translation universals**
T1: Podpisując niniejszą umowę, wnioskodawca oświadcza, *że nie ma żadnych nieuregulowanych zobowiązań* wobec […].	E
T2: Oferent przez podpisanie niniejszej umowy oświadcza, *że ma rozliczone zobowiązania* wobec […]	DT
T3: Ofert poprzez podpisanie niniejszej umowy oświadcza, *że nie posiada żadnych przeterminowanych zobowiązań* wobec […]	E
Comment: Translators T1 and T3 used a modulation technique in their translations, replacing an affirmative sentence with a negative one. They also made use of explicitation, expressing directly the message contained in the initial text, i.e., that the bidder is not in arrears with any payments to the contracting authority. Translator T2 used a faithful translation, translating the content of the source text literally.	
Example No. 14	**Context / text excerpt in Czech**
Tato smlouva nabývá platnosti a účinnosti dnem jejího podpisu *oprávněnými zástupci* obou smluvních stran.	
Proposals for translation:	**Translation universals**
T1: Niniejsza Umowa wchodzi w życie i obowiązuje w dniu jej podpisania *przez upoważnionych przedstawicieli* obu stron.	DT
T2: Niniejsza umowa wchodzi w życie z dniem jej podpisania *przez upoważnionych przedstawicieli* obu stron umowy.	DT
T3: Niniejsza umowa wchodzi w życie i staje się skuteczną z chwilą jej podpisania przez *umocowanych reprezentantów* stron.	R, N

Comment:
Translators T1 and T2 used a faithful, source-like translation. In contrast, translator T3 used not only a reduction (he omitted the lexeme *obu*, it is clear from the contract that there are only two parties to the contract, so the expression *reprezentantów* implicitly already contains the information that it refers to the representative of each party to the contract), but also a normalisation – in the Civil Code, expressions such as *wspólnik umocowany do reprezentacji* are most common, and there are numerous attestations in the NKJP for expressions of a similar nature: *był dobrze umocowany w partyjnym aparacie / bardzo silnie umocowany minister / odpowiednio umocowany urzędnik*.

3.1.8.1. Summary

1. What universals have been identified in translations of the cooperation agreement?

Example number	E (explicitation)	S (simplification)	N (normalisation)	R (reduction)	DT (discourse transfer)
1	•		•		•
2		•	•		•
3		•	•		•
4		•	•		•
5	•	•	•		•
6	•	•	•		•
7				•	•
8		•	•		•
9		•	•		•
10	•	•	•	•	
11	•		•		
12		•	•		•
13	•				•
14			•	•	•

2. Frequency of universals of a given type in translations of the cooperation agreement

Example number	E (explicitation)	S (simplification)	N (normalisation)	R (reduction)	DT (discourse transfer)
1	•		•••		••
2		•	•		•
3		•	••		••
4		•	••		•••
5	••	•	••		••
6	•	•	•		••••
7				•	••
8		•	•••		••
9		•	•••		••
10	•	•	••	••	
11	•		••		
12		•	•		••
13	••				•
14			•	•	••

3. Graph of the frequency of translation universals in translations of the cooperation agreement

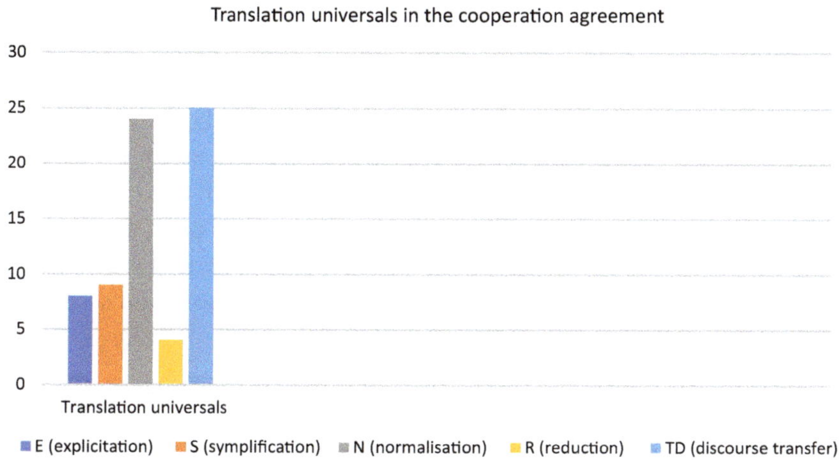

Source: Own elaboration

3.1.9 Conclusions and summary of the contract analysis

3.1.9.1. Summary of the study and conclusions

The main research objective was to answer the question of whether there are translation universals, as hypothesised by Mona Baker, in Czech-Polish translations of civil law contracts. Research on the peculiarities of translation has so far been carried out mainly in relation to translations made from Western European and Scandinavian languages, hence the research undertaken was an attempt to provide a new perspective on translators' decision-making behaviour in a group of (closely related) Slavic languages. The research carried out for this work was the author's own, and some of the author's initial assumptions about how it would be carried out had to be reviewed and changed. The following are some observations and comments on the research itself.

1. Initially, the author envisaged that, with the Sketch Engine, the analytical work would be highly automated. Having created the author's corpus of civil law contracts, amounting to more than 1 million words, the author was not entirely satisfied with the result. Making observations on translation universals required not only a collection of different translations of many types of civil law contracts but also some pictorial research material. The author, therefore, decided to select six types of civil law contracts (lease, donation, sale, commission, contract of specific work, and cooperation agreement). The authentic texts of these contracts, after prior anonymisation, were provided for translation. To ensure an equal level of translation competence, five sworn translators (from Poland and the Czech Republic) were commissioned.
2. The analysis of the translations was partly manual and partly automated. The author manually selected the analysed text passages and then, referring to the definitions of the various universals, attempted to pick up certain characteristic behaviours of the translators from the translations.
3. The reference corpora were NKJP, InterCorp, the EUR-Lex legislative database, and parallel texts. Parallel texts and the corpus of the Polish language were most helpful.
4. The greatest difficulty for the author was to make an objective assessment of the quality of the translation and to correctly identify

universals. The identified universals were sometimes intertwined (normalisation was accompanied by simplification and explicitation by normalisation). This part of the research was very arduous, full of uncertainties and the need to make decisions about the phenomena identified.

5. During her research, the author sought to follow the translators' thinking, follow their decision-making process, and make observations of the techniques and translation strategies they undertook.
6. Also, the initial concept of a supplementary survey in the form of an email questionnaire was modified. The questionnaires sent were not completed by the respondents promptly, sometimes the answers were too vague, and the results did not reflect the real translation services industry. The author decided to modify the research method. A scenario for a free in-depth interview was prepared and then, due to the epidemic situation, the interview was conducted by telephone. In the author's opinion, this method led to more reliable material and real and more honest opinions from respondents.

3.1.9.2. Summary of the research findings

As already noted, the Research Material consisted of translations of six civil law contracts from Czech into Polish by five different sworn translators, both Polish and Czech. A total of approximately 130 translation problems were selected from all contracts. These were discussed with reference to the author's Czech-Polish corpus of civil law contracts (numbering over 1 million words), reference corpora (the Czech and Polish national corpora), the Czech and Polish civil codes, and the EUR-Lex corpus of EU legal acts. By making observations in the selected examples, the author also tried to observe which strategies and techniques were used by the translators and to find out the determinants of these choices.

The universals observed include explicitation, normalisation, discourse transfer, reduction, and simplification. It should be noted that one of the universals – the distinctive distribution of lexical units – was excluded from the study due to the extensiveness of the research material required to investigate it. A chart summarising the frequency of universals in all the contracts analysed is presented below (Fig. 16).

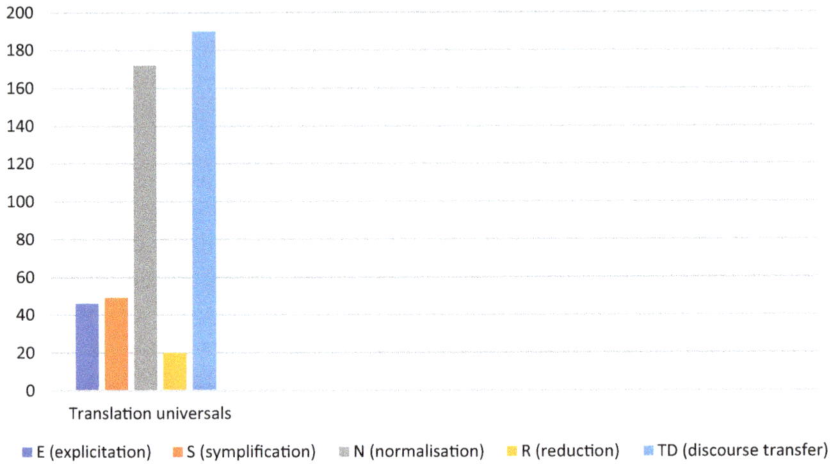

Fig. 16: Translation universals – a summary statement of all the agreements analysed
Source: Own elaboration based on the research conducted.

Out of the 477 total universals observed and recorded, discourse transfer was the most common (190 cases), followed by normalisation (172 cases), simplification (49 cases), explicitation (46 cases), and the least common was reduction (20 cases).

When analysing translations of civil law contract texts, the author noted the occurrence of discourse transfer wherever, in the example studied, the utterance being translated was constructed directly under the influence of the source text rather than in conformity with the norm of the target language. This phenomenon occurred, for example, at the level of syntax, as it was quite easy to recognise the translational character of a text by the very fact that the sentences in the target language retained, due to interference, the syntactic features of the sentences of the original language (cf. Kraskowska, 2018). Discourse transfer appeared most often at the level of sentence formation and structure when complex sentences occurred, punctuation was used sparingly in Czech source texts, and a high lexical density – a high saturation of specialised terminology and phraseology – could additionally be observed. It could be observed that the translators try to faithfully reflect the original text in the translation. It also happened that one or two translators used discourse transfer, while a third translator made a free translation using normalisation so that it sounded more natural in the language of the recipient. A greater familiarity with the terminology and genre conventions of the target language was then apparent in the translator who applied normalisation. According to the author, very often in such situations, one could get the impression that the translator who does not use discourse transfer works with parallel texts and has more familiarity with the legal system of the target language. Another conclusion is the observation that translations in the Czech-Polish pair are more prone to the phenomenon of interference, i.e., that the influence of the source language on the language of translation is visible. This is because Czech and Polish belong to the same group of West Slavic languages. Sometimes, as a result of interference, numerous linguistic calques or an unnatural copy of Czech sentence formation could be observed in the translations. It can also be argued that discourse transfer was evident wherever the translator employed a source-like translation strategy.

Normalisation was the second most common universal. The author noted this phenomenon wherever the translator adapted the translation to the standard of the target language. From the observations made, it can be concluded that standardisation has often been used when translating contractual clauses, as well as certain well-known phrases often found in civil law contracts. The use of this procedure demonstrates a certain linguistic erudition on the part of the translator and a very good knowledge of the usus of the target language. Translations made using this universal are characterised by their ease of reception and naturalness. According to the subjective opinion of the author, such texts are more acceptable to the recipients. For example, when law firms serving clients commission translations, Polish lawyers expect that the translation should be readable at the level of the Polish language standard.

Simplification was used by translators most often to simplify the syntax of complex sentences, as well as to make the message less complicated. The use of simplification had the effect of improving the textual fit of the translation. On the other hand, translators are very often apprehensive about using such a procedure for specialised texts, the translation of which requires a high degree of precision and accuracy, as well as care in preserving all the information contained in the source text. Simplification usually involved extended sentences or multi-word phrases in a foreign language that could be expressed more simply in Polish.

Explication did not appear very often in the translations, and if it was present, it usually occurred when the Polish linguistic norm required the content to be added. This was usually the addition of a pronoun, the repetition of a noun that in Czech had already been omitted from the syntax of the sentence, or the expression of the implicit content of the source text directly.

Reduction was used most often when there was repetition in the source text or sentences were overly elaborate. Observing the translators' behaviour in relation to the translations cited, it can also be concluded that translations rich in universals such as normalisation or simplification were made by translators of Polish nationality who were more familiar with the usus of the target language. They were bolder in their use of reduction and explicitation, while the Czech translators were far more cautious in their translation, attempting to faithfully convey the message contained in the source text.

The most important conclusion from this research, in the author's opinion, is that the specific behaviour of translators affects the quality of translation. Many of the examples given indicated the use of source translation, where there was an opportunity to use normalisation. Observing two, and sometimes three, different ways of translating the same text, one gets the impression that adapting the translation to the norm of the target language is possible and influences how the recipient reads the text in the target language. An example is the expression *kontaktní osoba*, which has been translated as *osoba kontaktowa* or with the use of explicitation as *osoba do kontaktów*. For the Polish reader – the entrepreneur who reads the contract – the second option is clearer (it is clear that it will be about the person with whom he or she will potentially be in contact on behalf of the counterparty). The Czech acronym *IČ* has several variants in Polish translations, of which the two most common are *numer identyfikacyjny* or *REGON* – it must be acknowledged that the use of the functional equivalent (option 2) makes it easier for the Polish public to understand the importance of the designation used. Translators should also reach for explicitation to exclude ambiguous or questionable understanding of the translation. In the example of *předmět smlouvy a jeho účel*, the importance of nuance can be seen. The options proposed by the translators (*przedmiot umowy i jego cel* and *przedmiot umowy i cel umowy*) show that the details matter a great deal. When looking at translations of contracts from Czech into Polish, it is easy to see that the Polish version is usually longer, often precisely as a result of the use of explicitation or the division of longer sentences in the source language into several shorter ones in the target language. The Polish law system and the Czech law system fall within the same continental law system, so theoretically, the incompatibility of the legal systems should be much less acute for translators of this language pair than for translators of English, as there is a significant difference between the Polish law system (statute law) and the British law system (case law) (cf. Kizinska, 2015: 7). But even this does not exclude numerous uncertainties for translators in their decision-making process when dealing, for example, with different semantic scopes of apparently the same concepts. Just to cite the first example: the Czech *jednatel* is most often translated as *prezes zarządu* in Polish. The Polish phrase *prezes zarządu* has the Czech equivalent *předseda představenstva*, and the Polish equivalent *członek zarządu* should be adequate for the Czech word *jednatel*. The trouble is that the Czech *jednatel* has a much broader remit than the Polish *członek zarządu* and is closer to the Polish *prezes zarządu*. Very often translators use the equivalent *prezes* as a functional equivalent, as Polish clients occupying the position of *jednatel* in Czech limited liability companies even expect to be shown in the registration documents as holding the position of chairman, not member of the management board.[157] The second important point is that the Czech Civil Code has not been translated into Polish, just as the Polish Civil Code has not been translated into Czech – in the case of English, there are translations into Czech and into Polish of English-language acts. Translators of the Polish-Czech language pair therefore very often have doubts that they are unable to resolve using reference materials. It remains for them to systematically improve their translation skills, do analytical work with parallel texts, and be active in the community of translation organisations. It is basically impossible for a good translator not to attend training courses

157 The above comment refers to the author's experience in cooperating with both Polish entrepreneurs and Polish law firms that use documents translated from Polish in legal transactions.

and conferences. Translation knowledge is dynamically evolving all the time, and only translators can keep their knowledge up to date and improve it. The question of the translator's path to experience is the subject of much academic and non-academic discussion. Marta Chromá (like Chris Durban, as discussed earlier in this paper) believes that it would be ideal for a translator of legal and juridical texts to do a work placement in an international legal consultancy firm. Daily contact with lawyers allows for immediate feedback on the differences in the legal systems of the countries of the translated language pair, gaining proficiency in the use of the correct legal terminology in both languages, as well as entailing continuous comparative analysis of the legal systems accompanying the daily work. Also, working in an environment with a larger number of translators solving problems of the same nature provides an excellent source of knowledge and an opportunity to exchange insights and experiences (Chromá, 2014: 37). This suggestion could also be applied to translators of specialised texts. Working in a particular industry provides an excellent source of knowledge for the translator in terms of specialised terminology or the opportunity to learn about the company's processes. All these factors are later reflected in the quality of the specialised translation. Referring to the results of the survey conducted as a free in-depth interview, such an idea of translators' training or work experience would meet the expectations of the principals. Still, quality and timeliness play a key role for companies commissioning specialised translations, while machine translation remains a question of future technological developments. Theory and practice complement each other in the translation industry – the pillars of a thorough knowledge of translation theory, the practical rules of the profession, and the translator's responsibility for the translation play an important role in his or her daily work. Clients expect a translation that not only reflects the message of the source text both in form and in content.

3.2. Environmental survey (email questionnaire and in-depth interview)Environmental survey

3.2.1. Survey characteristics

The purpose of the email questionnaire and the free in-depth interview was to find out the perceptions of translation by the principals (clients commissioning translation of a text into another language), the contractors (sworn and specialist translators), and the people who use translated texts in their professional work (notaries, lawyers, entrepreneurs). A separate group of respondents were translation agencies, which are both principals (they act as intermediaries in the transfer of texts to be translated to freelancers) and contractors (it is the agencies that physically settle the orders, which they do not carry out themselves, but for which they are responsible for the execution and final result). The original concept of the study was to obtain responses through a community interview. Subsequently, influenced by the global epidemic situation, the author decided to obtain responses by email by sending out questionnaires to respondents. Unfortunately, the response time of the respondents was getting longer. Their busy schedules made the author decide to conduct free in-depth telephone interviews. In both the email questionnaire and the in-depth interview, the questions were predominantly open-ended. The questionnaire was answered anonymously.

3.2.1.1. Email questionnaire

The following questions were included in an email questionnaire to principals and those who use translation in their professional activities:

1. The incompatibility of legal systems and non-equivalent terms pose a major challenge for the translator. In this area, do you perceive a problem with the quality of the translations you use?
2. In your opinion, what makes the reception of a translation difficult?
3. In your opinion, what should be included in the training programme for future translators to ensure that the translations they produce are of high quality?
4. What, in your opinion, has the greatest influence on the good reception of the translation performed – its high quality?
5. Machine translation is becoming increasingly popular. For many people, Google Translate, for example, is a convenience. Do you happen to use such tools, or in your opinion could they potentially replace a translator?
6. Have you had to deal with a mistranslation? How has this affected the quality of your work?

In the questionnaire addressed to the translators, the author of the study asked for the number of years of professional practice and the type of translations performed (specialist/certified, translation/interpretation). Respondents were then asked the following questions:

1. The incompatibility of legal systems and non-equivalent terms pose a major challenge for the translator. In this area, what strategies and techniques help you to deal with such difficult situations during execution?
2. What tools make your job easier?
3. In your opinion, what should be included in the training programme for future translators?
4. What, in your opinion, has the greatest impact on the quality of a translation?
5. Machine translation is a hot topic in the translation community. How do you see the potential automation of the translation process – as a threat to the translation profession or rather as an opportunity to increase the quality of translations?
6. Why do you think the work of a translator is interesting and worth undertaking? What predispositions does such work require?

3.2.1.2. Free in-depth interview

The questions in the email questionnaire were also used during the free in-depth interview. Respondents in these interviews were translators and businesspeople only (translation agencies only responded via questionnaires). When conducting these interviews, the author adopted the scenario presented below.[158]

158 The scenario was inspired by an individual in-depth interview scenario conducted with key representatives of NGOs, foundations, and associations actively involved in the social and vocational rehabilitation of people with disabilities, developed by the State Fund for the Rehabilitation of People with Disabilities, the Institute of Labour and Social Affairs, and the Social Opinion Research Centre in 2013. The scenario is available at www.ipiss.com.pl [15.06.2021].

Scenario for an individual in-depth interview with an entrepreneur or translation user		
Subject	**Specific issues (questions)**	**Comments**
Business area of the respondent	What industry do you operate in?	*Respondents include notaries, lawyers, and entrepreneurs.*
Scope of use of translations	What kind of translations do you deal with in your work?	*The question seeks to determine whether it is about translations of technical/specialist text, or whether this is about sworn translations.*
The problem of incompatibility of legal systems / non-equivalent terms	Do you perceive a problem of incompatibility of legal systems in the translations you deal with? ➜ <u>If not</u>, what is the cause? Do you use translations of legal/juridical texts? What kind of texts are these? ➜ <u>If so</u>, to what extent? What is the problem you experience with translations – does the translator not perceive the differences in legal systems and this is clearly visible in the translation, or does the translator perceive the differences in legal systems and highlight this issue in the translation? How can you see this issue? Do you perceive a problem with translations of non-equivalent terms? ➜ <u>If not</u>, what could be the cause? In your opinion, are there any non-equivalent terms in the texts you are dealing with? What is the nature of the translated texts you work with? ➜ <u>If so</u>, in which situations / for which texts / is it possible to give examples? Please give an example of a text in which an indefinite term appeared, and the translator had to find a solution to translate it in a way that was understandable to the audience.	*If the respondent uses translations of legal and juridical texts, the interview moves towards an analysis of the reception of texts of this nature; if the respondent uses translations of specialised texts – for example, technical texts – the interview focuses on real-life examples and the respondent's experience of the practical application of translations of such texts. If the respondent does not understand the expression 'non-equivalent term', the interviewer clarifies and elaborates so as to elicit a response. If the respondent is dealing with technical, specialised translations, the interviewer tries to ask what terms could potentially have been difficult for the translator to translate and how the translator dealt with them.*

Scenario for an individual in-depth interview with an entrepreneur or translation user		
Acceptance of a translation / quality of a translation	In your opinion, what makes the reception of a translation difficult? Please provide examples from your life. In your opinion, what elements are indicative of good translation quality?	*The aim is to get an accurate, precise answer supported by examples about what made the text they had to work with, which was a translation, incomprehensible to them, difficult to read, or questionable in terms of explicitness.* *The aim is to find out what the client values in the translation, what makes the text a good tool for their work and meets their expectations.*
Interpreter training	Using different types of translations, you may notice that sometimes the translator does better with the translation, but also that sometimes the translator has problems translating the text properly. In your opinion, what could further training/education of translators potentially look like, what do you think could help translators beyond their linguistic skills in their work?	*The respondent, through working with the translated text, may 'evidently' perceive some shortcomings in the translator's knowledge, perhaps he or she would have some ideas on how the translator could help themselves to do their work better.*

Scenario for an individual in-depth interview with an entrepreneur or translation user		
Machine translation	Machine translation is becoming more and more popular, with Google Translate making things easier for many people. Did you happen to use such tools? ➜ If so, in which situations? What kind of tool was it? Was the tool helpful? Was the translation obtained reliable? Was the resulting translation workable in practical use? Why did you choose to use such a tool rather than have the translation done by a translator? Do you regret your decision to use machine translation? ➜ If not, why have you never used Google Translate, for example? What is your opinion on machine translation, do you see the possibility of artificial intelligence displacing the translation profession? ➜ If so, what might such a process look like in the future in the industry in which you work? (The process of displacement of the translation profession by AI) ➜ If not, what, in your opinion, makes the translator's position still strong enough that it is not threatened by machines?	*Ask the respondent if he or she understands the concept of machine translation, and possibly explain and give examples of machine translation. The aim is to find out about the respondent's experience with machine translation, perhaps he or she has had an experience with a mistranslation that caused negative consequences in his or her work, or maybe, on the contrary, it provided a quick translation to speed up the process of signing a lucrative contract or solving a sudden fault on the work site? Ask for details, examples, and real-life experiences.* *It is important to ask how it is possible, with the popularity of Google Translate, that the respondent has never used this tool – perhaps there are specialist translators in the company, or perhaps the respondent speaks a language that is not included in Google Translate? Be more specific and ask what makes the respondent not reach for such a tool, maybe they have some concerns – what are they?*

Scenario for an individual in-depth interview with an entrepreneur or translation user		
Working with mistranslation – consequences	Have you ever been in a situation where a mistranslation directly affected your work? ➜ If not, potentially, if such a situation were to occur, what threats do you see to your work? ➜ If so, please give an example of what happened as a consequence of using the wrong translation. Have you suffered personal or professional consequences as a result, of what nature? How has your approach to translators changed as a result of this incident, do you now review the skills of a translator before commissioning a translation? How? In the end, is such verification effective – that is, have you not encountered more mistranslations as a result?	*The aim is to elicit the most detailed information from the respondent in terms of the consequences – professional, practical, and personal – if a mistranslated text is used in their work. If possible and not forbidden by company/trade secrets, we ask the respondent to provide the history and details of such an event – what the error was about, when it was verified, whether it was possible to undo the effects of using the mistranslation, etc.*

Source: Author's own elaboration.

When conducting free in-depth interviews with the translators, the author adopted the scenario presented in the following pages.

Scenario for an individual in-depth interview with a translator		
Subject	**Specific issues (questions)**	**Comments**
Activities of the respondent	What powers do you have to provide translations? What kind of translations do you do?	*The respondents are sworn and specialist translators.* *Translators may have a variety of specialisations, they may also do only translation or only interpretation, for example – the purpose of the question is to identify precisely what the respondent does, what they specialise in.*
Experience	Please indicate how many years you have been translating. If you are a sworn translator, please indicate the year of qualification.	*The aim is to determine the experience of respondents in terms of the number of years they have been translating. The respondents in this case are exclusively people who make a living from translation and are self-employed in this way.*
The problem of incompatibility of legal systems / non-equivalent terms	What strategies and techniques help you to deal with situations where you face the problem of incompatibility of legal systems / non-equivalent terms during translation? If possible, please provide an example of a text in which you encountered such a problem, cite the problem you had to solve, and state the solution you used.	*It is about talking about real-life situations from the translator's practice. Allow the respondent to tell as much as possible, in as much detail as possible, about real-life situations in which they had to think hard about solving a particular problem.*

Scenario for an individual in-depth interview with a translator		
Tools in the translator's work	What tools make your job as a translator easier? Do you use machine translation? ➜ If not, why not? ➜ If so, what are the tools? Do you use paid or free tools? How do you address the issue of personal data protection? Do you consider attending industry workshops and conferences to be an important tool in your work? ➜ If so, how often do you attend such events, please give the name of the event or the type of training; per year – how many such events do you attend? Does the charge for attending such a meeting determine your decision to attend? ➜ If not, why do you not attend such meetings? Do you create glossaries yourself? ➜ If so, how, with what tools? How do you archive them? ➜ If not, why not? Do you use CAT tools? ➜ If so, which ones? How often do you use them – daily, several times a month? What made you decide to buy a CAT licence and start using it? ➜ If not, why not? What tools do you lack at work and why? How could they potentially affect your work?	*The aim of the questions is to find out as precisely as possible what translators use in their daily work, what tools help them and why they are so keen to use them. Perhaps there are tools that are out of their financial reach, which translators would love to use in their work, but cannot due to lack of resources? Ask whether the translator works with a proofreader, consultant, or other translator who supports him or her in their daily work. Or perhaps there are tools that the translator must have due to signed cooperation agreements or qualifications – please ask and clarify.* *How does the translator perceive cooperation with other translators and mutual contacts/meetings/workshops in the translation community – is it a waste of time, an unnecessary expense, or rather a source of industry information and a stimulus to improve one's translation skills? Ask the interpreter/translator.*

Scenario for an individual in-depth interview with a translator		
Interpreter/translator training	How do you think translator training should be structured?	*The conversation on this point can start with the history of training and retraining the translator. Ask which part of his or her educational history he or she finds most valuable for his or her current job, and what the translator lacks in terms of knowledge and skills. Ask the translator what training or studies would help them in their work, you can ask if they have undertaken postgraduate studies or why they have not thought about complementary education at all. Perhaps the translator would have some valuable training tips and advice for students potentially thinking of pursuing the translation profession.*
Quality of translation	What, in your opinion, has the greatest impact on the quality of a translation?	*Steer the conversation in such a direction that the translator responds to the issues of high- and low-quality translation. The financial aspect, the time aspect, and the client's expectations may come up in the conversation. When is the translator satisfied with the translation and when is the translator aware that he or she has handed in a job with shortcomings; does the translator always carry out a revision of the translation? Do they work with a proofreader? Does the translator communicate with the client in his or her work and clarify concerns? Does the translator take on every job, or do they refuse when they are unsure of their competence?*

Scenario for an individual in-depth interview with a translator		
Machine translation	Machine translation is becoming more and more popular, with Google Translate making things easier for many people. Have you ever used such tools? ➜ If so, in which situations? What kind of tool was it? Was the tool helpful? Was the translation obtained reliable? Why did you decide to use such a tool? Do you regret your decision to use machine translation? ➜ If not, why have you never used Google Translate, for example? What is your opinion on machine translation, do you see the possibility of artificial intelligence displacing the translation profession? ➜ If so, what might such a process look like in the future in the translation industry? (The process of displacement of the translation profession by AI) ➜ If not, what, in your opinion, makes the translator's position still strong enough that the machines do not threaten it? How do you see the automation of the translation process?	

Scenario for an individual in-depth interview with a translator		
Translator's work – views and opinions	Why, in your opinion, is the job of a translator interesting and worth taking up, and what predispositions does such a job require?	*A question to close and summarise the whole conversation. Its aim is to find out the translator's opinion of his or her profession, how he or she perceives it. Does the translator enjoy his or her job? What is it about the job that they dislike and would like to change – can they do this and what would they need to do to do so? What factors hinder his or her work and what factors make it better?*

Source: Author's own elaboration.

3.2.2. Results of the study – conclusions and summary

A total of 45 respondents from both Poland and the Czech Republic took part in the survey. The breakdown of the respondents was as follows:

- 5 translation agencies – all agencies were interviewed via questionnaires;
- 2 notaries – one notary provided a questionnaire response, the other notary was interviewed by the author;
- 4 law firms – one law firm responded via a questionnaire;
- 4 accountancy offices – responses were mainly given in the form of an interview due to the lack of time of staff/owners of accountancy offices;
- 20 sworn translators – translators mainly responded via questionnaires;
- 10 entrepreneurs – the author interviewed all entrepreneurs.

In summary, the author managed to obtain 27 responses from email questionnaires and conducted 18 interviews. It should be noted that the responses varied widely – some were elaborate and detailed, while some were very concise and modest in volume – in the author's opinion, this is due to the amount of time respondents took to respond. Nonetheless, the material collected makes it possible to present a perspective on translation work and the work of the translator. The results of the analysis are presented below, broken down by type of respondent and question topic, such as the incompatibility of legal systems and non-equivalent terms and their meaning in translation, tools in the translator's work, the perception of the translation by the contractor, translator training, translation quality, machine translation, the translator's perception of the work, and working with mistranslation in the case of the contractor.

3.2.2.1. Translation agencies

Five translation agencies participated in the survey – two from Poland and three from the Czech Republic. These are nationwide offices (Czech/Polish), handling orders in around 50 different languages. Each office has between 2,000 and 4,000 translators, producing thousands of pages of translations per month. In assessing the quality of the responses provided, the author would like to emphasise that they were very precise, detailed, full of examples, and valuable in terms of evaluating the survey as a whole. Above all, agencies have a dual perspective – that of both principal and contractor – which adds to the value of their responses. At the outset, it should be stressed that each agency places a very strong emphasis on the process of verifying the **competence of the translators** with whom it works. This is not only because of the standards by which agencies are bound but also because of the responsibility, including financial, of the agency for the translation delivered to the client. In order to work with agencies, the translator not only has to prove his or her educational and professional background but is also required to translate sample texts, which are then assessed by proofreaders. In addition, agencies expect translators to be familiar with computer programmes that support translation and to have legal licences for these tools. In addition to CAT knowledge, agencies expect translators to know specialist terminology, as well as editing and proofreading skills. As a result of the advanced recruitment process and the clearly defined expectations placed on the translators, the agencies expressed in the questionnaires that the **problem of non-equivalent terms** and the **incompatibility of legal systems** were somehow alien to them. Respondents assume that they are working with experienced translators, highly qualified professionals who are well-versed in the above issues. In addition, when in doubt, translation agencies use the support of industry specialists, consultants, and proofreaders. Among the real problems mentioned by respondents concerning the reception of translations were linguistic calques, failure to use the correct specialised terminology, and sometimes sticking too closely to the source text, i.e., not being able to adapt the text freely to the needs and expectations of the audience. The result of such actions is a translation that sounds awkward, sometimes giving the impression of a machine translation. The lack of use of paraphrasing, the division of longer sentences into several shorter ones, and the use of non-existent equivalents are the main translation errors mentioned by respondents. Responses emphasised the relevance and importance of the translator reading the text after translation, as well as the role of final proofreading. The agency expects to obtain a text that is 'good to read', that 'reads well' and in which the graphic form of the original text is preserved. Both machine translation and translation support tools are a point of interest for the agency. As far as **machine translation** is concerned, respondents emphasise that the market situation has, in a way, forced them to adapt to the expectations of their clients – agencies use machine translation for large-volume texts.The post-editing service has now firmly established itself in the respondents' service portfolio. Translators, in turn, are expected to be familiar with translation support tools such as SDL Studio, MemSource, Wordfast, Across, or Xbench. According to the respondents, machine translation is already taking hold in some segments. Customers often opt to use machine translation themselves, assuming that post-editing is carried out by a qualified in-house employee. However, there are some industries where the use of automated translation will not be so straightforward – namely all commercial contracts, legal and juridical texts, medical texts, and highly specialised technical texts will always require the intervention of a human who understands what he or she is translating. The issue of **translation errors** is a hotspot of respondents' activities. The team working with the translators is responsible for carrying out final proofreading and revision of the translations to eliminate typing errors, typos, or factual mistakes. The stylistic side of the text is also subject to revision. Nevertheless, **mistakes** do occur. One agency cited an example of the mistranslation of a machine part number. If the component in question had been connected as instructed in the translation, human life could even have been endangered. Fortunately, the error was caught and corrected in time. Another example was when a translation underwent final proofreading, and the proofreader overlooked several errors. The client had the advertising leaflet printed and then, seeing the final form of the leaflet, had it disposed of, while the agency was charged with the cost of re-editing and reprinting the leaflets. This financial responsibility was repeatedly highlighted by respondents. In response to the question of what **translator training** should look like, the role of work experience after philological studies was emphasised. Knowledge of company processes as well as the practical use of specialised vocabulary is highly valued among agencies. Important values include the translator's specialisation in a specific industry, punctuality, and the ability to proofread and post-edit texts as well.

3.2.2.2. Notaries

The survey for notaries had a very narrow focus, as the author wanted to reach those of them who deal with translations in their work. The Czech notary who participated in the survey has a wealth of experience in this area, as he serves numerous Polish clients who carry out their activities in the Czech Republic on a daily basis. In his statements, he confirms that the **incompatibility of legal systems** is a key problem when working with Polish texts to be used in the Czech market. This respondent believes that it is an absolute requirement for a translator to have at least a basic knowledge of Polish and Czech law when carrying out translation assignments of legal and juridical texts, which is directly reflected in the **quality of the translation.** In this respect, the **training of sworn translators** in the Czech Republic, in the opinion of the respondent, is legitimate and well-developed (this refers to the requirement to complete a course/postgraduate study for sworn translators in the field of law). He repeatedly stressed that it is crucial to understand the terminology and semantic ranges of concepts operating in different legal systems. According to the respondent, the ability to grasp differences in legal systems as well as the ability to use the correct terminology are competencies that have a decisive impact on the quality of translation. The Polish notary did not have such extensive experience when it came to working with translations but nevertheless highlighted the problem associated with the different semantic scope of terms used in the Czech and Polish legal systems. During the interview, he recalled a situation where he had drafted a notarial deed in Poland using related documents translated from Czech. This notary saw such drastic differences in the legal provisions that he was forced to have a telephone conversation (consultation) with a Czech notary – the author of the deed that was used to prepare the documentation during the drafting of the Polish deed.[159]

Notaries did not take a position on the issue of **machine translation** and **working with mistranslation**, admitting that these issues are far from both their professional and private interests.

159 This concerned a situation in which a Polish entrepreneur, who was the president of a company and its sole shareholder, concluded a share sale agreement in the Czech Republic 'with himself'. In Poland, such a situation could not take place, while in the Czech Republic it was permissible at the time. The Polish notary needed to have clear and unambiguous confirmation that there was no mistranslation or misrepresentation in the documents, hence the need to consult the Czech notary.

3.2.2.3. Law firms

Four major law firms participated in the survey – two Polish and two Czech, including one specialising in Polish-Czech transactions. All unanimously confirmed that the translator must have knowledge of the law in order to cope with the challenges of **incompatible legal systems.** Lawyers confirm that in their practice they encounter translations in which the translator's lack of understanding of the meaning and differences in the legal systems of different countries is apparent. On a day-to-day basis, they mainly work with certified translations, however, this is not a requirement in all situations, as sometimes translations by specialist translators are sufficient for them. The answer to the question of who carries out the translations for the law firm and how the translator is selected was the same each time – the time taken to complete the translation was the determinant. Law firms work under immense pressure of time and client expectations, so any delay, including that caused by the untimely delivery of a translation of a text necessary to process a case, is unacceptable. The **training of translators** and the **quality of the translation** services provided go hand in hand in the opinion of lawyers. They believe that it is impossible to obtain a good quality translation of a legal or juridical text without adequate training in both philology and the basics of law. The ideal model for translator training, according to respondents, should include training in the concepts of the legal fields concerned and in the differences in legal systems. Without understanding the meaning of the text in the source language, the translator will never be able to correctly complete an assignment for a law firm. These two issues play a key role in the perception of the translation and thus affect the applicability of the translated text to the lawyer's work. Respondents admitted that they do not use **machine translation** because of the nature of their work – such translations require the work of a human being who understands and can interpret the text in the source language and then translate it with the needs of the recipient in mind. Regarding the **experience of mistranslation,** one law firm confirmed that there had been one occasion in their professional practice where the translator had mistranslated the opposing party's statements during the trial, potentially affecting the court's ruling. The error was caught during the trial and corrected, but it was a serious matter and could have ended with negative consequences for the represented party.

3.2.2.4. Accounting offices

In-depth interviews were conducted with four accounting offices specialising in Polish-Czech cooperation. For these respondents, the **issue of non-equivalent terms** was felt more than the **incompatibility of legal systems.** The different accounting systems and terminology used mean that accountancy firms place great emphasis on ensuring that clients understand the information provided correctly. Very often, seemingly obvious matters need to be clarified and explained (especially the semantic scope of the terms used – in practice, a term means something different in the Czech Republic and in Poland, the consequences of financial and economic actions are different, so the client should know exactly what a term means). A frequent phenomenon is the lack of counterparts of the institutions concerned on the other side of the border. An example is the *správce daně* – an official in the Czech tax office responsible for keeping the files of a given company; in Poland, the desk officers deal 'seamlessly' with taxpayers, they are not assigned to them, while in the Czech Republic, the situation is different. There is also different nomenclature for different types of taxes. Some taxes do not function in the other country at all, an example being the road tax – *silniční daň* – in the Czech Republic, which applies to every vehicle, while in Poland its equivalent is the tax on means of transport, which applies only to vehicles above 3.5 tonnes. Respondents admitted that they are very keen to employ people with Polish language skills but pointed out that their value on the labour market increases only after they have worked in the office for some time dealing with Polish and Czech clients, because only then are they really able to grasp the nuances of meaning and understand the differences in the accounting systems of both countries. In the opinion of respondents, the biggest problem is caused by linguistic calques and 'false friends', while the preservation of the graphic form of the translation is very often a key issue for the proper reception of the text (this refers mainly to the profit and loss account, the balance sheet, and all printouts in standardised form). The **quality of translation,** according to the interviewees, is closely linked to a proper understanding of the original text, but also to attention to the formal side of the text. **Machine translation** is used quite often when there is a need to translate simple terms and short economic phrases quickly (automatic translation works 90 %

of the time). Longer texts of a descriptive nature are always outsourced to translation agencies, but as far as possible, accounting offices use their own human resources. In terms of **translator training**, respondents would prefer people with a degree in economics or at least with experience working for an accountancy office. Respondents said that **translation errors** are relatively common and relate to the correct interpretation and understanding of the meaning of the original text – in such situations, it is clear that 'the translator has no idea what he is translating'.

3.2.2.4. Translators and interpreters

The survey was conducted on a group of 20 sworn and specialist translators with translation experience of between 10 and 25 years. All respondents declared that they do both translation and interpreting. When asked how they deal with **non-equivalent terms** and the **problem of incompatible legal systems**, the following answers were given:

- I use reference materials;
- I describe the term in question;
- I use the nearest available equivalent;
- I leave the name in the source language with the translator's explanation in brackets;
- I talk to the client and clarify any doubts;
- I call an interpreter friend and discuss the problem with him;
- I speak to a friendly lawyer.

One translator also replied that if he 'doesn't feel up to it', he doesn't take the assignment. Regarding the tools that translators use in their work; the following were cited in the hierarchy of frequency:

- dictionaries and terminology databases in CAT tools;
- CAT tools;
- internet resources: online dictionaries, encyclopaedic websites, translators' forums, multilingual materials, and dictionaries found on the European Union website.

Respondents also emphasised the role of cooperation within the translating community – any consultation, mutual support, and advice is a much-appreciated form of assistance in their work. Regarding the issue of the

training programme, all translators stressed the role of knowledge of the differences in legal systems, knowledge of the basics of law, and nowadays, increasingly, a better knowledge of the Polish language and the principles of post-editing texts. Knowledge of the use of **CAT** tools was highlighted by respondents each time, although those with more seniority (implicitly also slightly older) declared that it was not an indispensable tool in their work (some people are still much more willing to work 'analogue', using traditional dictionaries). The following factors influence the **quality of translation** in the opinion of respondents (in order of frequency mentioned by respondents):

- the time the client gives them to complete the order;
- rate per page of translation;
- availability of customer contact;
- the provision of terminology databases by the client (also known as *style guides* – a system of formatting the terminology resources used that has been developed over the years for a particular client);
- making translation memories available.

Generally speaking, time and money pressures were prioritised by respondents. Thus, translators also highlight concerns about the use of **machine translation.** According to them, they are increasingly being offered a post-editing service for the text, rather than the translation itself (this is mainly the case for popular languages like English and German). The earnings are considerably lower than if the translation is completed, while the time required for post-editing is practically the same as if the full translation is completed. Numerous respondents see machine translation as a trap lurking in the translation industry. Respondents are concerned about a decline in the quality of translations and a reduction in translation rates. They also see machine translation as a real problem in terms of compliance with data protection rules. Extremely comforting, however, was the fact that, when asked about job satisfaction, 90 % of respondents confirmed that they liked their job and found it interesting and thought-provoking, highlighting the opportunity to broaden their minds, and declaring a desire for continuous improvement and further training. In their work, translators also appreciate flexibility, although, on the other hand, they emphasise the high level of stress they are exposed to (for example, when interpreting).

3.2.2.5. *Entrepreneurs*

In-depth interviews were conducted with entrepreneurs operating in industries such as the:

- electrical industry (an international company involved in the construction of electrostatic precipitators);
- insurance industry;
- automotive sector;
- marketing industry;
- system services for large companies.

The respondents in the survey were companies that use translation daily, either because they provide services to foreign clients, or because they work closely with foreign suppliers and subcontractors. Regarding the problem of **choosing the right terminology** and dealing with the **issue of non-equivalent terms**, respondents emphasised that very often the process of developing a coherent system for using the terminology base adopted by both parties (respondent + its foreign partner) requires time and many completed translations. Companies confirm that they are very keen to work with a single, already-proven translator, although they do not rule out working with translation agencies. In their cooperation with translators, they value direct contact and the possibility of mutual consultation, ultimately leading to a uniform solution for the future (regarding the use of terminology). On the issue of the **incompatibility of legal systems**, respondents had very limited views, tending to focus their statements on issues strictly related to terminology. Entrepreneurs also expressed the view in interviews that, in the case of specialised translations, hiring a sworn translator is not a guarantee of success – they believe that a sworn translator does not necessarily have to specialise in technical vocabulary. Respondents value working with people who, in addition to their language skills, have experience in work other than translation. Specialists who understand the processes of companies, who can read technical drawings properly and who can grasp the differences between the parties involved in contracts are in great demand. These are individuals who have a broad perspective of the text being translated, and this is essential for proper translation. Factors determining the high **quality of translation** were timeliness, specialisation in a given industry, and openness to consultation, while price, paradoxically, was not so important here – respondents declared their willingness to pay adequate remuneration for high-quality translation. Regarding the issue of **machine translation**, entrepreneurs confirmed that they use Google Translate regularly when they need to quickly look up a word or phrase, or roughly understand what the text is about. In the interviews, it was emphasised that the human factor is essential for the proper translation of content. Virtually every respondent has had to deal with **mistranslations** – from errors on business cards to minor typos in page-long translations, to factual errors in contracts and machine manuals. Practical knowledge of the language, preferably supported by the translator's stay abroad, was considered crucial by entrepreneurs.

3.2.2.6. Summary

The survey revealed some views common to translators, businesses using translations, and those commissioning translations. Firstly, the translator must have the right training and a range of competencies, as well as sufficient time to be able to carry out the tasks correctly. Secondly, the translation must be done by a person (not a machine) who understands the meaning of the text he or she is translating. For the translation of legal and specialist texts, knowledge of the law and the industry to which the text relates is required. A translator's comfort level is determined both by his or her remuneration and the opportunity to discuss concerns with professionals, clients, and other translators. A good translator is a communicative and punctual person who can realistically assess his or her skills in the context of taking on an assignment and the amount of time needed to complete it. Both translators and customers strive to ensure that translations are free of errors – but if they do occur, they must be identified and corrected in time. Machine translation and post-editing are in a very strong position in some segments, but the future will show to what extent they will dominate the translation market.

Ending

In this work, the author has attempted to present both the theoretical and practical face of the translation profession and the most relevant aspects of translation. The considerations undertaken and the research carried out have shown that the translation business requires a thorough academic foundation as well as continuing education and qualification. Considering current legislation and standards, the profession carries considerable responsibility. The lack of translation of Civil Codes in the Czech-Polish pair hinders the translation of commercial contracts, business documents containing legal clauses, and documents in business circulation. The translator's task is to constantly seek knowledge and constantly work on his or her craft. As with other areas of professional life, it is important to keep up to date with current trends and the changing realities of practising the profession. Artificial intelligence is intruding into the lives of translators with increasing intensity, so the next few years will show whether it poses a threat to translators or offers an opportunity to develop and do more work. It should not be forgotten that the human factor in the translation process is indispensable and without it, translation could not exist. The question of translator training in the Polish-Czech language pair also remains open. While students of translation from Anglo-Saxon languages can count on a wide range of postgraduate studies and numerous training courses, Czech speakers specialising in translation into Polish are hardly offered any such opportunities. They are left to acquire knowledge through a 'third' language, provided their level of knowledge allows them to benefit from this type of study.

This work also opens up broader perspectives for the study of translator behaviour in the Czech-Polish language pair. Research carried out on a larger number of texts of civil law contracts (or other specialised texts), with the participation of a larger number of translators, could create the conditions for discovering new phenomena in the translation process and thus provide a field of discussion on the problems translators encounter in their work. The author supposes that the publication of such research or its presentation among translators could stimulate interesting discussion and exchange of experiences. Another idea is preparing a publication of

Czech-Polish parallel texts along the lines of the publications carried out for other languages by Translegis Publishing House.

One thing seems certain – it is in the interest of translators themselves to discuss translation problems and how they can be solved.

Resumé

Dizertační práce na téma „Jazyk občanskoprávních smluv v česko-polském srovnání“ [*Język umów cywilnoprawnych w komparacji czesko-polskiej*] se skládá ze dvou teoretických kapitol a výzkumné části. Hlavním cílem práce bylo potvrdit hypotézu Mony Bakerové o existenci překladových univerzálií, chápaných jako lingvistické rysy, které se v přeložených textech vyskytují znatelně častěji než v textech nepřeložených.

První kapitola práce představuje současný stav bádání překladu, představuje hlavní trendy v dějinách překladu a odkazuje na jména nejvýznamnějších lingvistů, kteří se ve svých dílech překladatelskému výzkumu věnovali. Jelikož se práce zaměřuje na korpusový výzkum, byla zpracována i problematika korpusového překladu jako metodologie translatologického výzkumu. Poté byly představeny hlavní nástroje pro korpusovou analýzu a tím byl vysvětlen pojem korpus a charakterizovány typy korpusů včetně charakteristiky referenčních korpusů – českého a polského národního korpusu. V této části práce je také představen způsob provádění výzkumu a použité nástroje – kromě autorského korpusu to byl také e-mailový dotazník a hloubkový rozhovor.

Ve druhé kapitole práce se autorka zaměřila na proces překladu odborných textů. Jsou popsána dilemata a výzvy, kterým moderní překladatel čelí, stejně jako perspektiva překladu z pohledu klienta/zadavatele (vnější perspektiva – *user's view*) a samotného překladatele (vnitřní perspektiva – *translator's view*). Byly přezkoumány nejdůležitější překladatelské strategie a techniky a také bylo naznačeno, které nástroje mohou být pro překladatele užitečné a cenné v dlouhodobé perspektivě jeho profesní praxe.

V této souvislosti byly nastoleny otázky spojené s tvorbou vlastních glosářů, a to i na základě paralelních textů. S ohledem na současné postavení překladatele na trhu překladatelských služeb je uvedena profesní odpovědnost překladatele vyplývající z příslušných zákonů (jak v ČR, tak v Polsku) a příslušných norem upravujících překladatelské služby.

Překladatelská a posteditační problematika je prezentována s ohledem na aktuální trendy na trhu a dynamicky se měnící situaci ve světě v důsledku rozvoje umělé inteligence, která zasahuje i do práce překladatele. Výčet a představení nejvýznamnějších organizací a sdružení soudních překladatelů obsažené v poslední části druhé kapitoly měly ukázat, kde může překladatel hledat pomoc ve formálních záležitostech souvisejících s profesí. Spolupráce v překladatelské komunitě, vzájemná pomoc a četná setkání a konference jsou podnětem pro sebevzdělávání a zkvalitňování překladatelské činnosti.

Třetí kapitola byla věnována výzkumu, který byl proveden dvěma způsoby. V první fázi výzkumu byl použit autorův srovnávací korpus s více než 1 milionem slov. Výzkum byl proveden na výzkumném vzorku šesti občanskoprávních smluv přeložených skupinou 5 soudních překladatelů. Cílem studie bylo potvrdit existenci nebo popřít existenci překladových univerzálií v chápání hypotézy předložené Monou Bakerovou. Bylo analyzováno téměř 130 příkladů, ve kterých byly prezentovány různé tlumočnické přístupy pro daný fragment textu občanskoprávní smlouvy, byly použity různé strategie a techniky a v rozhodovacím procesu byly učiněny různé volby překladu. V důsledku analýzy byla potvrzena přítomnost překladových univerzálií v překladu občanskoprávních smluv z češtiny do polštiny. Shrnutí pak uvádí nejdůležitější závěry a komentáře týkající se typu nalezených univerzálií a jejích základů.

Druhá fáze výzkumu byla zaměřena na poznání pohledu zhotovitele a zadavatele a probíhala formou e-mailového dotazníku a hloubkového rozhovoru. Výsledky provedených hloubkových rozhovorů potvrdily, že kvalita a kompetence překladatele jsou hodnoty, které nikdy nezestárnou, a i přes neustále se zvyšující časovou tíseň a náklady jsou zákazníky stále oceňovány a žádané. Zahájený výzkum poskytuje otevřený prostor pro diskuse o úloze překladatele v současné době, měnících se podmínkách jeho práce jak i sledování měnícího se chování překladatelů v rozhodovacím procesu a použité strategie či techniky.

Důležitá je otázka odpovědnosti překladatelů a v této souvislosti úloha profesních sdružení a organizací.

Summary

The doctoral work entitled *Language of Czech and Polish Civil Law Contracts: A Comparative Study* consists of two theoretical chapters and a research section. The main aim of the work is to confirm the hypothesis put forward by Mona Baker regarding the existence of universals of translation, understood as linguistic features occurring noticeably more frequently in translated texts than in texts which are not translations.

The first chapter presents the current state of translation studies and the main trends in the history of translation, discussing the most important linguists who devoted their work to studying translation. Since the work focuses on corpus analyses, corpus-based translation studies are also discussed as a translation studies methodology. The main tools of corpus analysis are presented: the concept of a corpus is explained, and its types are characterised, including a description of the reference text collections, i.e., the Czech and the Polish national corpora. This part also presents how the research analysis will be carried out and describes the research tools, including an original corpus and an e-mail questionnaire and in-depth interviews.

The second chapter focuses on the process of specialised translation. It describes the dilemmas and challenges faced by contemporary translators, as well as the different points of view on translation: that of the client / ordering party (external/user's view) and that of the translator (internal/translator's view). Key translation strategies and techniques are reviewed, with an indication of the tools which may prove helpful and valuable to the translator in the long term. The creation of glossaries, also based on parallel texts, is discussed in this context. As regards the contemporary position of translators in the translation services market, their professional liability resulting from the relevant legislation (both in the Czech Republic and in Poland) is indicated, along with the standards that apply to translation services. Translation and post-editing aspects are addressed, taking into account the current market trends and the dynamically changing global situation related to the development of artificial intelligence, which also affects translators' work. The final part of the second chapter contains a list and presentation of the most important organisations and associations of sworn translators, to show where translators can seek help with formal issues related to their profession. Cooperation within the translation community, mutual help, and numerous meetings and conferences constitute incentives for self-education and improvement of the translator's expertise.

The third chapter is devoted to the research, proceeding along two lines. The first stage was based on an original comparative corpus containing over 1 million words. A sample of six civil law contracts translated by a group of five sworn translators was studied. The aim was to confirm or deny the existence of universals of translation as defined in the hypothesis put forward by Mona Baker. Nearly 130 examples were analysed, with different translators' approaches presented for specific fragments of the civil law contracts, including different strategies and techniques applied, and different translation choices in the decision-making process. The analysis confirmed the presence of universals of translation in civil law contracts translated from Czech into Polish. The key conclusions and final comments are subsequently presented concerning the type of translation universals found and the bases underlying them.

The second stage of the research focused on exploring the translator's and the client's points of view, using an e-mail questionnaire and in-depth interviews. The results of the community survey confirm that translation quality and translators' expertise are assets that never become obsolete and, despite the constantly increasing pressure of time and money, continue to be appreciated and desired by clients.

This research opens the field for broader discussions on the role of the translator in today's world and on their changing working conditions, as well as for observations of the changing behaviour of translators concerning the decision-making process, the strategies used, and the techniques applied. The question of translators' liability is also important, and in this context, the role of professional associations and organisations is underscored.

Bibliography

Baker M., 1993. Corpus Linguistics and Translation Studies. Implications and Applications, [in:] M. Baker and others (eds.), *Text and Technology: In Honour of John Sinclair*, Amsterdam-Philadelphia, pp. 233–250.

Baker M., 1995. "Corpora in Translation Studies: An Overview and Some Suggestions for Future Research", *Target*, no. 7 (2), pp. 223–243.

Baker M., 1996. Corpus-Based Translation Studies: The Challenges That Lie Ahead, [in:] H.L. Somers (ed.), *Terminology, LSP and Translation. Studies in Language Engineering in Honour of Juan C. Sager*, Amsterdam-Philadelphia, pp. 175–186.

Baker M., 2006. *In Other Words. A Coursebook in Translation*, London.

Baker P., 2010. *Sociolinguistics and Corpus Linguistics*, Edinburgh.

Bassnet S., Lefevere A., 1998. *Constructing Cultures: Essays on Literary Translation*, Bristol.

Benjamin W., 2018. *The Task of the Translator*, Munich (Munich).

Berezowski L., 2018. *Jak czytać, rozumieć i tłumaczyć dokumenty prawnicze i gospodarcze*, Warszawa.

Biel Ł., 2010a. Corpus-Based Studies of Legal Language for Translation Purposes: Methodological and Practical Potential, [in:] C. Heine, J. Engberb (eds.), *Reconceptualizing LCP. Online Proceedings of the XVII European LSP Symposium 2009*, Aarhus, pp. 1–17.

Biel Ł., 2010b. „Terminologia i frazeologia reprezentacji spółki (pełnomocnik, prokurent i przedstawiciel) oraz ich angielskie ekwiwalenty", *Lingua Legis*, no 18, pp. 19–26.

Biel Ł., 2011. „Jakość przekładu prawnego i prawniczego w świetle normy europejskiej PN-EN 15038 oraz hipotezy uniwersaliów translatologicznych", *Rocznik Przekładoznawczy*, no 6, pp. 13–28.

Biel Ł., 2015. „Translatoryka korpusowa", *Rocznik Przekładoznawczy*, no 10, pp. 15–40.

Błaszkowska H., 2012. Praca tłumacza w świetle wyzwań współczesności, [in:] M. Guławska-Gawkowska, K. Hejwowski, A. Szczęsny (eds.), *Tłumacz: sługa, pośrednik, twórca?*, Warszawa, pp. 193–201.

Bogucki Ł., 2009. *Tłumaczenie wspomagane komputerowo*, Warszawa.

Bourdieu P., [1979] 2005. *Dystynkcja. Społeczna krytyka władzy sądzenia* [orig. *La Dictinction. Critique sociale du jugement*], transl. P. Biłos, Scholar, Warszawa [ed. orig. Minuit, Paris].

Bourdieu P., [1992] 2001. *Reguły sztuki. Geneza i struktura pola literackiego* [orig. *Les règles de l'art. Genèse et structure du champ littéraire*], transl. A. Zawadzki, Universitas, Kraków [ed. orig. Seuil, Paris].

Bukowski P., Heydel M. (eds.), 2009. *Współczesne teorie przekładu*, Kraków.

Chromá M., 2014. *Právní překlad v teorii a praxi. Nový občanský zákoník*, Praga.

Cieślik B., 2016. Ramy formalnoprawne egzaminu, [in:] M. Kuźniak (ed.), *Egzamin na tłumacza przysięgłego*, Warszawa.

Cronin M., 2010. "The Translation Crowd", *Revista Tradumàtica*, no. 8, pp. 1–7.

Czyżewska M., 2007. „Fałszywi przyjaciele tłumacza, czyli o pułapkach w czasie tłumaczenia", *Lingua Legis*, no 15, pp. 83–90.

Dąbrowski G., 2019. *Prawo cywilne. Zobowiązania. Spadki*, Warszawa.

Davies N., 1999. Przedmowa, [in:] E. Tabakowska (ed.), *O przekładzie na przykładzie. Rozprawa tłumacza z Europą Normana Daviesa*, Kraków, p. 7.

Dedecius K., 1974. *Notatnik tłumacza*, Kraków.

Dedecius K., 1988. *Notatnik tłumacza*, Warszawa.

Delisle J., Lee-Jahnke H., Cormier M.C. (eds.), 1999. *Translation Terminology*, Amsterdam/Philadephia.

Fabricius-Hansen, Cathrine, 2007. *Paralleltext und Übersetzung in sprachwissenschaftlicher Sicht*, [in:] *Übersetzung, Translation, Traduction. Eininternationales Handbuch zur Übersetzungsforschung*, ed. H. Kittel et al., Berlin/New York, s. 322–329.

Felber H., Budin G., 1994. *Teoria i praktyka terminologii*, Warszawa.

Gilewski W., 2020. *Stowarzyczenie Tłumaczy Polskich*, access from www.stp.org.pl [20.02.2021].

Göpferich S., 2005. Paralleltexte, [in:] M. Snell-Hornby et al. (red.), *Handbuch Translation*, Stauffenburg, Tübingen, s. 184–186.

Grabowski Ł., Hebal-Jezierska M., 2016. O różnych korpusowych metodach badawczych – próba krytycznej refleksji, *Komunikacja Specjalistyczna*, no. 11, pp. 65–85.

Grucza F. (ed.), 1981. *Bilingwizm a glottodydaktyka*. Warszawa.

Grucza F. (ed.), 1991a. *Teoretyczne podstawy terminologii*, Wrocław.

Grucza F., 1991b. Terminologia – jej przedmiot, status i znaczenie, [in:] F. Grucza (ed.), 1991, *Teoretyczne podstawy terminologii*, Wrocław, pp. 11–44.

Hebal-Jezierska M., 2021. *Terminologia lingwistyki korpusowej w języku czeskim, polskim i słowackim – wybrane problemy*, in: *Bohemistyka*, no 4, Warszawa.

Hejwowski K., 2011. „Wstęp do teorii tłumaczenia 'po pięćdziesięciu latach'", *Lingua Legis*, no 20, pp. 3–11.

Hejwowski K., 2012. *Kognitywno-komunikacyjna teoria przekładu*, Warszawa.

Hermans T., 1985. *The Manipulation of Literature. Studies in Literary Translation*, London.

Hermans T., 2007. Przekład, zazdrażnienie i rezonans, transl. M. Heydel, [in:] P. Bukowski, M. Heydel (ed.), 2009, *Współczesne teorie przekładu*, Kraków, pp. 297–315.

Heydel M., 2009. „Zwrot kulturowy w badaniach nad przekładem", *Teksty Drugie*, no 6, pp. 21–34.

Hulmák a kol., 2014. *Občanský zákoník V. Závazkové právo. Obecná část (§1721–2054)*, Český Těšín.

Imioło, I., 2014. Status prawny tłumaczy sądowych w Polsce, Republice Czeskiej i Republice Słowackiej – analiza porównawcza, *Lingua Legis*, no 22, pp. 20–38.

Jadacka H., 2005. „Po co tłumaczowi prawniczemu ‚Poradnik językowy'", *Lingua Legis*, no 13, pp. 95–96.

Jakobson R., 1959. On Linguistic Aspects of Translation, [in:] R.A. Brower (ed.), *On Translation*, Harvard, pp. 232–239.

Janikowski P., Krzemińska-Krzywda J., 2012. „ ‚Kim będziesz jak dorośniesz?' O postrzeganiu zawodu tłumacza przez młodych filologów", [in:] M. Gawkowska, K. Hejwowski, A. Szczęsny (eds.), *Tłumacz: sługa, pośrednik, twórca?* Warszawa, pp. 157–171.

Jedlikowska J., 2018. „O (nie)istnieniu efektywnych metod statystycznych w badaniach językoznawczych nad tekstem konstytucji", *The Peculiarity of Man – Granice ludzkiego świata: istniejące – nieistniejące (2)*, no 2 (28), pp. 193–207.

Jopek-Bosiacka A., 2019. *Teoretycznoprawne i logiczne uwarunkowania przekładu prawnego*, Warszawa.

Jopek-Bosiacka A., 2021. *Przekład prawny i sądowy*, Warszawa.

Kędzior Z., Karcz K., 2007. *Badania marketingowe w praktyce*, Warszawa.

Kędzior Z., Karcz K., 2010. *Badania marketingowe w praktyce*, Warszawa.

Kielar B., 1988. *Tłumaczenie i koncepcje translatoryczne*, Wrocław.

Kielar B., 1991. Problemy tłumaczenia tekstów specjalistycznych, [in:] F. Grucza (ed.), *Teoretyczne podstawy terminologii*, Wrocław, pp. 133–140.

Kierzkowska D., 2007. *Tłumaczenie prawnicze*, Warszawa.

Kierzkowska D., 2008. *Tłumaczenie prawnicze*, Warszawa.

Kierzkowska D. (elab.), 2009. „Zalecenia Forum Refleksji nt. kształcenia i statusu tłumaczy sądowych", *Lingua Legis*, no 17, pp. 3–5.

Kierzkowska D. (ed.), 2011a. *Dokumenty polskie. Wybór dla tłumaczy sądowych*, Warszawa.

Kierzkowska D., 2011b. „Odbiorcy tłumaczenia tekstu pragmatycznego, czyli teoria w praktyce", *Lingua Legis*, no 20, pp. 11–17.

Kierzkowska D., 2013. „Nazwy własne w tłumaczeniu dokumentów w świetle prawa polskiego i międzynarodowego", *Lingua Legis*, no 21, pp. 16–26.

Kierzkowska D., 2020. *Alchemia zawodu tłumacza*, Warszawa.

Kizińska A., 2015. Polskie ekwiwalenty terminów związanych z przysposobieniem (prawo rodzinne) – studium przypadku, [in:] J. Lubocha-Kruglik, O. Małys, G. Wilk (eds.), *Przestrzenie przekładu 3*, Katowice, pp. 259–269.

Konecki K.T., 2000. *Studia z metodologii badań jakościowych. Teoria ugruntowana*, Warszawa.

Konieczny P., 2006. „Rozwój komputerowych narzędzi wspomagających tłumaczenie i jego znaczenie dla rynku wydawniczego słowników", *Lingua Legis*, no 14, pp. 3–13.

Kraskowska E., 2018. „Uniwersalia przekładowe", *Forum Poetyki*, no 14, pp. 86–89.

Krzysztoforska-Weisswasser Z., 1995. *Wykorzystanie tekstów paralelnych przy tłumaczeniu wyroków w procesie cywilnym*, *Lingua Legis*, no 2, pp. 18–20.

Kubacki A., 2012. *Tłumaczenie poświadczone. Status, kształcenie, warsztat I odpowiedzialność tłumacza przysięgłego*, Warszawa.

Kubacki A., 2013. Teksty paralelne jako narzędzie pomocnicze przy sporządzaniu tłumacze (specjalistycznych), *Comparative Legilinguistic*, no 13, Katowice, pp. 145–159.

Kujawska-Lis E., 2008. „Ekwiwalencja przekładu wyrażeń opisujących chód w opowiadaniu G.K. Chestertona 'The Queer Feet'", *Prace Językoznawcze*, no 10, pp. 123–136.

Kuźniak M, 2015. *Egzamin na tłumacza przysięgłego w praktyce. Język angielski - analiza językowa*, Warszawa.

Kwieciński P., 2001. *Disturbing Strangeness. Foreignisation and Domestication in Translation Procedures in the Context of Cultural Asymmetry*, Toruń.

Labov W., 1966. *The Social Stratification of English in New York City*, Waszyngton.

Laviosa S., 2011. *Corpus Linguistics and Translation Studies*, in: *Perspectives on Corpus Linguistics*, pp 131–154, Amsterdam.

Lemnitzer L., 2015. "Semantic Modeling of Collocations for Lexicographic Purposes", *Journal of Cognitive Science*, no 16 (3), pp. 200–223.

Leńko-Szymańska A., Gruszczyńska E., 2016. Polskojęzyczne korpusy równoległe w Polsce i za granicą, [in:] A. Leńko-Szymańska, E. Gruszczyńska (eds.), *Polskojęzyczne korpusy równoległe*, Warsaw, pp. 1–23.

Levý J., 1967. *Umění překladu*, Praha.

Levý J., 2009. Przekład jako proces podejmowania decyzji, transl. M. Adamczyk, [in:] P. Bukowski, M. Heydel (eds.), *Współczesne teorie przekładu*, Kraków, pp. 71–85.

Lewandowska-Tomaszczyk B., 2005. *Podstawy językoznawstwa korpusowego*, Łódź.

Lewandowska-Tomaszczyk B., 2005a. Analiza języka z zastosowaniem korpusu, [in:] B. Lewandowska-Tomaszczyk (ed.), *Podstawy językoznawstwa korpusowego*, Łódź, pp. 133–174.

Lewandowska-Tomaszczyk B. (ed.), 2005b. *Podstawy językoznawstwa korpusowego*, Łódź.

Lewicki R., 2017. „Metody, techniki i strategie w procesie tłumaczeniowym: Próba porządkownia terminologii przekładoznawczej“, *Konińskie Studia Językowe*, no 5 (3), pp. 357–365.

Łomzik M., 2020. *Strategie i techniki przekładu niemieckojęzycznych nazw placówek medycznych w tłumaczeniu poświadczonym*, Kraków.

Lotko E., 1986. *Čeština a polština v překladatelské a tlumočnické praxi*, Praha.

Lotko E., 1997. *Synchronní konfrontace češtiny a polštiny*, Praha.

Lukszyn J. (ed.), 1993. *Tezaurus terminologii translatorycznej*, Warszawa: Wydawnictwo Naukowe PWN.

Malak P., 2011. „Metody statystyczne w komputerowym przetwarzaniu języka naturalnego“, *Toruńskie Studia Bibliologiczne*, no 1 (6), pp. 50–65.

Malinowski A., 2006. *Polski język prawny. Wybrane zagadnienia*, Warszawa.

McEnery T., Wilson A., 1996. *Corpus Linguistics*, Edinburgh.

Nagao H., 2005. „Sprawa z Melbourne: niewłaściwe tłumaczenie przyczyną oskarżenia o niepopełnione przestępstwa“, *Lingua Legis*, no 13, pp. 3–8.

Nartowska K., 2011. „Tłumaczenia sądowe w Polsce. Analiza rynku“, *Lingua Legis*, no 20, pp. 17–22.

Nerlicki K., 2003. Wiedza deklaratywna i proceduralna w kontekście rozwoju kompetencji translatorycznej, [in:] K. Hejwowski (ed.), *Teoria i dydaktyka przekładu. Materiały z konferencji zorganizowanej przez Wydział Filologiczny Wszechnicy Mazurskiej w Olecku. Olecko 28–29.05.2001*, Olecko.

Newmark P., 1981. *Approaches to Translation*, Oxford.

Newmark P., 1988. *A Textbook of Translation*, New York.

Nida E., 1964. *Toward a Science of Translating: With Special Reference to Principles and Procedures Involved in Bible Translating*, Leiden.

Okła J., 2011. „Podstawy wykonywania pisemnych tłumaczeń unijnych“, *Lingua Legis*, no 20, pp. 17–22.

Okulska U., 2006. Metody statystyczne w językoznawstwie, [in:] A. Duszak, E. Gajek, U. Okulska (eds.), *Korpusy w angielsko-polskim językoznawstwie kontrastywnym*, Kraków, pp. 351–386.

Pawlikowska A., 2012. „Zastosowanie metod językoznawstwa korpusowego i lingwistyki kwantytatywnej w analizie dyskursu", *Oblicza Komunikacji*, no 5, pp. 111–125.

Pawłowski A., 2003. „*Lingwistyka korpusowa – perspektywy i zagrożenia*", *Polonica*, no. 22–23, pp. 19–32.

Pawłowski, 2001. *Metody kwantytatywne w sekwencyjnej analizie tekstu*, Warszawa.

Perdek M., 2016. Tłumacz na tropie terminów, czyli w poszukiwaniu uparciuchów, patrzydeł i czynów przestępnych, [in:] B. Whyatt, Z. Nadstoga, A. Chmiel, P. Korpal, T. Kościuczuk, I. Mazur, M. Perdek, K. Stachowiak, M. Turski, M. Tymczyńska, O. Witczak, *Tłumacz – praktyczne aspekty zawodu*, Poznań, pp. 67–103.

Pęzik P., 2012. NKJP w warsztacie tłumacza, [in:] A. Przepiórkowski, M. Bańko, R.L. Górski, B. Lewandowska-Tomaszczyk (eds.), *Narodowy Korpus Języka Polskiego*, Warszawa, pp. 301–310.

Piątkowski Ł., 2018. „Zastosowanie analiz korpusowych w badaniach leksyko-gramatycznych. Perspektywa porównawcza niemiecko-polska", *Zeszyty Naukowe Towarzystwa Doktorantów UJ. Nauki Humanistyczne*, no 21 (2), pp. 131–150.

Pieńkos J., 1993. *Przekład i tłumacz we współczesnym świecie: aspekty lingwistyczne i pozalingwistyczne*, Warszawa.

Pieńkos J., 1999. *Podstawy juryslingwistyki. Język w prawie – prawo w języku*, Warszawa.

Piotrowska M., 2006. „Czy znajomość strategii jest w warsztacie każdego tłumacza niezbędna? (o strategii teoretycznie)", *Przekładaniec, Poezja i proza przekładu*, no 17, pp. 217–230.

Piotrowska M., 2007. *Proces decyzyjny tłumacza. Podstawy metodologii nauczania przekładu*, Kraków.

Pisarska A., Tomaszkiewicz T., 1996. *Współczesne tendencje przekładoznawcze*, Poznań.

Polański E. (ed.), 1999. *Encyklopedia językoznawstwa ogólnego*, Warszawa.

Przepiórkowski A., Bańko M., Górski R., Lewandowska-Tomaszczyk B. (eds.), 2012. *Narodowy Korpus Języka Polskiego*, Warszawa.

Puławska E., 2005. „Lokalizacja – nihil novi sub sole", *Lingua Legis*, no 13, pp. 90–95.

Pym A., 1992. *Translation and Text Transfer*, Frankfurt am Main.

Pym A., 1993. *Epistemological problems in translation and teaching: a seminar for thinking students*, Caminade.

Pym A., 2018. *A typology of translation solutions*, in: *The Journal of Specialised Translation*, Issue 30 – July 2018.

Pym A., 2021. *Competences of future interpreters*, access from https://usuaris.tinet.cat/apym/on-line/powerpoint/html [08.02.2021].

Radwański Z., Olejniczak A., 2016. *Zobowiązania – część ogólna*, ed. 12, Warszawa.

Reczulska H., 2010. „Terminologia i frazeologia reprezentacji spółki (pełnomocnik, prokurent i przedstawiciel) oraz ich angielskie ekwiwalenty", *Lingua Legis*, no 18, pp. 3–6.

Robinson D., 1997. *Becoming a Translator An Introduction to the Theory and Practice of Translation*, Ohio.

Rybicka-Nowacka H., 1991. Normalizacja polskiej terminologii technicznej, [in:] F. Grucza (ed.), *Teoretyczne podstawy terminologii*, Wrocław, pp. 141–156.

Šarcevic S., 1997. *Legal Translation and Translation Theory: a Receiver-oriented Approach*, Rijeka.

Šarčevič S., 1997. *New Approach to Legal Translation*, Hague.

Spillner B., 1981. Textsorten im Sprachvergleich: Ansätze zu einer kontrastiven Textologie, [in:] W. Kühlwein et al. (ed.), *Kontrastive Linguistik und Übersetzungswissenschaft: Akten des InternationalenKolloquiums Trier/Saarbrücken*, München, pp. 239–250.

Stefaniak K., 2012. Między sztuką, rzemiosłem a służbą publiczną, czyli co robią tłumacze DGT i co z tego wynika, [in:] M. Guławska-Gawkowska, K. Hejwowski, A. Szczęsny (eds.), *Tłumacz: sługa, pośrednik, twórca?*, Warszawa, pp. 203–212.

Steiner A., 2018. *Po wieży Babel. Aspekty języka i przekładu*, Warszawa.

Stolecka-Makowska A., 2016. „Triangulacja jako koncepcja pozyskania wiedzy o zachowaniach nabywczych konsumentów", *Studia Ekonomiczne. Zeszyty Naukowe Uniwersytetu Ekonomicznego w Katowicach*, no 261, pp. 50–62.

Stubbs M., 2004. Language Corpora, [in:] A. Davies, C. Elder (eds.), *Handbook of Applied Linguistics*, Oxford, pp. 106–132.

Szulc A., 1984. *Podręczny słownik językoznawstwa stosowanego*, Warszawa.

Tabakowska E., 1999. *O przekładzie na przykładzie. Rozprawa tłumacza z Europą Normana Daviesa*, Kraków.

Tognini-Bonelli E., 2001. *Corpus Linguistics at Work*, Amsterdam.

Tognini-Bonelli E., 2002. *Corpus Linguistics at Work*, Amsterdam.

Tomášek M., 1998. *Překlad v právní praxi*, Praha.

Tomášek M., 2007. *Antologie odborného překladu*, Praha.

Tryuk M., 1991. Stan organizacyjny działalności terminologicznej na świecie, [in:] F. Grucza (ed.), *Teoretyczne podstawy terminologii*, Wrocław, pp. 97–116.

Vermeer H., 1996. *A Skopos Theory of Translation (Some Arguments For and Against)*, Heidelberg.

Vinay, J.-P., Darbelnet, J. (1958/2000). *A Methodology for Translation.* [An excerpt from Comparative Stylistics of French and English: A Methodology for Transla-tion, trans. and eds. J. C. Sager & M.-J. Hamel, Amsterdam, 1995, first published in 1958 as Stylistique comparée du français et de l'anglais. Méthode de traduction] In L. Venuti (Ed.), The Translation Studies Reader (pp. 84–93). London.

Vinay J.P., Darbelnet J., [1958] 2003. *A Methodology for Translation*, [in:] L. Venuti (ed.), *The Translation Studies Reader*, London–New York.

Vinay J.P., Darbelnet J., 1995. *Comparative Stylistics of French and English. A Methodology for Translation*, Amsterdam–Filadelfia.

Voellnagel A., 2014. *Jak nie tłumaczyć tekstów technicznych*, Warszawa.

Waliński J., 2005. *Typologia korpusów oraz warsztat informatyczny lingwistyki korpusowej*, [in:] B. Lewandowska-Tomaszczyk (ed.), *Podstawy językoznawstwa korpusowego*, Łódź, pp. 27–41.

Weigt Z., 2012. „Tekst specjalistyczny w dydaktyce uniwersyteckiej", *Lingwistyka Stosowana*, nor 5, Warszawa, pp. 135–144.

Wilss W., 1977. *Übersetzungswissenschaft. Probleme und Methode*, Berlin.

Wilss W., 1996. *Übersetzungsunterricht. Eine Einführung: Begriffliche Grundlagen und methodische Optimierungen*, Tübingen.

Witczak O., 2016. Tłumacze kontra maszyny, czyli o tłumaczeniu wspomaganym komputerowo, [in:] B. Whyatt, Z. Nadstoga, A. Chmiel, P. Korpal, T. Kościuczuk, I. Mazur, M. Perdek, K. Stachowiak, M. Turski,

M. Tymczyńska, O. Witczak (eds.), *Tłumacz – praktyczne aspekty zawodu*, Poznań, pp. 66–100.

Wojan K., 2017. *Zjawisko homonimii międzyjęzykowej na przykładzie języków: polskiego, rosyjskiego i fińskiego*, Warszawa.

Wojnicki S., 1991. Subjęzyki specjalistyczne, [in:] F. Grucza (ed.), *Teoretyczne podstawy terminologii*, Wrocław, pp. 61–77.

Wojtasiewicz O., 1957. *Wstęp do teorii tłumaczenia*, Warszawa.

Wojtasiewicz O., 1958. *Wstęp do teorii tłumaczenia*, Warszawa.

Wróblewski B., 1948. *Język prawny i prawniczy*, Kraków.

Zarzycki Ł., 2016. *Dylematy tłumacza. Zastosowanie pięciu typów ekwiwalencji Kollera oraz modelu bezpośredniego i pośredniego Vinay i Darbelnet w tłumaczeniu terminologii medycznej z języka angielskiego na polski*, Warszawa.

Zieliński M., 1999. *Języki prawne i prawnicze, w: Polszczyzna 2000. Orędzie o stanie języka na przełomie tysiącleci*, W. Pisarek (ed.), Kraków, s. 50–72.

Zohar E., 2007. Miejsce literatury tłumaczonej w polisystemie lietrackim, transl. M. Heydel, [in:] P. Bukowski, M. Heydel (red.), 2009, *Współczesne teorie przekładu*, Kraków, pp. 195–252.

Zwierzchoń-Grabowska E., 2019. Oprogramowanie CAT w pracy początkujących tłumaczy, [in:] J. Lubocha-Kruglik, O. Małys, G. Wilk (eds.), *Przestrzenie przekładu 3*, Katowice, pp. 301–310.

Legislation and rulings

Act 2004, Act of 25 November 2004 on the profession of sworn translator (Coll. No. 273, item 2704 as amended).

Act of 23 April 1964 – Civil Code (Coll. No. 16, item 93 as amended).

Directive 2010/64/EU of the European Parliament and of the Council of 20 October 2010 on the right to interpretation and translation in criminal proceedings.

Judgment of the Supreme Administrative Court 1995, judgment of 4 December 1995, ref. II S.A. [Wyrok NSA 1995, wyrok z dnia 4 grudnia 1995 roku, sygn. akt II S.A.]. 1356/94.

Nový občanský zákoník. [online] https://www.justice.cz/novy-obcansky-zakonik.

Vyhláška 506/2020. Regulation No. 506/2020 Coll., on the activities of sworn translators and interpreters, in force from 1 January 2021*(Vyhláška č. 506/2020 Sb., o výkonu tlumočnické a překladatelské činnosti, účinná od 1. 1. 2021)*.

Vyhláška 507/2020. Regulation No. 507/2020 Coll., on remuneration and compensation for sworn translators and interpreters, in force from 1 January 2021*(Vyhláška č. 507/2020 Sb., o odměně a náhradách soudního tlumočníka a soudního překladatele, účinná od 1. 1. 2021)*.

Vyhláška 508/2020. Regulation No. 508/2020 Coll., on remuneration and compensation for sworn translators and interpreters, in force from 1 January 2021*(Vyhláška č. 508/2020 Sb., o odměně a náhradě hotových výdajů konzultanta přibraného pro účely trestního řízení, účinná od 1. 1. 2021)*.

Vyhláška 608/2020. Regulation No. 608/2020 Coll., on the determination of the necessary level of knowledge of the Czech language and equivalent language examinations to perform the activity of a sworn translator and interpreter, in force from 1 January 2021*(Vyhláška č. 608/2020 Sb., o stanovení potřebné úrovně znalosti českého jazyka a rovnocenných jazykových zkouškách pro výkon tlumočnické činnosti, účinná od 1. 1. 2021)*.

Zákon 2021. Act No. 354/2019 Coll., on sworn interpreters and translators in the wording of Act No. 166/2020 Coll. *(Zákon č. 354/2019 Sb., o soudních tlumočnících a soudních překladatelích ve znění zákona č. 166/2020 Sb., účinný od 1. 1. 2021)*.

Netography

BST: Bałtyckie Stowarzyszenie Tłumaczy, accessed from https://bst.org.pl [20.06.2021].

Český národní korpus, accessed from www.korpus.cz [12.12.2020].

NKJP: Narodowy Korpus Języka Polskiego (National Corpus of Polish Language), accessed from http://nkjp.pl [12.12.2020].

SJP, 2020. Korpus językowy PWN, accessed from https://sjp.pwn.pl/korpus/struktura [20.12.2020].

SJP, 2021. Glosariusz, accessed from https://sjp.pwn.pl/sjp/glosariusz;2559361.html [20.01.2021].

Sketch Engine, accessed from www.sketchengine.eu [12.12.2021].

Stowarzyszenie Tłumaczy Polskich, accessed from https://stp.org.pl [20.06.2021].

TEPIS: Polskie Towarzystwo Tłumaczy Przysięgłych i Specjalistycznych, accessed from https://tepis.org.pl [20.06.2021].

Zameo S., 2019. Neural Machine Translation: Tips and Advantages for Your Digital Translations, accessed from https://www.textmaster.com/blog/neural-machine-translation-guide/ [20.07.2020].

List of Figures

List of Tables

www.ingramcontent.com/pod-product-compliance
Ingram Content Group UK Ltd.
Pitfield, Milton Keynes, MK11 3LW, UK
UKHW021829100926
8556IPUK00004B/236

9 783631 908983